WONDERFULLY ALIVE

Holistic Insights for Your Health and Happiness

In our world of quick-fix solutions and health-wealth promises, Charlie Ong challenges us to lead a healthier and more holistic way of life. If our preferences are to avoid, deny, and suppress, Ong persuades us to face, accept, and integrate. With accessible content written in a way that we can all relate to, this book is for any soul seriously preparing to be wonderfully alive.

Mak Sue Ann
Faculty-in-development, Trinity Theological College

An excellent book. A brilliant piece of work with very helpful advice and it is definitely among the best 'personal development' or 'self-improvement' books I have come across. Very comprehensive but yet holistic and coherent. Most of all, I believe it will be an immensely impactful and life-changing book.

Koh Boon Long, M.Ed. (NTU), PPA, PBS
Educational Consultant at Educare International Consultancy
Former Deputy Director, National Education
Ministry of Education, Singapore

Wonderfully Alive discusses an important facet for our lives in modern society – holistic living. Charlie is not just an author but an experienced therapist who has helped many people to overcome challenging situations in their lives. He has skilfully written a much-needed book, which helps us look into all three different areas of our life, in order to find the balance in taking care of our body, mind and spirit, and keeping them strong so that we can live the life we truly desire to live. This book is for anyone who is looking to be Wonderfully Alive!

Shirley Woon
Counsellor/Psychotherapist
Author of Bleeding Hearts

Wonderfully Alive takes a very holistic approach and considers the biological, psychological, social and spiritual aspects of one's personhood as one seeks health and happiness - an interesting read.

Tony Ong
Senior Therapist and Clinical Supervisor
Counselling and Care Centre

Sometimes, what we don't have, we strive to achieve; and when we change our expectations, what we achieve becomes a bonus.

This book is about undertaking a life that is meaningful. It's about converting deficits into positives, understanding our emotions, having the discipline to learn the ABCs of transforming ourselves. All of us want to experience the gratifying sense of making progress in life. This book gives us the stimulus and path to move forward to become healthier and happier. What a useful companion as we journey from purpose to priorities, even as we re-calibrate and re-define our goals.

Simon Lee
Managing Partner & Master Executive Coach
BRIEF Academy

Highly recommended for anyone looking for both established and fresh insights about health and happiness all neatly put together in one place. As a cancer survivor, I found this latest book by Charlie very helpful in exploring life and health from a balanced viewpoint through the use of the Biopsychosocial–Spiritual (BPSS) Model.

Ho Hian Chye
Former Church Elder & current happy retiree

Charlie has an innate ability to transform complicated thoughts to this simple yet thought-provoking, absorbing read. As with his previous books, this book is Wonderfully Relatable, Wonderfully Relevant and Wonderfully Riveting with nuggets of wisdom and humour. Holistic Changes with Holistic Guidance for a Holistic Life - a must read as we move closer to the finish line, completing our journey unafraid as we are 'Wonderfully Made'.

Josephine Loo Yi
Lawyer/APAC General Counsel
Barrister-at-Law (UK) / Advocate & Solicitor (Singapore)

As Charlie's editor on this book, *Wonderfully Alive.* I was drawn to my study each morning over the course of a week to read each word, sentence and paragraph. It was an invigorating and rewarding experience. I could not make any suggestions on content, structure or any other Big Picture element of his book; he had written a whole, organised and complete manuscript. Effortlessly weaving relevant quotes from other thinkers on the subject of human health and happiness, Charlie's enthusiasm rubs off. He is representing years of his own therapeutic experience and a wealth of published academic research in this book which reaches out to the reader in a friendly and non-judgemental way. It is OK to experience all the complex feelings on the 'Feeling Wheel' and to experience suffering, yet we all have the capacity to change and live in better health and happiness. We are all human with a link to the divine. *Wonderfully Alive* is a book that does what it says. My work was absorbing but the author has mastered his messages.

Sarah Newton-John

Charlie Ong lives with his beautiful wife of more than three decades, Leng; their two lovely daughters, Charlene and Chessa, and a cat called Niu Niu. He enjoys his work and accepts his lot in life, believing that when people are busy enjoying their life, they will have no time to brood over the past; they will be too busy enjoying the gift from God, and God keeps them occupied with gladness of heart.

Charlie is Senior Counsellor at Agape Counselling Sanctuary, and has over 35 years of experience working with youth and families. He is a certified Solution-Focused Therapist and Coach (CSFT & CSFC), accredited by the Canadian Council of Professional Certification; and a certified Behavioural and Career Consultant (CBCC) by the Institute for Motivational Living, USA. Charlie is also the author of *Praying the Psalms for the Half-Full Soul* and *The Devil Goes for Life Coaching*.

In *Wonderfully Alive*, Charlie Ong has laid out a roadmap towards health and happiness through our multifaceted journeys of life. As an experienced mental health professional, Charlie demonstrates that mental wellbeing is not just a component of our existence, but rather the result of a conscious and realistic approach permeating and underpinning every aspect of our life. Recognising the complexity of our human condition, this book blends an impressive array of psychological perspectives, helping strategies and philosophical insights – humanising them into an accessible and engaging format. Charlie's wealth of experience from his years working as a counsellor is evident within these pages.

At first glance, this book appears to be written as a self-help guide intended for the lay reader who yearns to experience an enriched life in a holistic and healthy way. Anecdotes, analogies, and Charlie's personal reflections flesh out the variety of self-management strategies and helping models presented here. However, I can also imagine the book as a good resource for helping professionals, particularly those who have relatively recently embarked on their journey of development and growth. The counselling approaches given here will no doubt refresh and reinforce their appreciation of the many concepts and competencies they apply in their professional work – akin to receiving guidance and advice from a seasoned mentor.

This book also has a distinctly personal dimension. Charlie offers his own religious faith as a means of acknowledging the spiritual aspect of our human experience. Those who share Charlie's religious faith may find this enriching, while readers who have a different (or no) religious affiliation will find that the book is written so that the key helping strategies remain clear and distinct, from a secular perspective.

I am happy that Charlie has decided to encapsulate his considerable experience in this book. I warmly recommend it as a resource to anyone –lay reader and helping professional alike – who seeks a holistic approach to health and happiness, and wishes to draw upon the perspectives of an experienced helping professional to chart their own roadmap towards feeling 'Wonderfully Alive'.

Dr Jessica Leong
CEO/Clinical & Academic Director
Executive Counselling and Training Academy (ECTA)

CONTENTS

If you put wealth and health in front of people and ask them to pick one, most people will say they choose health. But in my work with people, while many rank family and health as most important, in the course of coaching or counselling they reveal decisions and habits that put the acquisition of wealth and fame as foremost in their life. Do not always listen to what people say – watch what they do.

Jack Ma Yun, the founder of Alibaba once said, 'If you put bananas and money in front of monkeys, the monkeys will choose bananas because monkeys do not know that money can buy a lot of bananas.' Monkeys are not necessarily foolish in choosing bananas, because if they choose money, how are they going to buy the bananas?

Jack's story about the monkeys may have helped some of us see the folly of our choice. For if you put wealth and health in front of people, while people may say they choose health, most choose wealth, judging by their lifestyles. This is because most people focus only on the immediate, and do not yet appreciate that health can offer us much more – happiness, freedom and the opportunities to create wealth. A. J. Reb Materi put it succinctly, 'So many people spend their health gaining wealth, and then have to spend their wealth to regain their health.'

The pursuit of health is paramount. But what is health? According to the World Health Organization (WHO), health is not merely the absence of disease or infirmity but a state of complete physical, mental and social well-being. Too often, we think only of physical health. That is why if you care to notice, you will find there are many physically healthy yet unhappy people. Likewise, there are people whose happiness is short-lived because they live such an unhealthy lifestyle.

Health is a holistic state – physical, mental, relational and spiritual. Where you find good health, you can also find the much-treasured happiness. Health and happiness are not twin peaks to be scaled separately, but a twin pack that comes together. The pursuit of health and happiness is therefore a single journey that ends in holistic wellness.

Welcome to your journey to health and happiness!

> *Health is the new wealth.*
>
> *Happiness is the new success.*

PART I

BEGINNING OUR JOURNEY

Beginning Our Journey

In our pursuit for health and happiness, let us begin our journey with some spring cleaning. How about we start by cleaning up our negative emotions? Why? Because negative emotions bother us. Does clearing them sound good? But as you shall soon see, negative emotions are great raw materials. So instead of sweeping them under the rug or emptying them out, let us turn these raw materials into positive energy.

`How is that possible?` you may ask. Well, turn the page.

TURNING NEGATIVE EMOTIONS INTO POSITIVE ENERGY

What are Negative Emotions?

Are you mad, sad or scared most of the time? If instead of being glad, you are feeling mad (angry), sad or scared, you are experiencing one of the three common negative emotions felt by humans. Close cousins of these three emotions are hate, frustration, jealousy, regret, despair, grief, depression, shame, guilt, doubt, anxiety, et cetera.

Persistent, pervasive and pointless negative emotions diminish joy, douse courage and snuff out hope. They also cause us to question our faith and ruffle our peace. Essentially, unchecked persistent negative emotions sap our energy.

Are Negative Emotions Bad?

Negative emotions are natural responses to stimuli, such as setbacks, failures, or other stressors. Though serving a purpose, negative emotions are never the destination. They are signposts leading us to greater self-awareness and higher perspectives, qualities which increase our resilience to face adversities. Important as they are, anger, fear and grief do not have the final say.

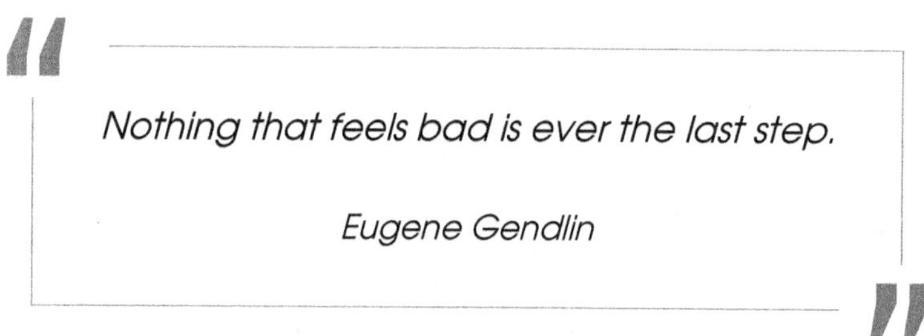

It may surprise you to learn that although negative emotions are horrible masters, they are good servants. For them to be profitable servants, you first need to accept them when they show up. When you are feeling angry or sad, allow yourself to experience your true feelings, without avoiding, restraining or criticising them. Acknowledge and identify them by their names. Often, when our self-worth is bruised, instead of naming what we feel as hurt, we react in anger. We confuse hurt with anger because we name our emotions wrongly. Be honest with your feelings.

Constantly remind yourself that negative emotions are natural emotional responses to your situations. Do not deny, avoid or suppress negative emotions, but allow yourself to feel your *genuine* emotions. Do not spiritually short-circuit your negative emotions. Like wild stallions, they can be tamed into submission, but not before you allow them to run their full course. Allowing your feelings to run their full course is not acting out your emotions in harmful ways. It has to do with you feeling your genuine emotion, naming it correctly, and turning it into positive energy.

For example, when we finally realize we have been using anger to cover up our low self-esteem, we start to work on improving our poor self-esteem instead of learning to manage our anger. In the same way, only when we finally acknowledge we have an anxiety issue, will we seek help to understand our anxiety and to manage it. Too many people hide behind their bottles or gaming consoles and blame the chemical hooks for their addictions, instead of admitting they have an anxiety problem.

It is understandable that a generation so used to fast food, instant coffee and food delivery would prefer quick-fix solutions by redirecting negative emotions to the junk mailbox. Hit with anxiety? No problem. Just escape into the world of computer gaming. Angry with your spouse? Drown out your annoyance with alcohol. Frustrated with the kids? Tune out by tuning in to Netflix. Escapism is a common way to cope with negative emotions, but unfortunately it is not the right way to deal with such feelings.

I once discussed negative emotions with a teenager. At the end of it, he called them fire alarms. Yes, they are fire alarms that give out warning sirens when the house is on fire. The siren calls out to us to put out the fire. Wouldn't it be silly to just turn off the fire alarm and not put out the fire? But that is what many would do – ignore the fire by switching off the fire alarm. Why? Because fighting the fire takes a lot of effort while switching the alarm off is very much easier to do.

Therefore, negative emotions are not bad in and of themselves. What matters is how we deal with them when they show up on our radar screen. If we persistently choose to avoid or ignore them, or condemn ourselves for having them, they will turn destructive over time. Let us walk with our negative emotions until we find a fertile ground to plant them, so that they can sprout and bear fruits.

Negative emotions are great teachers. They reveal to us our true self and real needs; and force us to deal with our latent problems. To name them as *negative* emotions does them a great disservice. It is destructive emotions that we are to avoid. As for negative emotions, we let them run their full course – we look in the direction they point and follow their lead until their hidden treasures are unearthed to us.

Kaitlin Robbs, an English teacher, came up with this Feeling Wheel[1] below. If you look at the outermost ring, these are the emotions that surface in response to an event. However, the negative ones are often smothered to death immediately, perhaps by poor upbringing, misguided moral or religious teachings.

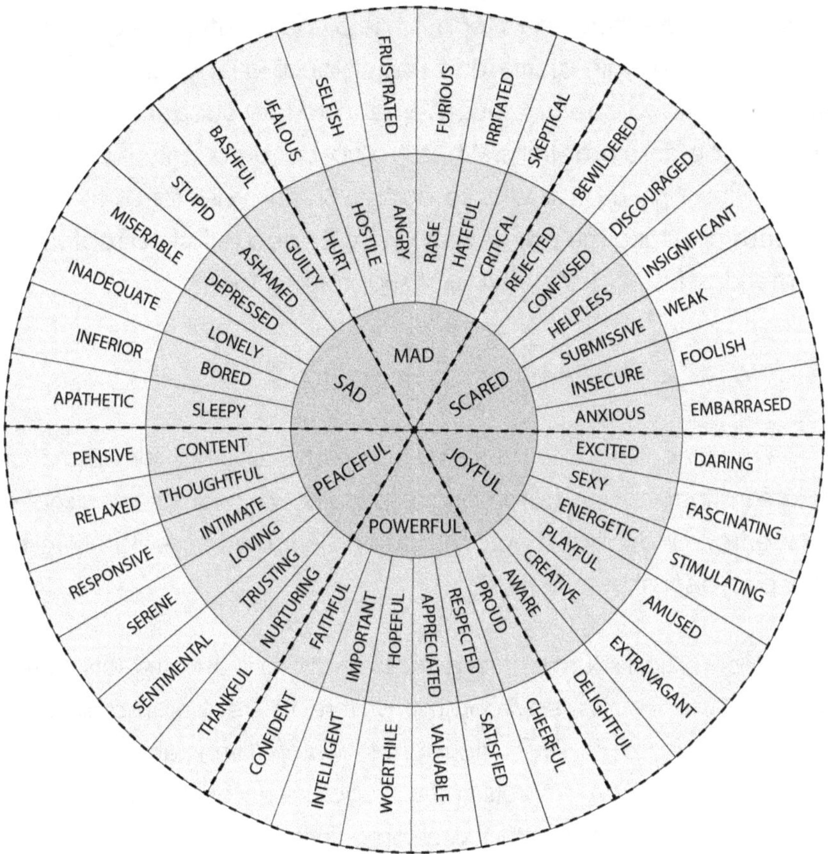

However, if you are honest with your negative emotions at this level, follow them to the secondary ring and all the way to the centre – you would be able to identify your core emotions. For example, you feel discouraged by your examination results. Instead of short-circuiting your discouragement by pseudo positive self-talk, you get acquainted with your discouragement and get to know it better. When you do, you could discover that at the core of your discouragement is *fear* – that you would end up as a failure in life. The discovery allows you to work on your fear, partly by dismissing its irrational component (failing an examination is not amounting to failing in life) and partly by overcoming the real fear with increased commitment and effort in preparing for future examinations.

When you experience negative emotions, use the Feeling Wheel to help you pinpoint your exact core feeling. Scan the outer ring, secondary ring and the core, back and forth, to help you identify all your emotions. In so doing, you gain clarity and understanding of your emotions and how they relate to one another. We need to feel our genuine emotions, especially the core emotions. When we do, our emotions help us to focus our attention and motivate us to action. But in order for us to have the right focus and take the correct actions, we need to first correctly identify our emotions, instead of denying or suppressing them.

Where do Negative Emotions Come From?

Emotions are our natural responses to external stimuli. At times, they are instinctive and automatic responses. For example, if a snake fell from the tree and landed on my shoulder, I would immediately respond in fear and disgust.

A common source of negative emotions is our stressors. Stressors, simply put, are events, environment or threats (real or imaginary) that trigger the release of stress hormones, which then lead to negative emotions. We all face stressors in life. Negative emotions are therefore a common life experience. What are some of the stressors in your life?

COMMON STRESSORS	NEGATIVE EMOTIONS
▶ Loss of a job	▷ Anxiety Anger ◁
▶ Excessive workload	
▶ Financial hardship	▷ Frustration Jealousy ◁
▶ Strained relationship	
▶ Conflicts	▷ Regret Depression ◁
▶ Death of a loved one	
▶ Poor health	▷ Shame Guilt ◁
▶ High expectations	
▶ Life transitions	▷ Grief Doubt ◁

In order to better understand the plausible causes of our negative emotions, we can adopt the Biopsychosocial–Spiritual (BPSS) Model. In this model, the biological, the psychological, the social, and the spiritual are different dimensions of the person, intricately interconnected with one another, and no one aspect can be disconnected from the whole.

An illustration of BPSS Model:

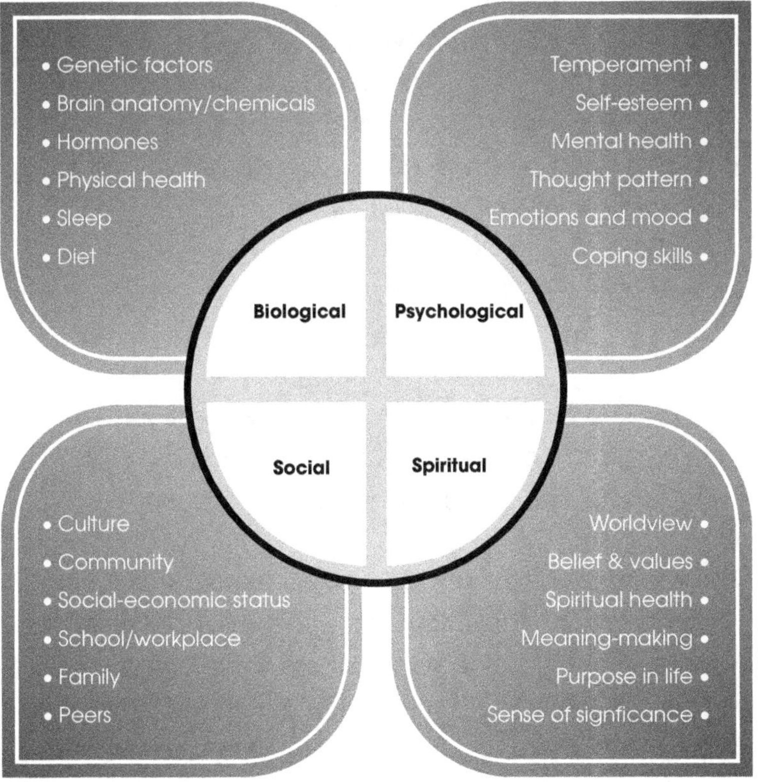

The BPSS Model is a simple yet holistic approach to understanding mental health. It enables us to have a broader and deeper understanding of negative emotions.

In his book, *In Search of Stones: A Pilgrimage of Faith, Reason, and Discovery,* Dr Scott Peck wrote,

> `It is a great principle in psychiatry that all symptoms are overdetermined. This means that they have more than one cause. I want to scream this from the rooftops: "All symptoms are overdetermined." Except that I want to expand it way beyond psychiatry. I want to expand it to almost everything. I want to translate it, "Anything of any significance is overdetermined. Everything worth thinking about has more than one cause." Repeat after me: "For any single thing of importance, there are multiple reasons."'*

This *great principle* applies to negative emotions. There is rarely a single cause for negative emotions. There is more than one, and usually several different causes for negative emotions.

For example, Jimmy lost his job and felt anxious and depressed. It seems easy and straightforward to attribute the negative emotions to his stressor – the loss of his job. This single cause model is too simplistic in fully understanding Jimmy's negative emotions and thus inadequate to help him turn them into positive energy. The BPSS Model enables us to take into consideration factors like his age, gender and health (**biological**); his self-esteem, personality and coping skills (**psychological**); his relationship with his wife, the needs of his family and the economic situation (**social**); and his beliefs and values (**spiritual**).

Once we prematurely conclude that there is but only one single cause for our negative emotion, we go around looking for that silver bullet. We are therefore likely to be blindsided by our desire to find quick-fix solutions. When we seek a simple and magical solution to a complicated problem, we are liable to fail. In reality, negative emotions have many roots and thus require a multi-pronged approach to turn them into positive energy.

What is Positive Energy?

Positive energy includes physical energy. It also encompasses positive *emotional* energy, *mental* strength and *spiritual* wellness. Below are some examples of positive energy:

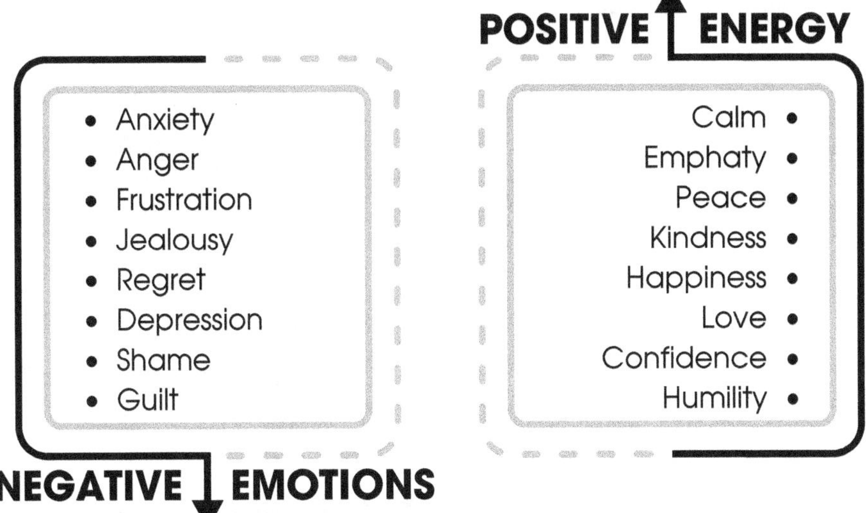

How Do We Turn Negative Emotions into Positive Energy?

If you had to pick one word to describe how you can turn negative emotions into positive energy, what *word* would you pick? I once asked an audience this question. Some of the answers they gave were:

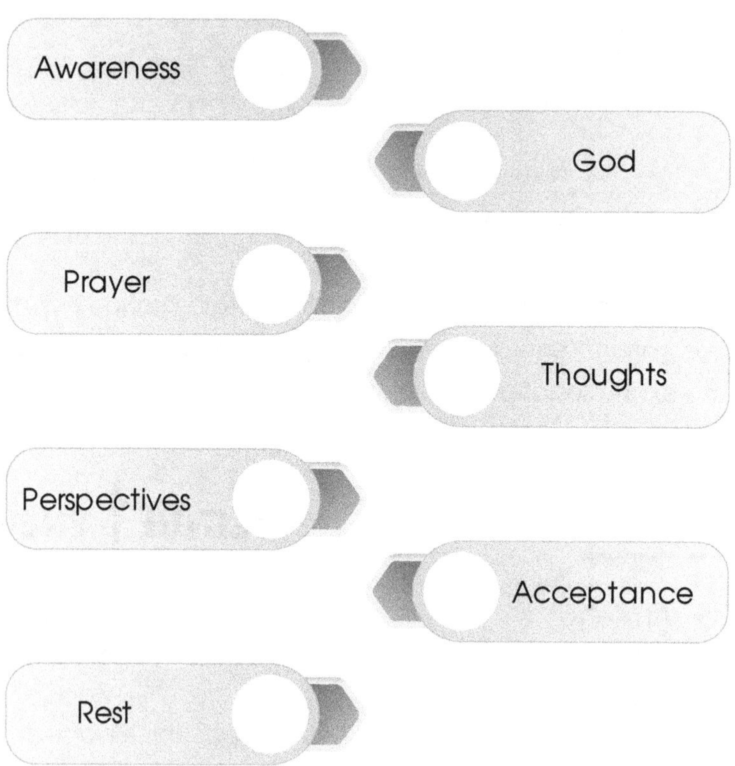

These are good answers. What about you? What word would you use to sum up how you can turn negative emotions into positive energy? Please do not turn the page until you have picked one word. 😬

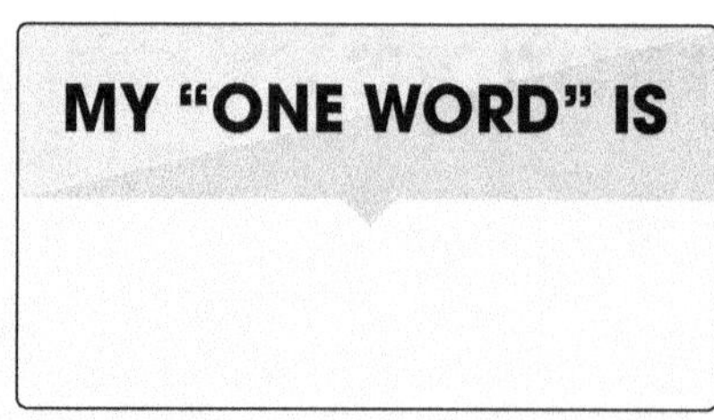

These words have been widely attributed to Albert Einstein, although there is no evidence that the genius wrote or spoke these words, and we might never find out who actually said them. But there is one thing we can be sure of – **these words are brilliant.**

If you want to turn negative emotions into positive energy, you cannot go on doing the same thing over and over again. You need to make changes in your life. Doing the same thing over and over again and expecting different results, is it plausible?

So, the next question that needs answering is this: **In what areas do I need to change?** There are three areas in which you can start to make changes in your life: Your **WOK**, **WALK** and **WATCH**.

CHAPTER ONE

CHANGING OUR WOK

Someone has noticed that 'stressed' spelled backwards is 'desserts', and light-heartedly suggested that to reverse being stressed, we could eat more desserts! So, are desserts the solution to fighting stress?

I can certainly see the humour in this suggestion and have personally experienced that an occasional timely dessert can indeed lift my mood! However, I seriously question using desserts to combat stress, especially when it is accompanied by indulgence and indiscretion.

One study published in the *British Medical Journal* found a possible link between sugary drinks and cancer. Commenting on this study, Ms Amelia Lake, an expert in public health nutrition at Britain's Teesside University, said that 'while this study doesn't offer a definitive causative answer about sugar and cancer, it does add to the overall picture of the importance of the current drive to reduce our sugar intake.'

If you regularly turn to desserts to combat stress, give heed to what Amelia further said: 'The message from the totality of evidence on excess sugar consumption and various health outcomes is clear – reducing the amount of sugar in our diet is extremely important.'

Almost everyone from my family of origin has diabetes. It is easy to deduce that my family probably has genes that are predisposed to diabetes. I therefore watch my sugar intake, including that of white milled rice. This is because **one bowl** of white rice has approximately the same carbohydrate content of **two cans** of soft drink.

The Harvard School of Public Health undertook a meta-analysis of four major studies, involving more than 350,000 people who were followed over four to 20 years. One of its findings showed that one plate of white rice eaten in a day – on a regular basis – raises the risk of diabetes by 11 percent in the overall population[1]. Diabetes experts are advising people to eat less rice.

If you have the habit of consuming beverages, snacks or food that are high in sugar content to boost your energy level, you might want to reconsider and think about the long-term side effects of this habit. By **WOK**, I mean changing to a diet that supports physical and mental health.

Some might question how a change in diet can turn negative emotions into positive energy. It is not difficult to see how a healthy diet could boost physical energy, but can it really produce positive energy, such as cheerfulness, enthusiasm or optimism?

I encourage you to watch the video on *How the Food You Eat Affects Your Brain* by Mia Nacamulli on TED-Ed. In less than five minutes, you will have a better understanding of how the food we eat can have an impact on our brain's functioning, development, energy and also **mood**.

Research has shown that proper nutrition can help reduce stress, anxiety and depressed mood. The link between food and mental health, as well as cognitive function, is strong. Studies show that foods containing serotonin, antioxidants, selenium, omega-3, vitamin D, zinc, magnesium, potassium and curcumin can reduce the symptoms of anxiety, stress and depression.

A diet that is high in vegetables, fruit, beans, nuts, whole grains, and lean protein is therefore helpful for your mental health. Changing your **WOK** is a good first step you can take to turn your negative emotions into positive energy.

A recent study[3] performed in Canada found that 'poor nutrition was linked to an increased risk of depression in middle-aged and older adults. Men who consume higher levels of fat and lower levels of omega-3 were more prone to depression. A diet low in fruits and vegetables was also associated with increased depression risks.' Your diet can put you at risk of depression!

My regular diet on weekdays includes turmeric powder, bananas, papayas, apples, oats, almonds, cashews, unsweetened soya milk, eggs, fish, pork and generous portions of vegetables. This is a part of my holistic approach to managing stress, anxiety and dismay in my daily life.

On weekends, I prioritize my meals around family and social needs. These are days off for me to enjoy the simple pleasures of life – while keeping an eye on excess.

I offer my 'menu' not as a template for you to follow but as an example for you to structure and then plan your own. To manage the symptoms of anxiety, stress and depression, you may use the food list in Appendix 1 to help change your **WOK**.

It is important to practise moderation when taking these foods. Excess may lead to side effects. And if you have health issues (allergies, diabetes or others) that require you to pay careful attention to your diet, consult a dietician or doctor before you rush to change your **WOK**.

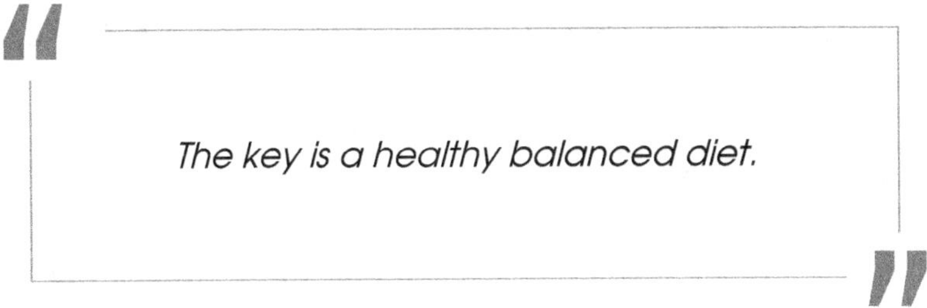

A mother once referred her son (in his early teens) for counselling. He was often stressed and anxious in the morning and would refuse to attend school because his stomach hurt. On days when the mother's persuasion or coercion prevailed, he would leave home for school, but his mother would end up having to pick him up from school before the morning break because his stomach pain would persist or worsen.

It was thought that her son's problem was psychosomatic, meaning that his bad stomach was caused by stress or anxiety. While he had stressors, they were common stressors faced by most teens, and they were insufficient to explain the disproportionate amount of stress or anxiety that he was experiencing. Furthermore, on 'good stomach days', the teen enjoyed school, and especially his co-curricular activity.

However, his irregular school attendance was a concern to his mother. She would use his father's frequent business trips and the days of particular subjects, tests and homework to speculate on his school 'reluctance' pattern. He was so frustrated that no one believed the reason for his stress and anxiety to be his bad stomach. He told me he was not as much refusing school as he was wishing for the pain to go away; and that he didn't need a counsellor but a doctor.

I believed him because of BPSS. Remember BPSS?

After several hospital visits, laboratory tests and reports, he was diagnosed to have poor gut health and eventually received the necessary treatment. And as his gut health improved, his school attendance improved as well.

At his last session with me, he told me that not only had his regular school attendance improved, but he had also even spent most of the school holidays in school to work with his friends to complete a school project. He no longer experienced excessive stress or anxiety. He was right – he did not need a counsellor; he needed a doctor.

This teen's story is a good anecdote on the link between gut health and mental health. What about scientific research? What does it say?

Researchers from Ohio State University did a study of 77 children aged 18 to 27 months and found that gut bacteria affect a toddler's temperament. 'There is definitely communication between bacteria in the gut and the brain, but we don't know which one starts the conversation,' said the OSU study's co-author, Dr Michael Bailey.

In 2015, *The New York Times Magazine* published an article 'Can the Bacteria in Your Gut Explain Your Mood?' Peter Andrey reported that the micro-organisms in our gut secrete chemicals, such as serotonin, dopamine, and gamma-aminobutyric acid (GABA). These are the same chemicals used by our neurons to communicate and regulate mood. Some neuroscientists are calling these gut microbes 'psychobiotics'.

> *It turns out that there's more to 'gut feeling' than we thought.*

Food scientist Heribert Watzke reminds us that the gut is connected to the emotional limbic system. Watzke tells the 'tale of two brains': one that is in our head, the other in our gut. He speaks of the gut being a full-fledged brain! And that these two brains speak with each other and make decisions.

It is fairly common knowledge that the way we feel affects our gut health. For example, protracted and excessive anxiety or stress can cause gastrointestinal problems. But now, the 'tale of two brains' adds to our understanding – our gut health can also influence the way we feel. Not only does the brain in our head talk with the gut, the 'brain in our gut' talks with the brain in our head[2].

Shilpa Ravella in her TED Ed video *How the Food You Eat Affects Your Gut* said, 'While we can't control all the factors that go into maintaining a healthy gut microbiome, we can manipulate the balance of our microbes by paying attention to what we eat.'

She recommends that 'dietary fibre from foods like fruits, vegetables, nuts, legumes, and whole grains is the best fuel for gut bacteria.'

So, you want to turn your negative emotions into positive energy?

Start by changing your WOK

I want to end this chapter by highlighting the danger of overplaying a healthy diet. While studies show that consuming foods rich in serotonin, antioxidants, selenium, omega-3, vitamin D, zinc, magnesium, potassium and curcumin can reduce the symptoms of anxiety, stress and depression, you should not **replace** your medication with these foods.

If you have been diagnosed with an anxiety disorder or depression, and have been prescribed medicine, you should not stop your medication without consulting your doctor. And if you have been wrestling with prolonged anxiety or depression, you should consult a psychiatrist or psychologist, instead of depending solely on a new diet. While not every case of mental illness needs to be treated with medicine, in some cases medicine is needed to kickstart and to support your recovery or to correct any chemical imbalances that perpetuate the symptoms of anxiety or depression.

Remember the BPSS MODEL we talked about earlier? We need a multi-pronged approach to mental wellness. There could be organic factors to your negative emotions, chemical imbalances, hormone deficiencies or other conditions.

For example, a man's level of hormones decreases with age. It decreases by about 10% every decade after age 30. A low testosterone level can lead to loss of muscle mass, weight gain and poor bone health. The decline in the testosterone production rate can also affect energy levels and mood, and cause loss of concentration, sleep disturbances and a decline in sex drive. If you notice these symptoms, consult a doctor to do a blood test to find out your testosterone level and whether some form of treatment is necessary. While every man will experience this hormone decrease that comes with age, not every man will suffer from testosterone deficiency or require treatment. It is good to find out whether your lower energy level, mood, concentration level and poor sleep are caused by testosterone deficiency. Similarly, for older women, if you are suffering from fatigue, anxiety or depressed mood, it is possible that menopause is the cause. Consult a doctor to ascertain if this is indeed so, and receive the right treatment.

The WOK of wellness has a wide spectrum that comprises a healthy diet that is necessary, health supplements if necessary and medicine when necessary. May you eat heartily and healthily on the journey to health and happiness!

In the pursuit of health and happiness, a common mistake that people make is to ignore, suppress or short-circuit negative emotions. Negative emotions are useful servants and helpful teachers. They are seedlings that can eventually bear fruits of positive energy. *If* we patiently cultivate them, we can turn negative emotions into positive energy.

Another common mistake that people make is to attribute a single cause to negative emotions. They examine their toxic social environment, scrutinise erroneous thought patterns or explore spiritual struggles. But they forget to take into consideration organic causes or biological factors that can contribute to emotional disturbance. The **WOK** of wellness is a good place to begin our journey of health and happiness.

CHAPTER TWO

CHANGING OUR WALK

In the preceding chapter, we discussed our **WOK**. Now we come to our **WALK**. By **WALK**, I am referring to the *way* we live. Our lifestyle is an important element in our emotional health. To come alive, we need to live well. This is a simple truth.

How can you improve your lifestyle? The answer is in two words: Make changes! Change begins when you start to act. It is crucial that you start, and not just think or talk about it.

> *You'll never change your life until you change something you do daily.*
>
> *John C. Maxwell*

When it comes to making lifestyle changes, we are more likely to succeed if we emphasize actions over thoughts, behaviours over beliefs and activities over feelings. John Bradshaw (a professional counsellor and a bestselling expert in addiction and recovery) shared one of the most important recovery rules for addiction: 'We have to act ourselves into the right way of feeling and thinking, rather than trying to think or feel ourselves into the right way of acting.'

Action begets good feelings, which in turn spur more actions. This creates a virtuous circle that becomes a habit over time. When you find it hard to overcome the inertia of laziness, goad yourself on with the saying 'Habits are first cobwebs, then cables.' You are not expected to churn out cables right from the start, just cobwebs. Cobwebs require you to only get off your seats and take that *first* small step. Do not demand of yourself the habit of cables right from the beginning. Be content with the habit of cobwebs – one action at a time, and one day at a time.

Laozi (老子), a 6th century B.C. Chinese philosopher, said, 'A journey of a thousand miles begins with a single step,' which in Chinese is '千里之行，始於足下'. Too often, we set our thoughts and feelings on the thousand miles. This deters us from even setting out. Yet we set out by taking the first step, and then following it with the second, and then the third and so forth. That is how every great endeavour gets accomplished. *Begin* to act by taking that *first* step. You would be surprised what that first step can do for you.

> *Life is like an ever-shifting kaleidoscope –*
>
> *a slight change, and all patterns alter.*
>
> *Sharon Salzberg*

Start by taking a first step. Make a slight change in your lifestyle in each of these three areas:

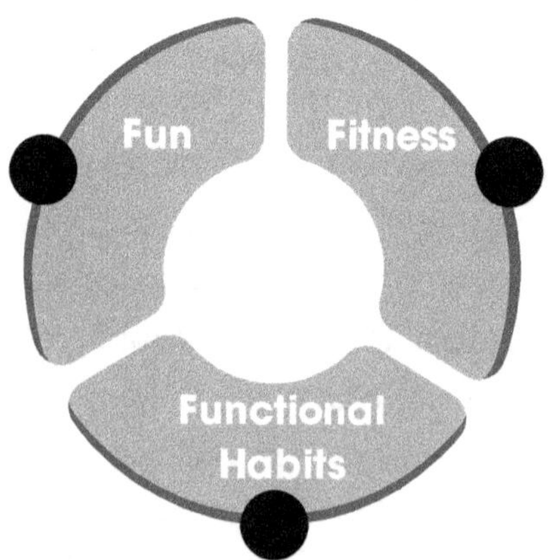

FUN

Delightful experiences break the monotony of life, and regular time-out frees us from the dullness of routine. Even though fun adds spice to life, many people hesitate to make time for fun. They think they have so much to do, but so little time. Perhaps, a timely reminder from Roald Dahl is helpful here: 'A little nonsense now and then is relished by the wisest men.'

Time spent on doing something fun is not wasteful. This is because joy rejuvenates us. This renewed strength will help us better manage our stress and make us more productive. The increased productivity more than makes up for the time we spend making fun. The Chinese have a saying, '事半功倍', which means 'expending half the effort yet achieving double the result'. Another saying is '休息是为了走更长远的路', and that is 'taking a break enables one to go even further'.

We need to change our mindset from 'I don't have time for fun because I am too busy with work' to 'I can achieve twice as much in half the time with increased productivity that comes from renewed energy'.

Now this relaxation of the mind from work consists on playful words or deeds. Therefore, it becomes a wise and virtuous man to have recourse to such things at times.

Thomas Aquinas

Not all jobs or tasks are fun though we yearn for them to be. Coming up with tedious reports is not fun; the jobs of security personnel (especially those guarding secluded army camps and coast guards on night watch, et cetera) and the many so-called dead-end jobs. It becomes even more important for the people in these unenviable jobs to make time for fun when they are off duty.

Make time for fun. This seems pretty straightforward. Or is it? A 2019 Straits Times report[1] says that taking a break does not seem to come easy for stressed-out Singaporeans. 31% of the 600 Singaporeans and permanent residents polled said that they did not know how to relax, and almost half of them were stressed by the thought of doing nothing.

How can we add fun to our life? What are some ways to break free from our monotonous routine and rejuvenate ourselves with positive energy?

'Retail therapy' is at the top of the list for some women. If you enjoy shopping, either alone or with friends, and it is the *experience* that delights you and not the *things*, 'retail therapy' may be an option.

In their book *Happy Money: The Science of Smarter Spending*, authors Elizabeth Dunn and Michael Norton, drawing upon years of quantitative and qualitative research, recommend that we buy experiences rather than things. Their research shows that spending money on material things is less satisfying than spending money on enjoying experiences. Instead of that new designer bag, a branded watch or an expensive pair of shoes, you might want to consider going for a dinner outing with friends, a holiday or a concert, et cetera.

> *To add fun to your life, buy experiences rather than things.*

If you are unable to make the time for a holiday, a concert or a movie right now, plan it and put it down on your calendar – even if it is a few months down the road. Study shows that when people think about watching their favourite movie, their endorphin levels rise by as much as 27%. So, when you need a boost of happiness, take a look at your calendar, and then daydream a little about that dinner, that holiday or that concert. And do you know that the most enjoyable part of an activity is often the anticipation, and that the happiest day for holiday-goers is the day *before* the trip?

What are some fun experiences that you can add to your life? I hesitate to share my list of fun experiences, as 'one man's medicine is another man's poison.' And truth be told, my wife would dissuade you from using my list, as she perceives them as boring!

In order to include a wide variety of fun activities enjoyed by people from different backgrounds, personalities, age groups and gender, I asked my diverse groups of friends this question, 'What are some fun experiences that you can add to your life?' Here are some of their answers:

With my girlfriend:

1. Go to Johor Bahru to eat and shop
2. Meet at a new food outlet
3. Enjoy high tea together
4. Volunteer to serve at a hospice once a month
5. Put aside one Saturday morning a month for a hospital or home visit
6. Learn a new hobby, recipe or art form

With my husband:

1. Exercise together
2. Walk from one park to another using the park connector
3. Spend an evening at a lounge drinking and listening to music

… joining a ukulele jam session, making pineapple tarts together with friends or playing a mahjong session with them

1. Do something you have never tried before? E.g. horse riding
2. Pick up a new hobby? E.g. ballroom dancing, balloon sculpting or painting
3. Visit a new place? A new mall? A local farm?
4. Surprise a stranger, a cleaner or a security guard with a free meal?

Surely from the examples of the above activities, you can get some ideas for fun activities that will suit you.

To add fun to life, many people turn to social media, computer gaming or online dramas and movies. These are undeniably fun. Playing computer games gives you an adrenaline rush, and watching a good movie helps you unwind at the end of a tiring day. Besides, they are easy, accessible and convenient. However, there is another side to them – they are also risky. You need to be aware of their pitfalls because it is easy to do them in excess.

> *Connecting online can disconnect you from life.*

A study[2] has shown that teenagers who spend more than three hours a day on social media are more likely to have mental health problems, such as depression, anxiety, loneliness, aggression and anti-social behaviour, than those who do not.

Another study[3] by KK Women's and Children's Hospital (KKH) and the National University of Singapore (NUS) shows that when children are exposed to electronic devices, computers and television at 18 months or earlier, they are more likely to experience disrupted sleep as well as emotional and behavioural difficulties. Kimberly Lim from *TODAY* newspaper summarized the following from the study: 'Basically, when the children spent time in front of screens, they had disrupted sleep, nightmares, insomnia and so on. This in turn caused them to have emotional and behavioural difficulties, such as tantrums, hyperactivity and an inability to focus.'

CNN Health also reported[4] that 'a new study scanned the brains of children 3 to 5 years old and found those who used screens more than the recommended one hour a day without parental involvement had lower levels of development in the brain's white matter – an area key to the development of language, literacy and cognitive skills.'

The WHO recognizes gaming addiction as a mental health disorder and added this disorder to the 11th revision of International Classification of Diseases **(ICD-11)** in mid-2018, the organisation's official diagnostic manual. The American Psychiatric Association (APA) did not include gaming addiction in its 2013 edition of the Diagnostic and Statistical Manual of Mental Disorders **(DSM-5)**. At the time of publication, the APA's view was that there was insufficient evidence. However, it recommended further research and included a section on the proposed symptoms of internet gaming disorder.

It is true that many people do not have any gaming addiction or disorders, but their excessive gaming undoubtedly is affecting their mental health, posing problems for their lives and those of their loved ones.

Adding fun to life does not come easily to some of us. However, this is no excuse to be lazy or unimaginative, and mindlessly connect to the internet for quick-fix pleasures. Neither should we follow the herd instinct or yield to peer influence on our choice of fun activities.

In choosing fun experiences, it is helpful to know the difference between pleasure and happiness (the meaning as used in this book). Pleasure is short-lived; happiness is deeper and longer lasting. Pleasure is a momentary feeling that comes from physical senses; happiness touches the heart and outlasts the moment through the memory of its meaningful impact.

Moments of pleasure do not last; like flowers, they are here today, gone tomorrow. Pleasurable activities are like clouds without rain; they cannot satisfy and will leave you thirsty for more. This can lead to indulgence or addiction. The Chinese have a saying, '玩物丧志', which means 'pleasures blunt the edge of a person's ambition and sap a person's spirit.' We need to exercise caution and restraint when it comes to the choice of our pleasure-seeking activities.

There is nothing wrong with having pleasure. Happiness provides us with much pleasure. The problem is if we seek pleasure in and of itself, that is, for the sole purpose of sheer pleasure – disregarding everyone and everything else – we will end up disillusioned and disconnected. Happiness eludes us and we end up living from a moment of pleasure to the next. Pleasure-seeking always ends in emptiness.

Having sex is pleasurable. Making love is also pleasurable. The latter involves pleasurable sex in a *loving* relationship and gives you happiness. Sex without love can give you momentarily pleasure but not happiness. The sensual gratification is short-lived, and the pleasurable experience vanishes after the act. In its place, you often find shame, guilt, hollowness or insatiable passion. The key difference between making love and having sex is the presence of love.

It is the same with computer gaming (or any other pleasurable activity). When computer gaming is set in the context of responsibility, self-control and prudence, it gives you much happiness. However, when you engage in it for its sheer pleasure, that is what you will get – sheer pleasure. Sheer pleasures are like passing clouds. They do not last. Like clouds without rain, they are not able to satisfy you with the happiness you long for. And because they do not satisfy, many keep returning for more and end up with an addiction.

The key difference between happiness and pleasure is the presence of love. Love forms the basis of a happy relationship. Pleasure-seeking in the context of a loving relationship leads to happiness. However, let us not erroneously conclude that loving others excludes the love of self. Loving yourself is not 'me first' or 'me only', but 'me too'. You can derive much happiness from reading a book while sipping iced tea on a scenic beach, as long as this act of self-care does not prevent you from loving others. That is why love is sometimes known by its other names – kindness, responsibility, consideration, respect, giving, self-sacrifice, compassion, et cetera. Your computer gaming or golfing cannot cause distress for others. But without love, it only brings you pleasure, not happiness.

Besides knowing the difference between happiness and pleasure, taking an integrated approach to **fun**, **fitness** and **functional** habits can also lead us to healthier choices of fun activities. These **Three Fs** are interconnected, and it is best not to see them as separate compartments in our lives. Therefore, we will now turn our attention to the second **F: Fitness**, followed by **Functional Habits**.

FITNESS

Physical fitness[5] improves our focus, memory and mood. It also lowers the risk of dementia. A recent study[6] shows that physical exercise not only improves physical health, but also reduces episodes of depression, even in those who have a higher genetic risk.

When we exercise, our body releases endorphins[7] which trigger a euphoric feeling in our body, similar to that of taking morphine. But do not worry; though structurally similar to morphine, endorphins do not lead to addiction. The good feeling that follows after a good run is called 'runner's high'. Anecdotally, some claim this 'high' to be addictive and this is what got them hooked on running.

Even if this were true, go for it! The 'endorphin rush' is good for you. Get your regular 'high' from this 'endogenous morphine' (internally produced morphine) by exercising regularly. This regular 'exercise high' helps to reduce stress and anxiety, raises self-esteem as well as improves sleep. When you put on your running shoes to go for a run, you are running towards positive energy!

What could be better than regular physical exercise? Well, actually there is something better – it is engaging in **sports**[8] with friends. It turns out that if you can find a sport that you enjoy and play it together with a team that you like, the benefits go beyond the physical and mental benefits of exercising alone. Being in a team places you in a supportive community that can give you a sense of belonging and acceptance. As you improve in performance, gain more confidence and build your self-esteem in the process, you also learn commitment, trust and teamwork. Study has shown that these additional benefits can reduce the risk of depression. To me, the biggest prize of team sport is the long and lasting effects it has on a person – resilience and a growth mindset. Both of these attributes not only support mental health, but also promote personal growth. Continual personal growth is essential in the journey to health and happiness.

I understand that team sport is not always feasible for some of us. Minimally, find a group of friends with whom you can run, exercise or go to the gym with. I used to run with a group of friends from my neighbourhood on Saturday mornings. However, after I moved to a different neighbourhood, we stopped our Saturday morning runs. I still run or walk on Saturday mornings but sadly, it is no longer as much fun.

FUNCTIONAL HABITS

The third **F** stands for functional habits. By this, I am referring to habits that are functional (*workable or feasible*) and help us function (*work*) better. Functional habits improve our functionality, which *The Cambridge Dictionary* defines as 'the quality of being useful, practical, and right for the purpose for which something was made.'

> *What does a fully functional human being look like?*

Human beings are more than just living organisms. There is more to life than just being alive! The seed of eternity is sown in every human heart. No forces, natural or unnatural, can stop it from germinating. Its shoot will break through the soil that buries it in darkness to meet the sun, sky, mountains, trees, pasture, animals and birds. The eternity that humans desire is not measured by the length of time alone, but more by the breadth and depth of life. It is pointless to live forever unless there is a point to it.

We are wired with both the desire and capacity for a full life. A fully functional person finds meaning, purpose and significance in his or her work, play and relationships, and engages in continual growth, and fruitfulness with vigour. However, we need *health* to lead this full life.

The WHO defines health as 'a state of complete physical, mental and social well-being and not merely the absence of disease or infirmity.' The absence of sickness does not necessarily mean you are healthy. Think about that. Furthermore, WHO advocates *holistic* health (not merely physical health) as 'a resource for everyday life'. Without the resource of holistic health, it is hard to live everyday life well, let alone pursue a full life.

Holistic health enables us to live a full life. And as our lifestyle determines our health, a full life therefore requires that we lead a healthy lifestyle. Makes sense? Besides food, fitness and fun, it is vital that we support our healthy lifestyle with *functional* habits.

Brian Tracy (a top-selling author on self-development) says that 'successful people are simply those with successful habits.' If 'successful people are simply those with successful habits', then healthy people are simply those with healthy habits. A fully functional person is simply the person with functional habits. Our habits set us on a course to our destiny.

> *Functional habits are habits that are functional (work-able) and help us function (work) better.*

So far, we have discussed that to begin living a healthy lifestyle, we start with eating healthy **food**. Then we make time for **fun** and exercise regularly to improve and maintain our **fitness**. It is also important to have **functional** habits to support and sustain the healthy lifestyle.

You probably have noticed that at the beginning of a new year, gyms are mostly packed with people charged up by new year's resolutions; but by Lunar New Year or Valentine's Day, attendance has dropped to its usual level. To kickstart a new lifestyle, begin with activities that are *workable* for you, that are practical and doable. For example, do not start with unrealistic plans, such as a daily 10-kilometre run. Instead, start with a 3-kilometre jog two or three times a week. Gradually increase the distance and frequency when the momentum kicks in. It is also helpful to identify someone who will run with you and encourage you on the new endeavour. Trading success stories with this person regularly will also help you sustain your new habit.

At this point, I would like to remind you of the BPSS (Biopsychosocial-Spiritual) model of health which we introduced earlier. In pursuing a holistic approach to wellness, we need to include habits that contribute to our total well-being – body, mind, social and spiritual. In this vein, I would like to suggest three functional habits: **SLEEP, MEDITATION** and **GRATITUDE**.

SLEEP

'Sleep is a non-negotiable biological necessity. It is your life-support system, and it is Mother Nature's best effort yet at immortality,' says sleep scientist Matthew Walker, a professor of neuroscience and psychology at the University of California. In his TED *talk Sleep is Your Super Power*, Walker shares 'the wonderfully good things that happen when you get sleep, but the alarmingly bad things that happen when you don't get enough, both for your brain and for your body.'

Let us start with the 'alarmingly bad things' insufficient sleep can do to the body. 'Men who sleep five hours a night have significantly smaller testicles than those who sleep seven hours or more', says Walker. Women are not spared – lack of sleep causes equivalent impairments to female reproductive health.

Not only does sleep have an impact on the size of a man's testicle, it also affects his testosterone level. If you are surviving on five to six hours of sleep a night, your testosterone level is the same as your friends who are ten years older than you. Yuck! Lack of sleep will age you by almost a decade!

The data from Walker's research also shows that sleep has an impact on our learning, memory, immune system and cardiovascular system, and the lack of it can even erode our genetic code! Insufficient sleep also increases our risk of getting dementia, cancer of the bowel, cancer of the prostate, cancer of the breast, heart attack or stroke. This is rather serious stuff. I strongly recommend that you watch Walker's talk on TED to learn the importance of sleep on our physical and mental health.

So, how much sleep do we need? Sleep experts, Dr Rebecca Robbins and Dr David Rapoport, recommend seven to eight hours of sleep for adults. They debunk the myth[10] that many adults need only five hours of sleep or less. Epidemiological data and data from sleep labs show that five hours is insufficient for most adults. Our brain and body do not adapt to less sleep. Studies show that our performance deteriorates when we don't get sufficient sleep. I have heard men who boasted that they were able to perform well despite having only five or six hours of sleep. They were probably right. But can you imagine the much higher level of performance that they could have attained if they had slept longer?

To improve our sleep, Walker recommends that we avoid the damaging and harmful impact of alcohol and caffeine. I have heard people claim that alcohol helps them fall asleep. While intoxication does help you fall asleep faster, it unfortunately lowers the quality of sleep, particularly in the second half of your sleep duration. A small glass of wine can be good for health, but you would do well to avoid intoxication and of course abuse, and stay away from the pitfalls of using alcohol as a sleep aid. Regular use of alcohol to help you fall asleep can lead to alcohol dependence. You might be surprised to know that alcohol abuse ranks as the second most common mental illness in Singapore[9] and affects one in 24 Singaporeans.

Now that you have been made aware of the damaging and harmful impact of alcohol on sleep, let us move on to coffee. What about coffee? Aren't there reports[11] about the health benefits of coffee? Yes, there is increasing evidence that *moderate* coffee consumption might be good for our health. Besides being linked with a longer lifespan, studies have found that its consumption (in *moderation*) may also reduce the risk of heart attack, heart failure, gout, stroke,

Type 2 diabetes, Parkinson's disease, cirrhosis, liver cancer and uterine cancer.

As always, an important keyword to take note here is moderation. What is the moderate consumption of coffee? Well, the 2015 Dietary Guidelines Advisory Committee (commissioned by the US Department of Health and Human Services and the US Department of Agriculture) recommends three to five cups per day as the 'moderate coffee consumption' for 'a healthy dietary pattern'.

The concern here is not coffee per se but caffeine. While coffee is a common source of caffeine, other beverages, such as tea, soft drinks and energy drinks, as well as chocolate, also contain caffeine. The European Food Safety Authority (EFSA) in their *Scientific Opinion on the Safety of Caffeine* advises a maximum intake of 400 mg per day and single dose of up to 200 mg. While a cup of instant coffee contains about 60 mg of caffeine, commercially brewed coffee can contain more than 150 mg per serving. We need to bear in mind these facts in order to guard against excessive caffeine intake.

Over-consumption of caffeine increases feelings of anxiety, hyperactivity and nervousness, and it also impairs sleep, especially when the coffee is consumed close to bedtime. Hence, it is good to regulate your coffee consumption. But what if this seems insurmountable? We will ask the Kiwis to help us here. New Zealanders are very creative with their road signs. Their speed limit sign reads '**IT'S NOT A TARGET. DRIVE TO THE CONDITIONS.**' Similarly, three to five cups of coffee or 400 mg of caffeine per day is not a target. You need to be aware of your own conditions. The real issue here is not to let caffeine affect a good night's sleep. Personally, over time, I have found that keeping to two cups of coffee a day (and drinking them by noon) works best for me. To do otherwise will affect my sleep. What about you? Find out what works best for you regarding your daily caffeine intake, and regulate it accordingly. 400 mg of caffeine is not a target. Drink to your conditions.

If you continue to struggle with getting adequate sleep after avoiding the negative impacts of alcohol and caffeine, take note of another recommendation by Walker: Avoid naps during the day. In addition, Dr Robbins recommends that you avoid exercising within four hours of bedtime as this might also disturb your sleep.

Besides the avoidance list for better sleep, Walker gives two other pieces of advice to get 'a full night of sleep': 'The first is regularity. Go to bed at the same time, wake up at the same time, no matter whether it is the weekday or the weekend. The second is keep it cool. Your body needs to drop its core temperature by about two to three degrees Fahrenheit to initiate sleep and then to stay asleep, and it's the reason you will always find it easier to fall asleep in a room that's too cold than too hot. So, aim for a bedroom temperature of around 65 degrees, or about 18 degrees Celsius. That's going to be optimal for the sleep of most people.'

In a 70-year study of more than 70,000 children across five generations, scientists in Britain have been studying the children's lives to find out the reasons why some of them grow up happy and healthy, while others maladjusted and rebellious. Using the data from this study, Helen Pearson, a science journalist, shares her findings about good parenting on TED[12]. She lists the following as good parental behaviours associated with improved outcomes for children, even the at-risk kids:

- Talking to and listening to your kids

- Making it clear you have ambitions for their future

- Being emotionally warm

- Teaching them letters and numbers

- Taking them on excursions

- Reading to them daily (and encouraging them to read for pleasure)

- Maintaining a regular bedtime.

Did you pick up on the last item – 'maintaining a regular bedtime'? Pearson says 'they looked at the bedtime routines of about 10,000 children born at the turn of the millennium. The data showed that those children who were going to bed at different times were more likely to have behavioural problems, and that those that switched to having regular bedtimes often showed an improvement in behaviour, and that was really crucial, because it suggested it was the bedtime routines that were really helping things get better for those kids.'

Sleep scientist Matt Walker recommends regularity for better sleep for he said, 'Regularity is king, and it will anchor your sleep and improve the quantity and the quality of that sleep.' Place Walker's recommendation side by side with Pearson's findings and it is not difficult to conclude that *regularity* not only improves the quantity and quality of our sleep, but also improves our behaviour!

Maintaining good sleep hygiene – avoiding excessive alcohol and caffeine, and adhering to a regular bedtime – is important to improve our physical and mental health. Make it a priority to improve your sleep hygiene if you are serious about your wellness.

MEDITATION

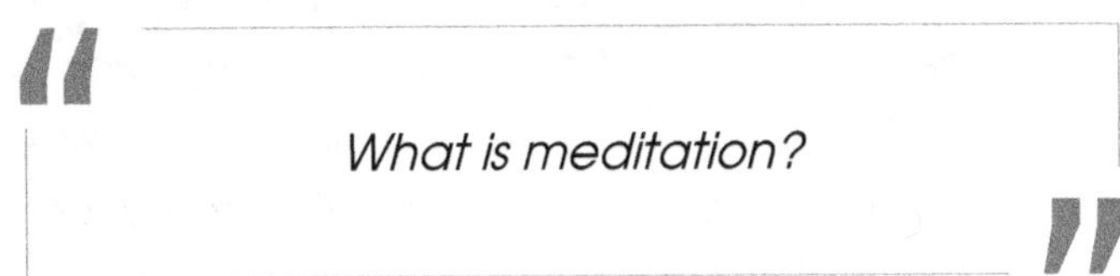

The Cambridge Dictionary defines meditation as 'the act of giving your attention to only one thing, either as a religious activity or as a way of becoming calm and relaxed.'

I like Wikipedia's version: 'Meditation is a practice where an individual uses a technique – such as mindfulness, or focusing the mind on a particular object, thought or activity – to train attention and awareness, and achieve a mentally clear and emotionally calm and stable state.'

Joyce Meyer, an American Christian author and speaker, says, 'If you know how to worry, you know how to meditate. It means to think of something over and over.' The Hebrew word for meditation, 'siach', is the same word for 'concern', 'complaint' and 'occupied'.

In meditation, instead of occupying your mind with a concern or complaint, you occupy it with thoughts that calm you down and give you peace. Slow, deep abdominal breathing exercises and an enhanced sitting posture can accompany meditation for better focus and relaxation.

> *If you know how to worry, you know how to meditate.*
>
> *It means to think of something over and over.*
>
> *Joyce Meyer*

In her study[13], Sara Lazar, a neuroscientist, shows that 50-year-olds can maintain the brains of 25-year-olds if they meditate daily. The cortexes of most people shrink as they age, but her research found that 50-year-old 'meditators' had the same amount of grey matter in the frontal cortex as participants half their age. The frontal cortex is the brain region that is linked to decision-making and working memory.

Lazar found that people who had no prior experience in meditation had their brains changed for the better in just eight weeks of participation in a meditation programme. In just eight weeks, there were developments in several regions of the brain that are linked to learning, memory, emotional regulation, empathy and perspective-taking ability. In addition, for these 'new meditators', the regions in their brains associated with fear, anxiety, aggression and stress levels shrank.

Participants in Lazar's study averaged about 27 minutes of meditation a day, but other studies have shown that you can make significant changes in just 15 to 20 minutes.

Whoa! These are incredible results for an investment of just 15 minutes every day! Meditation is definitely one functional habit you should consider if you desire wellness of the body, mind and spirit.

For those who want to start meditation but are clueless as to how to begin, I have included instructions on meditation in Appendix 2.

GRATITUDE

If meditation is essentially thinking of something calming over and over again, I would like to highlight *a form* of meditation that is profoundly helpful for the well-being of our body, soul, mind and spirit.

I once went away for a 36-hour spiritual retreat. One of the activities I engaged in was to sit in an empty church or cathedral for an hour to do some reading, praying and meditating. In the chapel of a small church, I decided to write out one hundred things for which I was grateful. Listing the first twenty or so was relatively easy. After that, it was an uphill task. Surprisingly, as I drew near the end of list, it became easy again. In that one hour, I learnt that I had so many things to be grateful for. I also noticed my spirit becoming lighter and my happiness baseline going up. It was a truly delightful reflective exercise. I recommend that you engage in this 'gratitude meditation' regularly.

> *Happiness isn't complicated. It is a humble state of gratitude for simple pleasures, tender mercies, recognized blessings, and inherent beauty.*
>
> *Richelle E. Goodrich*

As I write this section, I realize that my heart has been feeling sad lately. My thoughts have been on certain relationship difficulties, my personal health, hearing loss and declining memory, as well as my concern for my mother's cognitive impairment and deteriorating health. With my focus on these distressing matters, my mood has been dipping.

I keep a gratitude journal in which I do not make entries often enough. Upon reflection, I realised I could have focused on things that have gone well – instead of things that have gone wrong – had I been more disciplined in making regular entries in my gratitude journal. In order to keep my focus on what I *have* instead of what I do *not have*, I need the habit of gratitude.

Giving Thanks Can Make You Happier[14] by Harvard Health Publishing says, 'In positive psychology research, gratitude is strongly and consistently associated with greater happiness. Gratitude helps people feel more positive emotions, relish good experiences, improve their health, deal with adversity, and build strong relationships.'

The Harvard article recommends the following ways to cultivate gratitude on a regular basis:

- **Write a thank-you note**. Writing a thank-you letter or card to express your appreciation of a person's impact on your life not only makes you happier, it also nurtures your relationship with the person. A good guide is to send at least one 'gratitude' letter a month. Send it or deliver and read it to the person, if possible. If the convenience of using text messages will encourage you to write – by all means, use them.

- **Thank someone mentally.** Even if you have no time to write, it is still helpful to think about the person who has been kind or nice to you, and mentally thank the individual.

- **Keep a gratitude journal.** Make it a habit to write down, or share with a loved one, your thoughts on the gifts or kindness you have received at the end of each day.

- **Count your blessings.** Pick a time to sit down and write about your blessings once a week – reflecting on what went well or what you are grateful for. As you write, be specific and think about the sensations you felt when something good happened to you.

- **Pray.** For people who are religious, prayer is a good way to cultivate gratitude.

- **Meditate.** Mindfulness meditation involves focusing on the present moment without judgment. Although people often focus on a word or phrase (such as 'peace'), it is also possible to focus on what you are grateful for (the warmth of the sun, a pleasant sound, et cetera).

> *Gratitude is the healthiest of all human emotions. The more you express gratitude for what you have, the more likely you will have even more to express gratitude for.*
>
> *Zig Ziglar*

CHANGE OUR WALK BY CHANGING OUR HABITS

Shawn Achor spent over a decade researching and lecturing at Harvard University. In his book, *The Happiness Advantage*[15], Achor listed seven activities that can improve mood and raise happiness.

'Each activity listed below not only gives us a quick boost of positive emotions, improving our performance and focus in the moment; but if performed habitually over time, each has been shown to help permanently raise our happiness baseline,' wrote Achor.

1. Meditate

2. Find something to look forward to

3. Commit conscious acts of kindness

4. Infuse positivity into your surroundings

5. Exercise

6. Spend money (but not on stuff)

7. Exercise a signature strength (e.g. playing a sport, painting, photography or playing a musical instrument)

I like Achor's approach because it is *activity* based. In cultivating functional habits, the key lies in carrying out the activities. When we engage in the activities, we experience 'a quick boost of positive emotions, improving our performance and focus in the moment.' The positive experience makes it more likely for us to repeat the activities, eventually repeating them until they become habits.

The promise that these activities will raise our happiness baseline permanently should dangle like a carrot in front of us. Besides, the seven activities are based on well researched studies, and have proven to be very effective.

The hardest habit to break

is trying to break the habits of others.

Dr. Edwin Howard Friedman

However, take note of a caution here. Deal with your own habits only; do not try to change those of your spouse, parents or children, et cetera. They have to make the changes themselves. I agree with Dr Friedman (a rabbi, family therapist and leadership consultant) on how hard it is to change another person's habits. As a helping professional, I have learnt that enforcing rules, reasoning and coaxing are inadequate to help change a person's habits. Nothing I can do will change the habits of another person. Only the person can do it themselves.

No one can change your habits. Only you can do it.

And when you do, you change your life

What can stand in our way of changing our habits? Surprisingly, sometimes it is our minds. Our minds are often torn between 'doing what's right' and 'doing what I like'. The latter will form a resistant force to create inertia. It will whisper into our ears that we need to be *completely* persuaded or convinced before we act. We believe the lie that says, 'If it is not from the heart, it's not worth doing,' or another one that goes, 'You are a hypocrite; that was all an act.'

Adopting a new way of thinking is difficult. Thinking traps will sabotage our efforts and have us firmly in their grip. To change habits, I suggest we simply adopt Nike's slogan of '*Just Do It*', and simply do not think too much! Or in the words of Millard Fuller: 'It is easier to act yourself into a new way of thinking, than it is to think yourself into a new way of acting.'

On 'becoming a better person, we simply have to just do it', a young aspiring lawyer shared with me the following helpful information:

'In Neo-Confucian philosophy, there are traditionally two schools of thought. The Lu-Wang School is one of them. Practitioners believe that there are no elaborate steps that are needed to take towards self-cultivation. One simply has to focus on the tasks at hand. It was Lu Xiangshan, one of the founders of this school, who said that "There are no affairs outside of the Way, there is no Way outside of affairs". This means that our path to enlightenment (or the Way), can solely be found in the daily events that we face. Mastery of these daily ins and outs, like controlling our emotions, being filial, and having good habits are all steps towards becoming a better person.

Lu's philosophy draws heavily upon Zen Buddhism, where the element of perfecting daily tasks is also found. Zen Buddhists believe that enlightenment is found in performing everyday actions well. It is not found in absorbing all the tomes of wisdom, nor is it found through grand displays of sacrifice. But rather, the message of Zen Buddhism is to find the Buddha-nature in all of reality, which comprises of everyday actions like sweeping and cleaning. Similarly, if we are to become better, we should commit ourselves to performing our daily actions with good intent.

Incidentally, modern self-help remedies prescribe starting with small tasks like doing laundry and getting groceries to overcome conditions like depression and anxiety. By achieving these small victories, one would be further encouraged to live their life, one day at a time. Thus, there is value in performing daily tasks as therapy is found in action.'

> *It's the small habits.*
>
> *How you spend your mornings.*
>
> *How you talk to yourself.*
>
> *What you read and what you watch.*
>
> *Who you share your energy with.*
>
> *Who has access to you.*
>
> *That will change your life.*
>
> *Michael Tonge*

Before you turn the page to the next chapter, list down some action steps you will take to cultivate two new habits. If you are still hesitant (or resistant), let the words of the Persian poet Rumi jumpstart you: 'As you start to walk on the way, the way appears.'

New Habit	Action Steps
	1. 2. 3.
	1. 2. 3.

"

You don't have to be great to start,

but you do have to start to be great.

Zig Ziglar

"

CHAPTER THREE

CHANGING OUR WATCH

We have learnt that to turn negative emotions into positive energy, we need to make changes to our **WOK** and **WALK**. In this chapter, we will discuss another area, **WATCH**.

WATCH? Change my **WATCH**? What is this about? Before we talk about the next change, let us take a look at self-esteem first. It will help unravel the mystery of what changing our **WATCH** is all about.

> *Too many people overvalue what they are not and undervalue what they are.*
>
> Malcolm S. Forbes

WHAT IS SELF-ESTEEM?

Self-esteem (in simple terms) is how we value ourselves. It is often seen as a personality trait and is classed as a 'psychological factor' in the Biopsychosocial-Spiritual (BPSS) model of health. Self-esteem is such an important factor to well-being that it has been called "the measure of mental health".

BPSS Model of Health

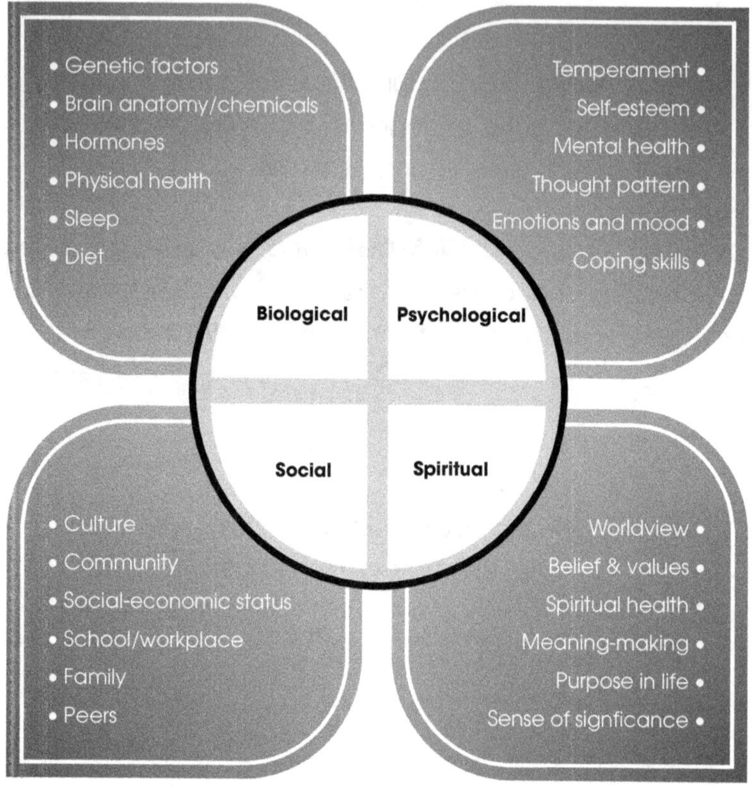

A few years ago, Simon, a Junior College student, sought my help for his depressive mood. Simon had an elder brother who was a high achiever as well as a good looker. Simon felt the need to equal, if not surpass, his brother's feats. Being average in appearance and ability, he compensated for this lack by working extremely hard, putting in long hours in his studies and taking up multiple leadership roles and many co-curricular activities. His plate became too full for him; he overcommitted himself. In the end, he had a meltdown. His self-confidence plunged and he ended up deeply depressed. When he began putting his life back together, he confessed that it was his poor self-esteem that started his path down into the abyss.

Low self-esteem can cause a person to be stressed, anxious or depressed, while an overblown self-esteem can make a person arrogant, egoistic and inconsiderate. In contrast, a healthy self-esteem is neither poor nor overblown. Maintaining a healthy self-esteem is crucial, for a person's self-esteem influences his performance[1], relationships and emotional health.

As one of the personality traits, self-esteem is thought to be stable and consistent. Well, it should be. However, as self-esteem is constantly influenced by two interactive forces – nature and nurture – it is often in a state of flux for many people – and at times – turbulent for some. This can cause emotional instability and relationship difficulties. For self-esteem to be healthy, it needs to be stable.

The Interacting Forces on Self-Esteem
- Basic temperament
- Physical health & physical disabilities
- Biological strengths & weaknesses
- Physical attributes

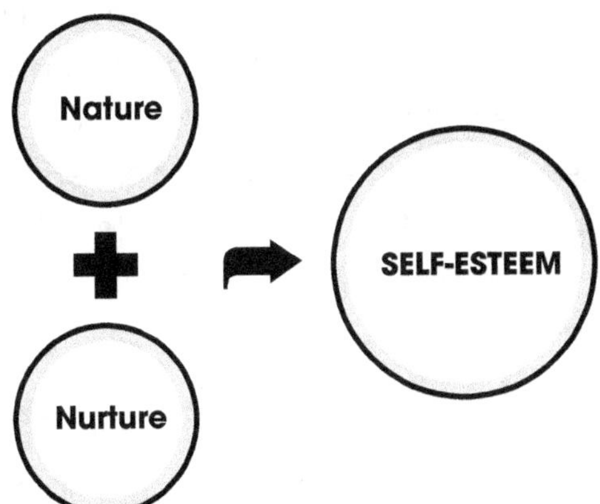

- Childhood (experience with caregivers)
- Family & friends (sense of belonging & acceptance)
- Social environment (society, media, school or work environment)
- Beliefs & values (identity, locus of control, faith)
- Competency (achievement & performance)
- Socio-economic status

The simple model above serves to illustrate the contributing elements of nature and nurture, and the impact they have on self-esteem. Of course, in reality, self-esteem is much more complex than the simple model represented above.

'Nature' and 'nurture' are not independent of each other but are in fact, interactive. For example, while poor physical health or physique affects our confidence level, regular exercise and a healthy diet can strengthen our physical health or improve our physique, and subsequently raise our confidence.

16-year-old Thomas was sent to me for mandatory counselling. Appearing overweight and shy, Thomas wouldn't maintain eye contact and was remorseful for his aggressive behaviours towards his classmates. His gentle manners and soft voice in the counselling room did not match his violent behaviour on the soccer field. It turned out that Thomas struggled with poor body image and low self-esteem, and whenever someone made fun of his body size, he got angry and turned aggressive. When Thomas realized that his aggression had its roots in his low self-esteem, he opted to work on improving his physique and body image. He started to eat healthily and exercise diligently. In less than a year, he succeeded in building his physique, together with his confidence and self-esteem. He became gentle in his ways on the soccer field, and off the field as well. Besides learning the difference between anger and aggression, Thomas's change is largely due to his improved self-esteem.

Our self-esteem does not depend on either nature or nurture alone. These two factors interact with each other, and together affect our self-esteem. In addition, while the two interactive forces of nature and nurture affect our self-esteem, an improved self-esteem can also positively influence these two very same factors (nature and nurture) in return. When there is a link between two factors, usually they work both ways in influencing each other. A more accurate depiction of their relationships is thus as follows:

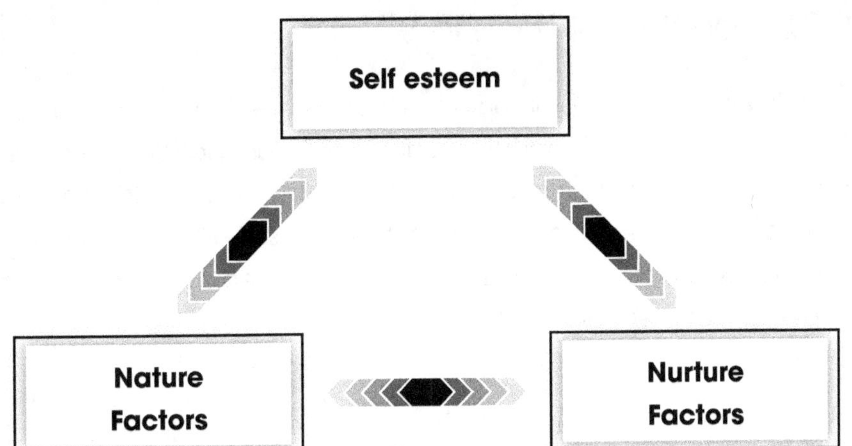

A deterministic or fatalistic mindset is not helpful in our efforts to build a healthy and stable self-esteem. Although we may have little or no control over the genetic or biological factors, through nurture we can make changes. We need to remind ourselves that 'predisposed does not equal predetermined'. You probably know of someone who did not have the best starting point in life (nature) or have the best nurturing environment, but turned out to be a person with extremely healthy and stable self-esteem. How is that possible? Let us turn our attention to the 'pillars' of self-esteem.

THE EIGHT PILLARS OF SELF-ESTEEM

There are eight common pillars that we erect to support our self-esteem. Most of us are unable to manage all eight because of nature factors, but we try to build as many as possible. One would think that the more pillars a person has, the healthier their self-esteem is, and that the reverse is also true. Well, we shall see. Let us begin by taking a brief look at each of these eight pillars.

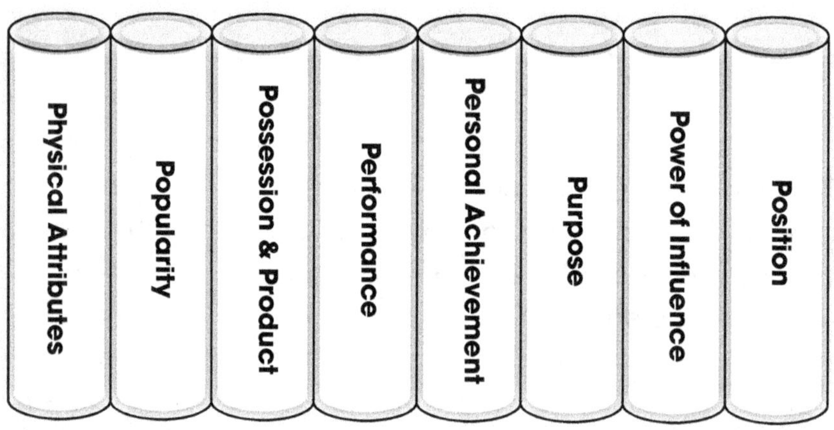

1. Physical Attributes

This refers to a person's physical characteristics which are visually apparent, or what we can see on the outside – a person's skin colour, height, physique, facial features, hair, et cetera. If you possess the set of physical attributes which your society happens to value, you are rewarded with admiration and esteem. Praise and approval can significantly shape your self-esteem, especially during your childhood. However, you cannot build your self-esteem solely upon this pillar. Suppose you are not endowed with the set of 'socially desirable' physical attributes – are you done for then?

Even if you are endowed with them, what would happen to your self-esteem when age eventually strips you of them? No wonder ageing is such a dreaded season in human life.

2. Popularity

Some believe what you lack in physical attributes, you can make up with personal attributes. Qualities, such as wittiness, eloquence, brilliance, generosity, kindness, honesty, sincerity and empathy can endear you to people. And as people are being drawn to your character, charm and charisma, you experience acceptance and warm relationships. Your popularity can greatly influence your self-esteem, especially during your formative years.

More and more people, both young and old, are increasingly dependent on social media likes, comments, number of followers or friends to build their self-esteem. Yet, you need to be aware that there are risks in depending on people's approval or comments to establish self-esteem. If you want a stable and consistent self-esteem, you cannot depend on popularity for your value and worth. People may say nice things about you one day, but criticize you on another. And what would happen to you should your friends one day abandon you, turn against you or betray you?

3. Possession & Product

Material possessions do not necessarily have a positive impact on self-esteem. But thanks (or no thanks) to the media, we are constantly bombarded with the message that material goods will bring us happiness and fulfilment. This influences us to place great importance on purchasing power, brand names and our property type and size. In my work with teens, I have learnt that teens often peg their self-esteem on material goods. Adults are not off the hook either. Guess who the teens' role models are?

In reality, possessions and products do not build self-esteem. Instead, they are often used to compensate for our low self-esteem and to cover up the void in our heart. Material possessions (at best) form a thin sheet of ice over the water of our deep emotional needs. They can neither withstand the weight of emptiness nor the test of time. The day will come when you will fall through the ice sheet into the deep cold icy water. When that day arrives, how would you survive?

4. Performance

Performance has to do with how well a person does a piece of work. Research[1] shows that high self-esteem does not necessarily lead to good performance; instead, high self-esteem is partly the result of good performance. Being able to perform a task well improves our self-confidence and self-perception of competency. These tend to increase a person's self-esteem. However, while research results indicate that the relationship between self-esteem and performance is positive, it is not a perfectly positive correlation[2] (or 100% of the time). Many good performers suffer from low self-esteem. You probably know of at least one person with high performance but low self-esteem. Why is that so?

Building self-esteem on good performance can be rather tricky and is not as straightforward as you think. If your good performance does not meet the endorsement of society or the approval of your significant others (for example, parents, spouse or children), it can have a negative impact on your self-esteem. Think of a kid who's very good at soccer, but has parents who disapprove of the sport. Or picture a teen who is a high performing gamer, but sadly defeated by poor self-esteem. If performance does not guarantee positive self-esteem, what would? Achievement?

5. Personal Achievement

If performance is how well a person does a piece of work, then achievement is what this good performance is achieving for them, such as a successful career or financial reward. Studies show that success in career tends to boost a person's self-esteem[3].

Appreciation and rewards turn good performance into achievement. Accolades and recognition of a person's achievement strengthen self-esteem. So, does personal achievement build self-esteem? Well... yes, but again, it is not a perfectly positive correlation. Many high achievers suffer from low self-esteem. Think of those famous celebrities[4] who confess to low self-esteem. Some of you might have also suffered at the hands of high achieving bosses with very low self-esteem, and were therefore extremely insecure.

Suppose we build our self-esteem on our successful career – what would happen when we retire or are made redundant? People who derive their self-esteem from their jobs are likely to experience the loss of purpose and worth when they no longer have their jobs. People who fail to find a replacement after losing their jobs struggle with more than just the loss of income, but the loss of self-esteem as well.

Some parents place their hopes (or rather self-esteem) so much on their children's performance, that their entire world revolves around the children, and the children's results drive their reason for existence, mood and self-worth. This will not only exert excessive stress on their children, it will also lead to the loss of meaning and worth when their children do not perform as expected.

6. Purpose

When *'that which you are good at'* (**proficiency**) *and 'that which you love'* (**passion**) happen to be *'that which the world needs'* (**practicality**) and *'would reward you for'* (**payoff**), your good performance and personal achievement collide to become that sweet spot which the Japanese call *'ikigai'* (a reason for being). Being able to live out one's purpose can be extremely fulfilling for any individual.

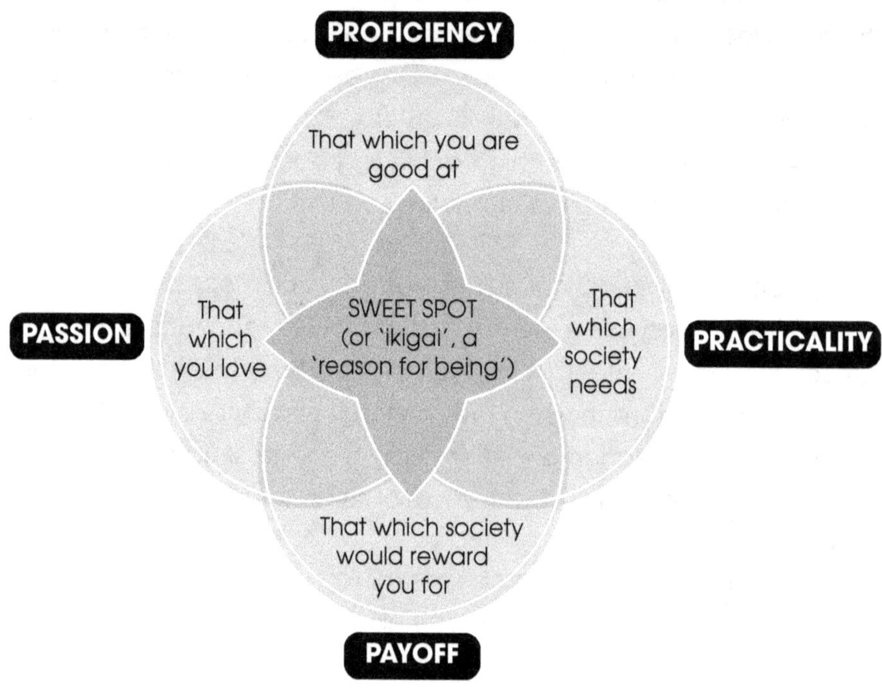

Surely when a person hits the sweet spot of *'ikigai'* and hence discovers their 'reason for being', they would have succeeded in building a healthy self-esteem, wouldn't they? In many cases, they do; but unfortunately, the 21st century economy does not always support a lifelong career (one life, one job). There are people who build their self-esteem on their job, but this works only when you still have your job.

The day you retire or are made redundant, your self-esteem collapses. Simply put, could your 'reason for being' withstand the test of time, or your retirement?

7. Power of Influence

From our very first years, whether innate or learned, we discover the power to influence those around us. Some common forms of power we use to exert our influence are cries, charm, charisma, carrot and stick, coercion, criticizing or convincing others, et cetera.

Closely related to the power of influence is the concept of locus of control. Locus of control is the belief that we have control over the outcome of events in our life. A person with an *internal* locus of control believes he has control over his life, as opposed to *external* forces beyond his control. Whereas a person who has an external locus of control attributes his success or failure to external forces that are beyond his control.

For example, if Mary has an internal locus of control and she tops her company quarterly sales record, she would attribute her success to the hard work she puts in. However, if Mary has an external locus of control, she would probably attribute her good results to luck, timing, other people's efforts or divine intervention.

Does the extent of our control – whether our control over other people, or the belief that we have control over our life – whether perceived or real – raise our self-esteem? When it does, would this elevated level of self-esteem be stable and sustainable?

8. Position

Positional leadership is a form of power of influence. For example, a formal position in a hierarchical organization allows a person to wield significant authority or influence over others. However, most societies and organizations are structured like a pyramid, top light, bottom heavy. As a result of this structure, positional leadership is out of reach for many people.

No worries; if positional leadership is beyond our reach, let's go for social position. Our social position (determined by factors such as education, occupation, income, age, gender and race) gives us our social status. If we lack the *ascribed* factors (age, gender or race), we surely can, with hard work, attain the *achieved* factors (education, occupation or income) to win the esteem of others, can't we?

But would our social value improve how we actually value ourselves? Research that studied the relationship between social class and self-esteem found that there is virtually *no* association for younger children, a modest association for adolescents and a moderate association for adults. Well, it looks like position, whether it be positional leadership or social position, is also not a sure bet as a strong pillar for self-esteem.

WHY CALL THEM PILLARS?

By now, you are probably wondering why these are called pillars if they are not a sure thing in building or maintaining a healthy self-esteem? I agree. We should not call them 'the eight pillars of self-esteem'.

Self-esteem needs to be built on firm foundations. Physical attributes, popularity, possession, performance, personal achievement, purpose, power and position are common and readily available resources people use to build their self-esteem. However, these crumble too easily. A healthy self-esteem needs to be *both* stable and *sustainable*. Even if we succeed in erecting *all* eight pillars to make our self-esteem *stable*, is it *sustainable* over time? I have seen peoples' self-esteem shatter to pieces because of cancer, bankruptcy, divorce, ageing, retrenchment or retirement.

As pillars, these '8 Ps' are not sturdy enough because they erode with time or can be rendered useless owing to changes in life. Nonetheless, these '8 Ps' are important aspects of our formative years and developmental stages. We should not totally disregard them. We simply have to regard them as what they really are – scaffolds – but never as pillars. As scaffolds, the '8 Ps' are *temporary* structures we erect to aid us in the construction of the real pillars. Scaffolds are important and necessary in the construction process. Nevertheless, when it is time, let us rid our lives of the need to depend on scaffolds, and work instead towards erecting the true pillar. That begs the question – 'What then is the true pillar of our self-esteem?'

> *Your personal attributes, popularity, possession, performance, achievement, purpose, power and position are scaffolds, not pillars, of self-esteem.*

THE TRUE PILLAR OF SELF-ESTEEM

What is the true pillar of self-esteem? Truth is often so obvious, but we are so blind that we often miss what's right in front of us. Well, the true pillar of self-esteem is – you, the **PERSON**! This is so important that I have to say it again: The **PERSON** is the true pillar of self-esteem. Whoever you are – regardless of your ethnicity, gender, age, health, stature, bank account and property, the level of your performance, achievement or social status, et cetera – you are a **PERSON** of immeasurable intrinsic value!

The true pillar of our self-esteem is our *self*-worth. Self-esteem is how we value ourselves. Self-worth is the belief that we are innately invaluable. Self-esteem that is built on what is outside of us will not survive changing times and circumstances. What is outside of us, or the world we have known so far, will not endure forever. One day, when this world of ours falls apart, our self-esteem will plummet and hit rock bottom.

How then can our self-esteem weather the storms of life? Well, that will depend on whether you have succeeded in building your self-esteem upon your self-worth. If you sense your value by your intrinsic worth, then even when you feel sad, disappointed or forsaken, you will continue to believe in your innate worth. And your self-esteem remains stable at all times, regardless of your feelings.

In our growing and developing years, we need scaffolds while our true pillar is still a work in progress. However, before these scaffolds corrode or become obsolete, the true pillar of our self-worth needs to be firmly in place. It is therefore vital that we work towards becoming a **PERSON** with a strong conviction of our intrinsic worth.

Many people continue to struggle with their self-esteem into their middle age or even seniority. Having depended on the scaffolds in their younger days, they now reach the stage in their life where the scaffolds are gradually being stripped away by the passage of time. Fortunately, no matter how old you are, it is never too late to believe that you are innately valuable.

THE SOLE PILLAR OF SELF-ESTEEM

So, if the intrinsic worth of a **PERSON** is the true pillar of self-esteem, is it also the *sole* pillar? Does it mean that if I have become a person with strong conviction of my intrinsic worth, there is no need for scaffolds since my true pillar is in place? And therefore, there is no place for purpose, personal performance or achievement et cetera?

Well, while the person *is* the true and sole pillar of self-esteem, there is a room for the other eight Ps, or so-called scaffolds. A person with healthy self-esteem will exude character, charm and confidence, as well as excel in areas of personal performance and achievement, that are distinctive to their unique personality and purpose. The question here is that of *attachment*. He does not attach his self-worth to them. Instead, they flow out of his sense of self-worth.

In a world that is unpredictable, rapidly changing and even perilous, there will be failure and setbacks. However, for a person who believes in his innate worth, when the world around him falls apart, his world does not. For he has built his world on the true and sole pillar of self-esteem.

ERECTING THE PILLAR OF SELF-ESTEEM

How can we strengthen the belief that we are innately valuable? One approach is to realign our understanding of self-worth. Jamie Daniel-Farrell, a marriage and family therapist, listed some 'truths about self-worth'[6]:

- **You don't have to prove your worthiness.** Yes, it's a myth you have to earn your worthiness. The truth is that you were born worthy.

- **External measures do not add or take away from your worthiness.** Since you are born worthy, successes and failures don't add to or detract from your inherent worthiness.

- **Comparing yourself to others is a waste of time and energy.** You don't have to prove your worth. It's already there, so it doesn't matter how you compare to others.

- **YOU are enough just as you are.** Right here. Right now.

Rick Warren, a Christian pastor and a bestselling author once spoke at a prison to about 5,000 inmates. He recalled:

'Nobody was paying attention except a couple of hundred people right up front. I was standing on the ground with no stage, just a microphone, but the microphone could be heard through the entire yard. I pulled out a $50 bill, held it up, and said, "How many of you would like this $50 bill?" Five thousand hands went up. I had everybody's attention. Then I crumpled it in my hands, tore it a bit, and said, "How many of you would still like this $50 bill?" Five thousand hands went up. (Then) I spat on the $50 bill, threw it on the ground, stomped it into the dirt, held it up, and said, "How many of you would like it now?" Five thousand hands went up.

Then I said, "Now for many of you, this is what your father did to you. You've been mistreated. You are abused. You are misused. You were told that you wouldn't amount to anything. You've done a lot of dumb things too. You sinned. You've done some crimes, and you're paying for them. You've been beaten. You've been torn. You've been dirty, but you have not lost one cent of your value to God."'[7]

Religion can certainly help us learn our intrinsic worth. Paul Sohn, an award-winning blogger, leadership coach, and speaker, in discussing the topic about men and women being the workmanship of God, wrote, 'The word workmanship means that we are handcrafted by God. In Greek, workmanship is *poeima*, which means "work of art".

This is where we get our English words poem and poetry. In essence, we are God's poem in motion. How beautiful is that!'[8]

Knowing that we are an art piece made by God that is being continuously and intricately handcrafted by Him helps us recognize our innate worth.

However, you can attend a religious meeting, learn your true worth and be inspired for an hour or two, but if you fail to guard your life the rest of the week, you will eventually lose the battle on your true worth.

The great evangelist, Billy Graham, told this story, 'An Eskimo fisherman came to town every Saturday afternoon. He always brought his two dogs with him. One was white and the other was black. He had taught them to fight on command. Every Saturday afternoon in the town square the people would gather and these two dogs would fight and the fisherman would take bets. On one Saturday the black dog would win; another Saturday, the white dog would win – but the fisherman always won! His friends began to ask him how he did it. He said, "I starve one and feed the other. The one I feed always wins because he is stronger."' (*The Holy Spirit: Activating God's Power in Your Life*, 1978).

There are two dogs in our life. One dog constantly snarls at us: 'you are not good enough', 'you will never amount to anything', 'if only you were better, stronger, smarter, more good-looking', 'life has dealt you a bad hand or taken away a good hand', 'you are not loved', 'there's no meaning in life', et cetera.

The other dog snuggles close to us with assuring messages of love: 'You are loved', 'I love you for who you are', 'I want to be with you', 'You are important to me', 'Come, spend time with me', et cetera.

What does it say about our worth if we are constantly reminded that God chooses to lavish His inexhaustibly abundant love on us?

Which dog will win the fight in your life? It depends on which dog you have been feeding! Interesting, isn't it? In the end, whether you are able to erect the true pillar of self-esteem depends on which dog you have been feeding! If you feed the good dog once a week by attending a weekly religious service but feed the other dog throughout the week with negative messages from social media, movies, dramas or commercials, it is little wonder that your self-esteem is so fragile. To start changing how you value your worth, you need to start changing what you watch. It is as simple as that.

> *To change how you value your worth,*
>
> *change what you watch.*

'So simple?' you ask. Well, like I said earlier, the truth is often so obvious, but we are so blind that we often miss what's right in front of us. However, truth is no use to us unless we start to act on it.

So, start changing how you value your worth by changing what you watch. **WATCH** is for changing what you watch – the list includes what you watch on your computer, television, Netflix, YouTube, Facebook and Instagram. **WATCH** is also for changing **what you read**.

For a start, to help you change what you **WATCH**, I am suggesting a few good books that you might want to start reading: *The Road Less Travelled* by M. Scott Peck, *Tuesdays with Morrie* by Mitch Albom and *What the Dog Saw* by Malcolm Gladwell. For more suggested reading, you can refer to Appendix 4.

PART II

CONTINUING THE JOURNEY

CONTINUING THE JOURNEY

'The beginning is the most important part of any work.'[1] We begin our pursuit of health and happiness by making changes – changes to our **WOK**, **WALK** and **WATCH**. As you have seen, these changes are important, for when we make changes in these areas, we start to turn the negative emotions in our life into positive energy.

However, changes can be cosmetic and temporary, and externally driven changes can be reversed easily. We need more than superficial changes. We need changes that are radical, thorough and lasting. We are, in fact, looking for *transformation* – a deep-rooted, complete and permanent renewal.

To achieve transformation, we must continue our journey by making more changes – changes that go deeper into the inner core of our being. But before we look at this, let us explore the different levels of changes.

TURNING CHANGE
INTO TRANSFORMATION

LEVELS OF CHANGE

There are three levels of change. As we move from one level to the next, we move towards transformation – not just of appearance but of character, and not just of form but of substance. Instead of seeing change as a single decision or act, it is better to see change as a journey, made of many decisions and actions along the way.

Level 1: External Change

At this level, the change is behavioural and it is characterized by *approval-seeking* and *appearance-driven* conduct. Even so, it is not to be sneered at, but rather to be outgrown. Growth takes time, patience and nurturing.

Behavioural changes are often motivated by 'carrot and stick', or cajoling and coercion. Generally, we do so in order to please, or not to antagonize someone. When a couple comes in for counselling, often you will find that one of them is the not-so-willing party. For example, the husband may be oblivious that his behaviour is also causing the marital problem, and therefore lacks the motivation to change. But when he realizes his wife is considering divorcing him, he sits up and pays attention. The risk of losing his wife and children prods him to change. Instead of gluing his face to the mobile phone or computer the minute he gets home, the husband now agrees to spend the first two hours helping with household chores. This change improves the spousal relationship and repairs their sexual bond. These improvements delight the husband and give him the incentive to continue his efforts. Of course, this is an oversimplified example, but it does illustrate that 'carrot and stick' can bring about behavioural change.

However, if behavioural change remains superficial and externally driven, other kinds of problems are likely to surface sooner or later. For example, the husband could be watching the clock constantly, and once the 'contractual two hours' are up, he returns to his video games immediately. The wife may fume over his inflexibility and want him to spend more time coaching the children during the examination period. The husband sees this as an unreasonable demand from his wife. The sense of inequity sets him on a lookout for opportunities to cut corners in order to maintain his sense of fair play. So, when the wife is required to work overtime, the husband sees it as a God-given opportunity to take a break. He orders a McDonald's delivery for the kids, and while the kids have a TV dinner, he works hard at advancing his video game to the next level. Imagine his wife's reaction when she finds out!

When changes are superficial and externally driven (versus self-driven), there is a need for reminders, constant monitoring and renegotiation. Parents who have used contractual agreements with their children would know how frustrating and painful this can be. One mother worked out an agreement with her teenage son that there would be no usage of the internet when he returned home from school. In exchange for that, he would get additional iPad time on weekends. She observed his compliance and rewarded him with the extra hours. However, she also noticed he began to arrive home later, sometimes up to two hours later. When she found out that he had been staying back in school to use the library computer to access the internet, she confronted him. Nonchalantly, he countered that the agreement did not say he could not stay back in school to use the internet.

The mother complained to me that using a contractual agreement with her son had not worked very well. The teen always managed to find a loophole to the agreement. She and her husband found the cost of monitoring and enforcing too high; it was exhausting and time-consuming. They always ended up exasperated and disappointed.

Perhaps this is an extreme example of a teen stuck at Level 1 change. While the true example may be extreme, it is not uncommon. I once conducted a counselling workshop for social workers helping school dropouts in China. A common frustration experienced by these social workers was this: working with school dropouts was like pulling a horse and cart. When the horse pulled, the cart moved; but when the horse stopped pulling, the cart stopped too. They felt more like horses than social workers.

Level 1 change is characterized by *approval-seeking* and *appearance-driven* behaviour. Change at this level is usually showy, skin-deep and inconsistent. Religious followers, including leaders, can remain at this level for a long time. Spiritual leaders need to help devotees grow beyond carrying out a pretentious and infantile form of religion, which gives the illusion of being pious, humble and ascetic. But really, such a practice of religion is just another way of showing off, with devotees making themselves look important[2].

However, let us not be too quick or harsh to dismiss Level 1 change. It is a necessary stage for most people. The growth process takes time, and requires patience and nurturing. Level 1 change becomes a concern only when we ought to have moved on to the next level, but stubbornly refuse to grow, perhaps because of laziness or contentment with the pretence of growth.

Level 2: Internalised Change

When a person progresses to this level, the change starts to be internalised. What that means is that the person begins to understand with his *mind* the reasons for change and becomes convinced in his heart that change is both necessary and good for himself and others. Rooted in reason and commitment, the change is more likely to last, even when the going gets tough.

Since the change that comes from the mind and heart is internally driven, it tends to be proactive. Returning to the example of the couple, when the husband undergoes internalised change, he will now not be constantly watching the clock. Instead, he will be thinking of ways to improve his family life. He spends time and does things for his children not because he wants to fulfil a contractual agreement, but because he genuinely cares for them. In the same way, the teen who is internally driven will not be looking for a loophole to beat the system, but instead will be seeking out what is genuinely best for his life. And school dropouts who are at Level 2 change have a better chance of getting their lives together. Even if they do not return to school, they seek to advance their lives in other ways, instead of hanging out with other runaway kids or loitering aimlessly in the malls.

When it comes to having a religion, a person who has undergone internalised change is convinced and therefore wants to work out his or her repentance, which is a change of mind and heart that leads to a change in direction. There is a turning away from the old life towards living the new life more and more. Repentance (*metanoia*), meaning 'a change of mind', is an important step towards transformation (*metamorphosis*), which is 'a change of form in keeping with inner reality'.

However, as Level 2 change is **internalised** and primarily s*elf*-driven, we need to be mindful that the "*inner self*" is also a human entity and therefore subject to human weaknesses. While it is true that 'when the going gets tough, the tough get going', it is also true that 'the tough' is as good as the soundness of his reason, the depth of his commitment and the level of his consistency.

The human *will* is susceptible to external influences and internal contradictions. It can cave in to the weight of pressure and the allure of pleasure. Many honest men and women who started off being committed to change, reverted to their old ways under the strain of external influence and momentary weakness. Change is never a linear progression or a one-way street. Even at Level 2, we can give up the progress we have attained and make a U-turn to our former lifestyle. Families, friends, social workers and counsellors of addicts can fill you in with story after story of relapse. Our own stories probably tell the same tale.

At Level 2, the internalised change comes from an informed *mind* and a reformed *heart*, but unfortunately, we can still experience the revolt of our heart and mind. The Jews are familiar with this, as it is written in their holy scriptures that 'The *lev* (heart, mind) *akov* (is deceitful) above all things, and *anush* (incurable (in wickedness)); who can know it?'[3]

The revolt of the heart and mind is often very subtle because we have the tendency to explain away our bad behaviour. For example, we may tell ourselves that it is okay to order our favourite milk tea with 100% sugar level because we went for a run this morning. Or the husband may think to himself, 'I have been so good these days, helping with the chores and coaching the kids in their homework. I have even taken the family to the zoo last weekend.' And so, while his wife sleeps, he rationalises that it is all right for him to chat with his online girlfriend.

We engage in this psychological bargaining called 'moral self-licensing' because buried deep in the recesses of our psyche, we harbour the belief that we can balance out our questionable actions by our past good deeds. Studies have shown that when people initially behave in a moral way, they are more likely to engage in behaviour that is immoral or unethical later. It is almost as if people believe that by behaving well in the past, they have earned the licence to behave badly later. 'Moral self-licensing occurs because good deeds make people feel secure in their moral self-regard. For example, when people are confident that their past behaviour demonstrates compassion, generosity, or a lack of prejudice, they are more likely to act in morally dubious ways without fear of feeling heartless, selfish, or bigoted.'[4]

Human weakness, the deceitfulness of our heart and mind, and our inclination for moral self-licencing are some reasons why we should not end our journey at Level 2. We need to continue our journey until we arrive at transformation, where change is complete, thorough and permanent.

Level 3: Transformational Change

Transformational change is radical. By radical, I do not mean 'extreme', but I am referring to the Latin origin of the word, *radicalis*, which means 'of or relating to a root'. A root is the basic cause, source or beginning of something. Changes at the root level are fundamental and deep-seated, affecting the elemental nature of a person, and are far-reaching and thorough. Come to think of it, seen in this light, transformational change is extreme!

More will be said about transformational change when we discuss spiritual health in Part III. For now, suffice it to say that at Level 3, transformational change is characterized by **RICE** (**R**elational, **I**dentity, **C**ontinual and **E**nigmatic).

Relational

If you are fond of reading inspiring turnaround stories of rebels and renegades, you would notice that the one significant factor that turns people around is love. 'Carrot and stick' can *alter* human behaviour. A change of mind and heart *reforms* a person. But love *transforms* a person as well as his life.

The journey to recovery for drug addicts is often long, bumpy and arduous. Those who eventually make it will testify that while Levels 1 and 2 changes are necessary, they are insufficient. In the end, what transforms them is a caring and loving relationship. Often, the relationship is a *spiritual* one.

One huge difference between change of reformation (Level 2) and change of transformation (Level 3) is that in transformational change, the reformed often becomes the reformer! There are numerous examples of former drug addicts who not only reformed their own lives but became reformers of other lives. The late Pastor Philip Chan was a former addict who led a self-described 'havoc' life of drinking and doing drugs up to his early 20s. Two significant relationships transformed him – he encountered Jesus and he married his wife. As a result, he kicked his drug habit and co-founded The Hiding Place, a Christian halfway house, to help other drug addicts, gamblers and alcoholics turn their lives around[5]. Listening to the testimonies of those whose lives Pastor Philip turned around, one thing stood out – he was like a father to them.

A mistake made by many parents and educators is trying to change a young person without first having a relationship with the youth. I have seen parents struggle to force change on their children and fail miserably. There are many reasons for the failure but typically the chief reason is a breakdown in the relationship with the child. In the absence of a loving and trusting relationship, 'carrot and stick' does not work very well, and neither does more reasoning or persuading. When there is a relationship breakdown, you need to focus on repairing the relationship *first*. Unless safety is a concern, reduce to a minimum your efforts to bring about Levels 1 and 2 changes. Only when the relationship is restored, will you then gradually resume the changes.

> *Rules without relationship lead to rebellion.*
>
> *Josh McDowell*

However, in cases where the relationship will take a longer time to be restored for whatever reasons, boundaries need to be firmly put in place and consequences clearly spelt out while we work at restoring the relationship. This is for the safety and well-being of that individual, the family and perhaps even the community.

In working with young people, it's good to bear in mind this motto: '*When they like you, you can do no wrong; when they don't like you, you can do no right.*' Begin your work with young people by building strong relationships with them. Come to think of it, I think this principle applies to our work with any age group.

Identity

What is identity? There is no standard definition for it. If you google for a definition, you will find many versions and they do not seem to fully unify into a coherent idea.

Wikipedia offers this definition: 'Identity is the qualities, beliefs, personality, looks and/or expressions that make a person or group.' Cambridge Dictionary defines identity as 'who a person is, or the qualities of a person or group that make them different from others.'

From these two definitions, we see that identity is largely concerned with the question, 'Who am I?' When this is so, the search for self often leads to an identity or existential crisis. Perhaps the problem lies with the 'postmodern' Western cultural phenomenon that *overemphasizes* individuality.

'*Ubuntu*' is an African word meaning 'humanity' and is often translated as 'I am because we are'. This is a view of life that emphasizes 'I am' only because 'we are'. This African philosophy is counter to the glorified personal autonomy of the West and serves as a healthy counterweight to the unchallenged overemphasis on individualism.

Identity that is rooted in 'I am because we are' is stable and settling. This is in contrast to being rootless and tossed and blown about by every wind of new influence. For example, a devout Muslim or Jew does not eat pork. That is part of their identity. They do not struggle with the decision as to whether to eat pork or not. They simply do not.

Similarly, a person who identifies himself as a Buddhist or Hindu keeps to his non-beef diet. Once the identity is formed, the way of life follows.

Continual

Our identity needs to be bookended by '*Who am I?*' and '*Whose am I?*' Firmly propped up by both, the space in between creates a safe haven for the *personal* identity to be continually clarified and refined by the *community* identity. This strong identity provides certitude for continual transformation.

A person who undergoes a spiritual experience often assumes a new identity because of the 'new life'. Expressions such as 'the old life is dead' and 'you are alive in your new life' are being used to describe the continual transformation. All living things grow. And as with all living things, a 'new life' that is 'alive' will continue to grow.

Christians receive their identity in a special person, Jesus Christ, whom they believe to be God Incarnate. These believers collectively make up the Church (literally meaning 'assembly'), which is called the Body of Christ. Christ and the Church give Christians their identity, which continually shape and mould them, until the image of Christ is formed in them. For Christians, this is the ultimate transformation or full maturity[6]. But until full maturity is attained, Christians continue to grow[7].

Enigmatic

I love the story of the Chinese Bamboo Tree[8]:

'To grow the Chinese Bamboo Tree, you'd water it, make sure that it gets enough sunshine – all the usual stuff. But even if you do everything right, you won't see any visible signs of growth in the first year. Nor the second, third, or fourth year.

But in the fifth year, something magical happens. Your plant, which has been dormant all this time, suddenly shoots up by 80 feet in just six weeks, and it becomes virtually unrecognizable over that short span of time.'

Of course, you can try to explain away the 'magic' by pointing out that for the first four years, the bamboo was growing underground to develop its root system in order to support the height and weight of the fully-grown tree, and that even without any visible sign, it was growing nonetheless. Still, the explanation does not take away the mystery of why the bamboo does not develop its tree and root system the way other trees do.

Transformational growth is often as mysterious as the growth of a bamboo tree – if not more. In exchanging stories with fellow therapists, the enigmatic change of a person is a topic that often baffles us. We could work with a client for a long period of time, try just about everything we could think of, and yet see no noticeable change. Then one day the client shows up – excited and smiling broadly. Even before you can settle down, he is already gesturing enthusiastically and laughing intermittently as he shares how everything came together for him in an instant – when he was looking at the rain one day!

Human growth is a mystery. We can go through a spell of dryness in our life. A season of fruitlessness. A period of darkness. And when we least expect it, 'everything comes together' serendipitously – 'things clicked', 'we get it', and we find ourselves at the start of a new chapter.

Growth can feel like a seed that is buried underneath the soil. We see no light but darkness. We feel no life but death. And when everything around us smells like decay, we lay our pride down and relinquish our knowledge and understanding. Strangely, the point of surrender is also the point where one turns the corner. The wisest Jewish teacher of all once said, 'I tell you the truth, unless a kernel of wheat is planted in the soil and dies, it remains alone. But its death will produce many new kernels – a plentiful harvest of new lives.'[8]

Level 1 change is what we would expect, and Level 2 change is explicable, but Level 3 change is enigmatic. Some have likened Level 3 human growth as a gift, or grace (both come from the same Greek word, *charis*). Others have used 'chaotic change' to describe transformational change.

While recognizing the mystery of transformational change, we do not, however, leave things entirely up to chance and fate. Returning to the analogy of a seed, it does no good at all to keep the seed in a jar; no growth will ever take place. But if we bury the seed in good soil, water it and expose it to the sun – by grace, the gift of life will cause the seed to sprout and grow a tiny seedling. And if you continue to care for it diligently, a fruitful tree awaits you.

Just as we can provide the right conditions for a seed to grow, we can also provide the right conditions for transformational change to emerge in our life. I would like to recommend the following three changes as offering these right conditions:

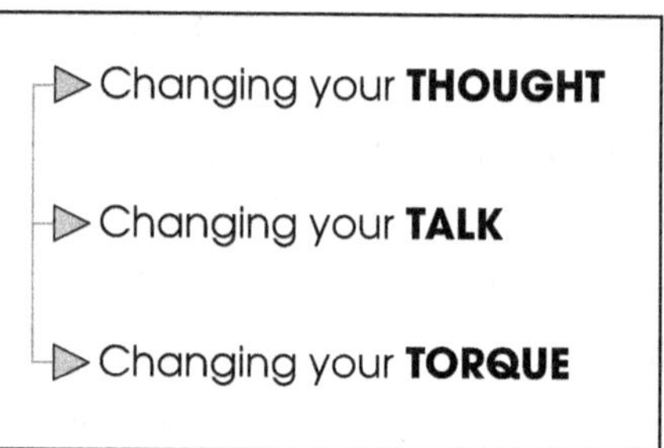

To harvest growth that is full of **RICE** (**R**elational, **I**dentity, **C**ontinual and **E**nigmatic), turn the page to unravel the mystery of transformational growth.

"

Change can be hard. It requires no extra effort to settle for the same old thing. Auto-pilot keeps us locked into past patterns. But transforming your life? That requires courage, commitment, and effort. It's tempting to stay camped in the zone of That's-Just-How-It-Is. But to get to the really good stuff in life, you have to be willing to become an explorer and adventurer.

John Mark Green

"

CHAPTER FOUR

CHANGING OUR THOUGHT

Have you ever wondered why we feel the way we do? What makes us feel sad, scared or mad at times, but glad, confident or calm at other times? In an earlier chapter, we looked at how the food we eat can affect the way we feel. Someone may respond in jest, 'But I don't remember eating anxiety!' Though in jest, this point is rather valid. The best of diets certainly helps but does not save us fully from negative feelings. Besides dopamine, oxytocin, serotonin and endorphins, there must be other reasons why we feel the way we feel. What are they?

One thing that stood out in the Feeling Wheel[1] of Kaitlin Robbs is the equal numbers of positive and negative emotions.

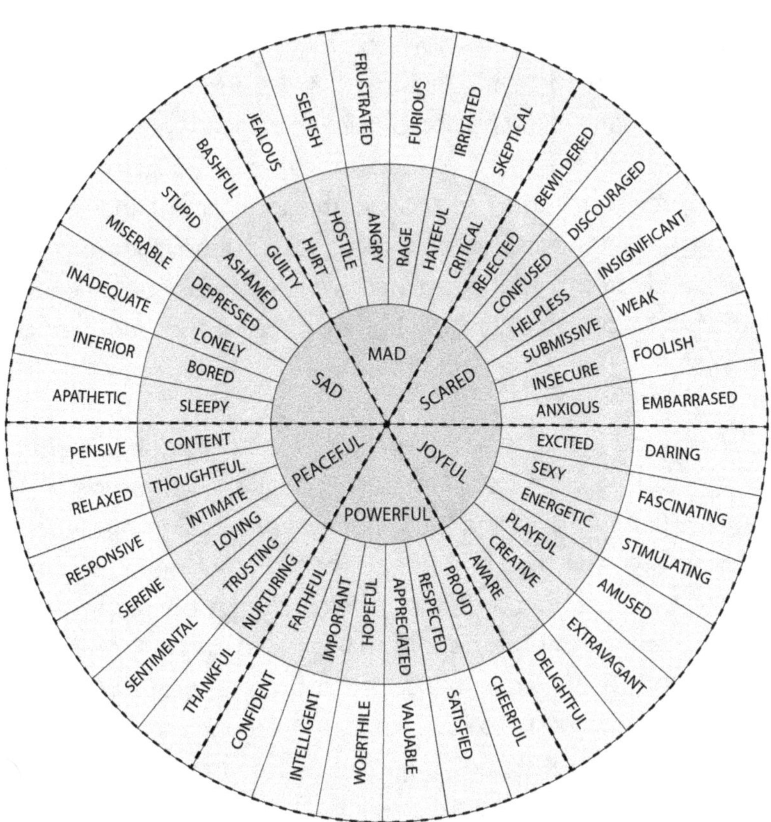

Negative emotions are natural human responses and are not bad in and of themselves. It is what we do with them that matters. As fire alarms, they call out to us to act constructively – feeling our genuine emotion, naming it correctly, processing and turning it into positive ones. If we fail to act constructively, negative emotions can degenerate into destructive emotions. Destructive emotions wreck lives, for they are like wild stallions that run amok. Out of control, they lead to destructive or self-destructive behaviours – aggression, violence, cruelty, insomnia, self-harm, addiction, et cetera.

Supposing we could unravel the mystery even further of why we feel the way we do – wouldn't we have learnt how to turn negative emotions into positives? And experienced more positive emotions and less of the negatives? We would be happier, and thus healthier, wouldn't we? That being the case, wouldn't you like to invest some time into unravelling this mystery deeper?

Let us imagine you got home at midnight after a long unproductive meeting at the office. Tired, sleepy and grumpy, you turned in immediately after having a quick shower. In your deep slumber, you were rudely awakened by a loud knocking on your bedroom door. You looked across the bed at the alarm clock and it showed five in the morning. You let out a grunt, walked toward the door and threw it open, ready to scream your head off at whoever was behind your door. The single best word to describe your emotion at that moment would be **anger**.

When you pulled open the door, standing behind it was your landlord. 'Fire! Run! Fire! Run! Get out of here!' she screamed. It would not be too difficult to imagine that your **anger** would immediately turn into **fear**. And as you followed her out of the apartment, you realised how close you were to death when thick smoke enveloped both of you and you felt the intense heat from the fire raging in the kitchen. As you ran down the stairwell, your **fear** turned into **gratitude** that your landlord had risked her life to save yours. In that one minute or less, your emotions have changed from **anger** to **fear** to **gratitude**. What has caused your feelings to change?

WHY WE FEEL THE WAY WE DO?

Suppose you were caught by the teacher for putting a lizard tail in the pencil case of your cute female classmate, and the teacher called your father. When you got home from school that evening, your Dad yelled his head off at you while huffing and puffing with uncontrollable anger. Just when you were thinking, 'Uh-uh… nothing will ever calm him down,' his mobile phone rang. He answered the phone, and you witnessed a miracle – an angry face turned instantly into a smiling one, and with the politest tone, your Dad said, 'Yes, Mr. Tan. We have completed the final draft of the contract and we will deliver it to your office first thing in the morning. Yes, Sir. That's right. Thank you, Sir.'

Before you call your Dad a phony, you will do well to recall the incident when you angrily slammed the bedroom door in your younger brother's face while answering the ringing phone. You immediately replied with the greatest tenderness when you recognized the sweet voice of the girl you met at a recent party.

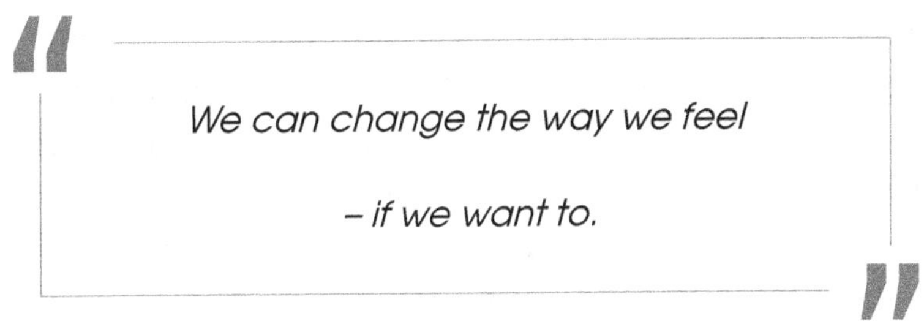

When an unpleasant event (*Antecedent*) occurs, we may immediately feel angry, anxious or sad (*Consequence*). As the two events are sequential, the *antecedent* event is often thought of as causing the *consequence*.

However, if this were true, then it would be difficult to explain why the same antecedent often produces different consequences in different people. The same antecedent might even produce a different consequence in the same person on a different occasion. The reason is that we have confused correlation with causation.

Let us suppose the parents of 16-year-old Tommy wanted to motivate him to work hard for his GCE Ordinary Level examination. They promised him a month-long holiday to Europe after the examination. For what seemed like forever, Tommy slogged like never before as he imagined himself skiing in the Swiss Alps and floating in a hot-air balloon across the castles, forests and the French countryside and over the Eiffel Tower in Paris. The day he finished his examination, he and his classmates celebrated by playing a game of soccer, but it unfortunately ended in Tommy sustaining a broken leg. It was lamentable no doubt, especially when Tommy's parents had no choice but to cancel the trip, as the surgery to fix his broken bone was scheduled on the day of their flight departure.

'It's pretty pointless to continue with the trip. You are not going to learn how to ski with a broken leg,' his father said to him after the surgery. The word 'pointless' sank Tommy's heart and regrets began to overwhelm him. For the next few weeks, he kept blaming himself for not turning down the invitation to the game, and for not going home to pack his luggage instead. The broken leg led to a broken dream, which in turn led to a broken heart that ended up in depression.

It is easy to attribute the broken heart (*consequence*) to the broken leg or dream (*antecedent*). On the surface, it does seem that the antecedent has indeed caused the *consequence*. This common perception has caused many people to throw all their resources to avert or alter undesirable antecedents. For example, constantly seeking approval to avoid criticism, or refusing to accept that a breakup is final and insisting on reconciliation. However, when it fails, their lives are thrown into disarray. The harsh reality of life is that it does not always go the way you plan it, or want it. You will never be able to avert or alter all unwanted antecedents. What are you going to do with this harsh reality?

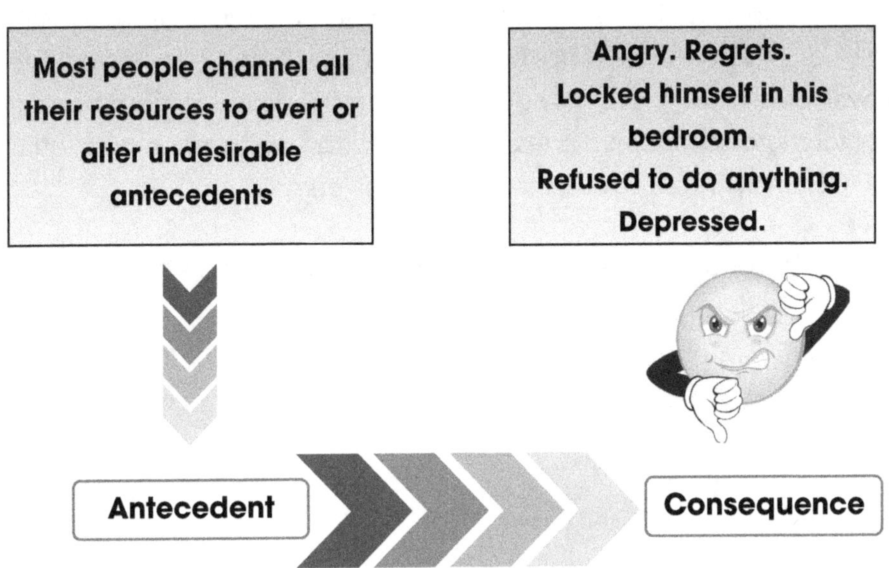

Let us suppose the parents of Tammy, another 16-year-old, promised her a month-long holiday to Australia and New Zealand after her major examination. The thoughts of cute penguins on Phillip Island, hot-air balloons across the Yarra Valley and the magnificent 'Lord of the Rings' scenery kept Tammy motivated as she prepared for her GCE Ordinary Level examination. Misfortune also struck Tammy on the last day of the examination. She broke out with a bad case of chickenpox and the family had to cancel the much-anticipated holiday. Naturally, Tammy was disappointed that instead of being on holiday, she was being quarantined in her room; instead of feeling the cool mountain breeze on her face, she felt the super-itchy rashes on her face. The first three days were the hardest for Tammy. She did nothing but sleep, and ate nothing but drank soup and water. After three miserable days, she gained sufficient strength to start learning how to play the guitar through YouTube. She also began to read. By the end of the month, she had learnt to play the guitar at a basic level and finished the books she had always wanted to read, but didn't have time to before.

'I still would love to have gone for the holiday, but this wasn't so bad. In some ways, it has been a blessing in disguise. I would have never learnt how to play the guitar or finished reading all those books if not for the chickenpox. I guess the holiday can wait until perhaps after my GCE Advanced Level,' she wrote in her journal.

Similar antecedents but different consequences. Why?

HOW DO YOU EXPLAIN SIMILAR ANTECEDENTS WITH DIFFERENT CONSEQUENCES?

If consequences were caused by antecedents, then similar antecedents would produce similar consequences. The fact that they produce different consequences in different people means that there must be something else that is causing the consequences. Something is missing in this **A** causing **C** sequence. What is missing?

Antecedents are triggers – not the causes of consequences. They trigger automatic thoughts that arise from our assumptions and attitudes. But what is really feeding these assumptions and attitudes is: our belief. Hence, the missing link in the **A** and **C** sequence is **B**, our belief.

It is not what happens that upsets me. It is what I ***believe*** about what happens that upsets me. Make sense? William Shakespeare put it this way, 'There is nothing either good or bad, but thinking makes it so.' As early as the first century, the Greek philosopher Epictetus recognized this, 'Men are not worried by things, but by their ideas about things. When we meet with difficulties, become anxious or troubled, let us not blame others, but rather ourselves. That is: our ideas about things.'

The very good news is that it lies within our power to change our beliefs. We need to reclaim control. We have more influence over our thoughts, feelings, and behaviour than we realise. When we change our belief, with its corresponding assumptions and attitudes, we can change our sad feeling, anxiety or anger.

If someone woke you up for no good reason (or the reason was not good enough to disrupt your sleep), you would feel angry. But when you realised that the person had woken you up to save your life, you would feel grateful. The **A** (antecedent), that is, being interrupted from your sleep, has not changed, but your **B** (belief) has. The change in **B** produces a change in **C** (consequence).

ANTECEDENT remains → **BELIEF changes** → **CONSEQUENCE changes**

Changing our belief can make a whole world of difference for us. Unfortunately, we often stubbornly hold on to our belief that is negative or destructive. We choose familiarity over change and refuse to change irrational beliefs and destructive thinking patterns that perpetuate negative and self-defeating emotions and behaviour.

Why insist on the familiar, and choose misery over happiness? For the sake of our well-being, let us have the courage to let go of our irrational beliefs. Moreover, we have to let go of our negative thought patterns. Studies have also shown that our thoughts can make us sick[2]. We will deal with this topic in detail in the next section. Though familiar and comfortable, irrational beliefs and negative thought patterns land us in misery in the first place. It is therefore crucial that we learn to replace our old beliefs and patterns of thinking with new and effective ones. While it might be frightening to say goodbye to these familiar ways initially, we will be glad when we do so. And you know what? Stop giving yourselves excuses that you are much too set in your ways, and that it is too late to change – that is utter nonsense!

WE CAN CHANGE THE WAY WE FEEL
BY CHANGING THE WAY WE THINK!

As mentioned earlier, studies have shown that our thoughts can make us sick[2]. The good news is if our thoughts can make us sick, they can also make us well. Changing our thought is absolutely necessary for us to improve our health. But for thoughts to make us well, we need to change the way we think and learn to think things through.

To have effective and functional thoughts, you need to first of all: *identify* your thinking distortions; second, *dispute* your distorted thoughts; and finally, *replace* them with effective ones.

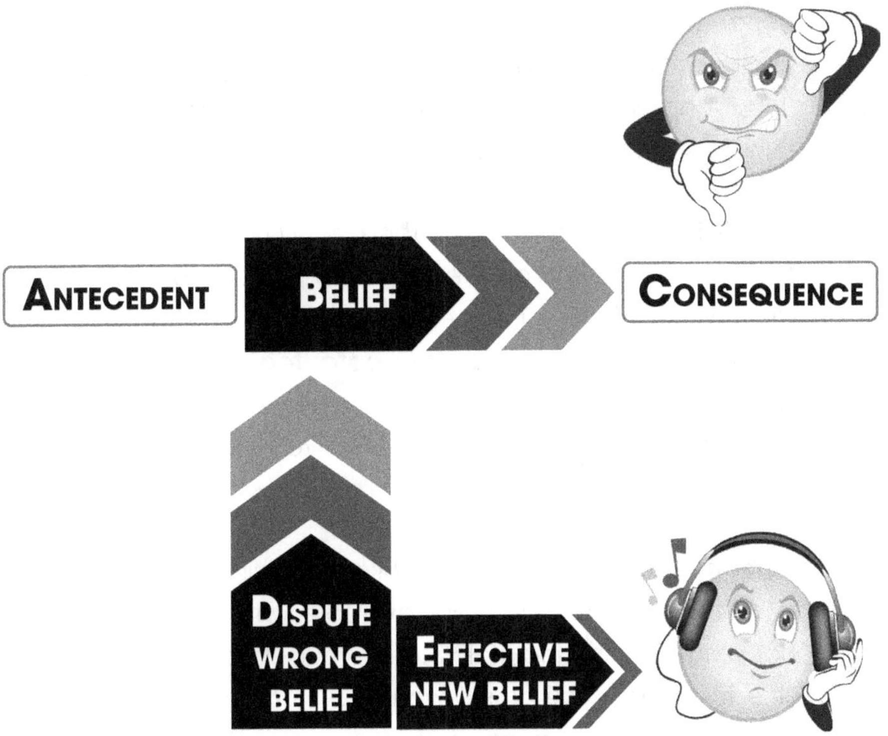

All of us are susceptible to thinking distortions which become more exaggerated when we are stressed or depressed. In order to identify our distorted thinking, it helps to know the common thinking distortions. Trevor Powell, a clinical psychologist and clinical neuropsychologist, listed six of them[3].

1. **All-or-Nothing Thinking.** This is when you think in binary terms: '0' or '1', 'black' or 'white', and create a world where things are either good or bad, with nothing in between. For example, the boss is either a good boss or a bad one; or you condemn a person on the basis of a single event, decision, or personality trait. There is no room for a good person with certain bad habits or traits. When you apply this distorted thinking to yourself, you condemn yourself as a complete and utter failure because of a single failure. You have to be perfect, or you are 'hopeless', a 'loser' and an 'idiot'. In your relationships with others, you often think 'either it's their fault, or it's mine.'

2. **Awfulising-Catastrophising.** This cognitive distortion assumes the worst outcome of an event and then goes on to overestimate the severity of the outcome. For example, you woke up with a dry throat and immediately 'catastrophised' that it would develop into a bad flu, which would then cause you to fail your examination. And as a result, your entire life is over. A concern quickly escalates into a catastrophe with awful consequences.

3. **Personalising.** This is when you take everything that goes wrong in your life – personally. For example, when something bad happens, you immediately blame yourself for it, even if it has little to do with you or is beyond your control. Automatically and overly assuming responsibility for everything can produce enormous amounts of guilt, shame and inadequacy. If you engage in personalising, you may also literally take everything

personally and wrongly assume that everything others do or say is directed at you. You often imagine that you have been intentionally targeted or ostracised. However, what if things are not really targeted at you? You will learn later the steps you can take to evaluate your thinking in a more objective way.

4. **Negative Focus.** If you have this thought distortion, you discount the positive and engage in negative-biased thinking. Your focus is on the negatives while disregarding or dismissing the positives. When something good happens, you explain it away as sheer luck or attribute it to an anomaly, rather than recognizing your contributions to the good outcome. This negative mindset zooms in on weaknesses and problems while ignoring strengths and resources. Shackled by a negative outlook, you look for evidence to support your negative-biased conclusion, thus ending up pessimistic and cynical. 'Argue for your limitations and sure enough, they're yours,' Richard Bach would say.

5. **Jumping to Conclusions.** We are familiar with fill-in-the-blank test questions and probably can recall how creative we were when we did not know the answers. Life too comes with similar fill-in-the blank moments – when we don't have the facts, when we don't know what others are thinking or saying about us, or when we don't know what will happen, et cetera. This thinking distortion fills the blanks with negative interpretations or predictions in the absence of evidence. It also comes in the form of 'mind reading', that is, assuming the thoughts and intentions of others, with the worst possible conclusions. For example, you walked into the office and heard your colleagues laughing. You immediately decided that they were laughing at you.

6. Living by Fixed Rules. When you regularly think in terms of 'shoulds', 'oughts' or 'musts' and have an ironclad rule of how you or others 'should', 'ought' and 'must' be, you are living by fixed rules. Having unrealistic expectations, rigid views or rules are sure ways to make you feel angry, resentful, depressed, disappointed or guilty. For example, 'I must never fail', 'my kids ought to be respectful at all times', 'the sales assistant should always be polite to the customer' or 'the management have to be fair'. The reality is that we or others are unable to meet such high or even unattainable standards. Adhering to and emphasizing such high or unattainable standards will cause us much misery.

Step Two: Disputing Thinking Distortions

How many thinking distortions do you identify yourself as having from the previous section? Most of us will have a few. It is a matter of how many, how frequent and how firm we hold on to our thinking traps. When we choose to do nothing with our dysfunctional thoughts, they affect our happiness, as well as our health (remember 'our thoughts can make us sick'?) What then should we do with our thinking distortions? Well, you dispute them or argue with them to loosen their grip on your mind. To help you win the debate with your own mind, I am offering you a framework to engage in a Socratic dialogue with yourself.

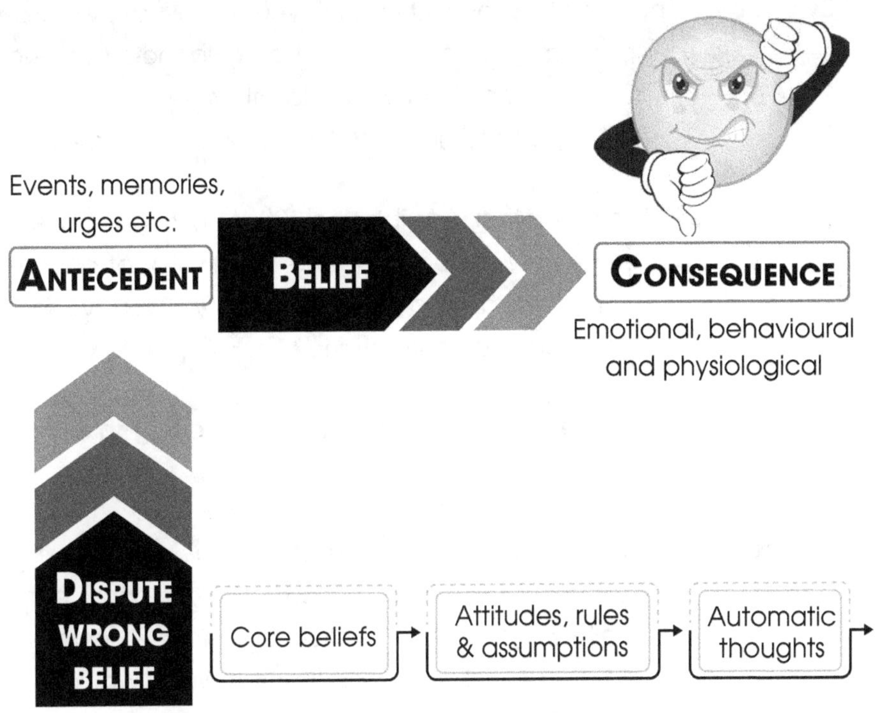

A Socratic Dialogue with Yourself

Engage in a conversation with yourself to discover whether there may be conclusions or viewpoints which better reflect reality, or which are more helpful for you.

Pause   You catch yourself thinking in a negative manner or having feelings of negativity and pessimism. Hit the 'PAUSE' button immediately.

Relax   Where it is possible, find a quiet place to do the 4-2-6 breathing for three to five minutes. Otherwise, just do it wherever you are.

Evidence Engage in a conversation with yourself: What evidence supports my conclusion? What evidence may not support my conclusion? Would other people consider my evidence convincing? Or irrational? Extreme?

Alternative Is there another possible view? Who might have a different view? Can someone I trust think of another way of understanding this situation? Would I have seen things differently another time?

Cost and What are the costs and benefits of seeing things this way?

Confront What are the costs and benefits of seeing things in a more positive or less critical way? How consistent is my belief? If I were to publicly defend my viewpoint, would I be able to convince others? Why? Would they think my conclusion is too extreme? What are some possible errors in my thinking?

Helpful What might be a more helpful way to think in this situation? What are some helpful ways to improve the situation? If my thought is true, how can I change my thinking to make things work? If my conclusion is true, how can I cope with the situation?

This way of challenging your own thinking distortions does not come naturally or effortlessly. It requires discipline and practice. Your core beliefs, which are basic convictions about yourself, other people and your world have been formed since early childhood. These beliefs are deeply rooted in early formative experiences and therefore so fundamental and inherent that you regard them as absolute truths, or as the way things are. It is hence not easy to modify dysfunctional beliefs and thinking distortions. However, with determination and commitment, they can be unlearned and replaced with effective and functional thoughts and beliefs? So, the next time you feel sad, mad or scared, take a moment to identify your thinking distortions. Then take a small step – but a great leap forward – by engaging in a Socratic dialogue with yourself. **PREACH** to yourself – **P**ause. **R**elax. **E**vidence. **A**lternative. **C**ost/confront. **H**elpful.

Step Three: Replacing Thinking Distortions

After we have identified and debated with our irrational thoughts, we replace them with new effective and functional thoughts. The ABCDE framework below provides us with easy-to-remember steps to help us change the way we think.

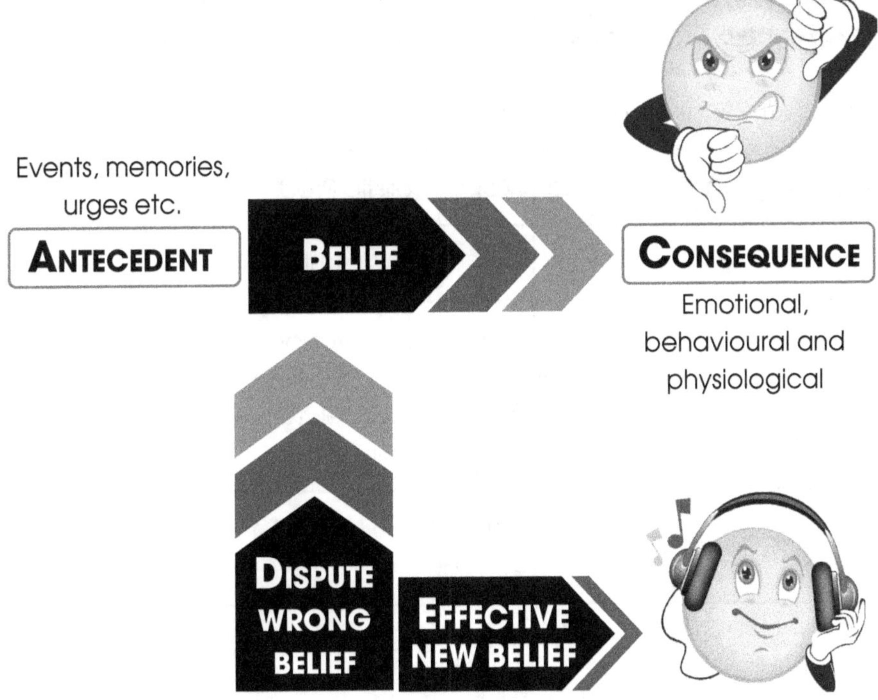

Someone might say, 'Okay, I get it. I need to change the way I think in order to change the way I feel. But what's this new way of thinking? What are these new effective and functional thoughts?' Fair questions, I must say.

Identifying common thinking distortions is a big first step. After which, you need to run in the opposite direction of these thought distortions. For example, instead of thinking in terms of 'should', 'must' or 'ought', you can think or use words such as 'I *would* prefer', 'it *would* be great if she' or 'if I *could*'. In our earlier example of Tammy, instead of thinking that 'this shouldn't have happened to me,' she was telling herself that 'I still *would* love to have gone on the holiday...'

Kim Pratt, a licensed clinical social worker, came up with ten Cognitive Clarifiers[4] (the opposite of cognitive distortions). I tabulate some of Pratt's Cognitive Clarifiers below.

Cognitive Distortions	Cognitive Clarifiers
All-or-Nothing Thinking	Practice 'Rainbow' Thinking
Awfulising-Catastrophising	Make Realistic Predictions
Personalising	Don't Take Anything Personally
Negative Focus	Balance Positives and Negatives
Jumping to Conclusions	Be Curious. Seek to Understand (rather than assuming)
Living by Fixed Rules	Remove the word "Should" from your vocabulary

Engaging in a Socratic dialogue in which we **PREACH** to ourselves will also lead us to self-discover effective and functional thoughts. As we come up with these thoughts ourselves, they are usually the best fit for our particular situations and are likely to enjoy 'longevity', that is, stay with us longer.

In his growing years, William was a hyperactive and impulsive child who was also very mischievous. Needless to say, he had difficulty fitting into the traditional classroom and was perceived as a troublemaker. He was often taken to task by the teachers and punished by his parents for his undisciplined behaviour and impulsivity. He had poor self-image and always said to himself, 'I am a bad person.' William's parents reinforced his negative self-image by overly criticising his impulsive and mischievous behaviours, and openly doubting his sincerity and integrity.

By the time William reached mid-teen years, he had become an angry young man who was easily provoked to aggression. He spoke rudely to his teachers, yelled at his parents and hit his classmates. His anger, which escalated to aggression instantly, usually stemmed from his perception that he had been misunderstood, falsely accused, treated with disrespect or unfairly.

William eventually learnt to **P**ause and **R**elax by taking deep breaths whenever he felt his temper rising. He further slowed down his angry thoughts by examining the **E**vidence that supported or contradicted his perception of injustice, and considering **A**nother way of looking at the incident. But according to him, what really helped him was thinking about the likely **C**onsequences of his aggression, and coming out with other more **H**elpful ways to deal with the situation. Of course, it was also helpful that the school's Principal had suspended him thrice for aggressive behaviour, and had issued him with an expulsion ultimatum.

Whenever he ran into situations where he considered the evidence and felt that his angers were justifiable, he kept repeating to himself his 'personalised' coping statements: 'It's okay to be angry but I do not have to be aggressive'; 'I can talk it out in the counselling room instead of acting it out'; 'I have walked away before, I can walk away again'; 'Instead of getting mad, I would get even and there are better ways to get even.'

William came up with these coping statements by engaging in a Socratic dialogue (**PREACH**) in the counselling room. Although they might not be the most polished or perfect functional thoughts, they were all his. As he came up with them himself, they were a good fit for his situations and worked well for him.

> *A happy person is not a person in a certain set of circumstances, but rather a person with a certain set of attitudes.*
>
> *Hugh Downs*

THE RELIGIOUS TRAP

Books of philosophy or positive thinking are good viable options to develop effective and functional thoughts. Many people turn to religious teachings for functional thoughts. This is a good choice as many religious teachings provide good alternatives to dysfunctional thoughts.

Unfortunately, some people turn to religions not to replace their thinking distortions, but to avert or alter their antecedents. Remember we mentioned most people channel all their resources to avert or alter undesirable antecedents? Seekers of religion can fall into this group. By becoming a devotee, they think the gods will protect them from all undesirable antecedents such as misfortunes and miseries; or through religious piety that sickness and poverty will be replaced by health and wealth.

The focus of prosperity theology is not necessarily the acquiring of new effective functional thoughts, but the averting or altering of undesirable antecedents. Its devotees' attention is not on personal growth or spiritual development in terms of right actions, right thoughts and right words, but on the growth of wealth, power and improvement of health.

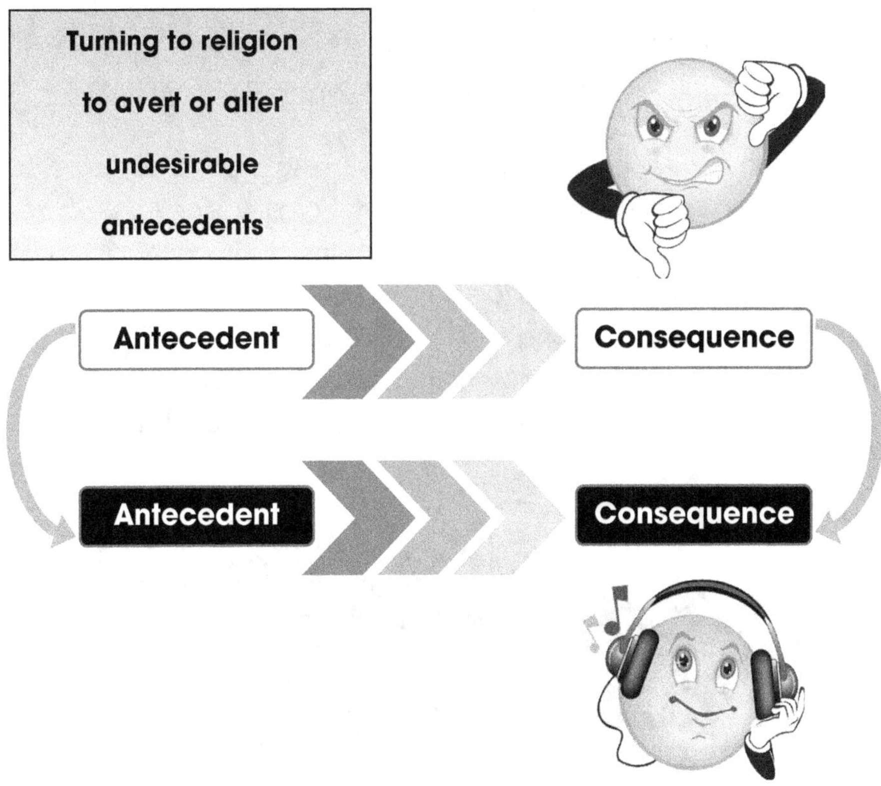

We are becoming a generation of less learning and reading, and of more entertainment and distractions. Our short attention span, coupled with our compulsion for social media, draw us to memes and quotes. Many who turn to religion (or philosophy) do not spend enough time to read, study or understand their religious teachings. Mimicking their teachers or circulating inspiring quotes may give them an appearance of wisdom but does not root them in true wisdom and understanding. It is not surprising that while they can word the right thoughts, they continue to languish in dysfunctional thoughts and behaviour. This is perhaps an indication and indictment that we lack depth and profundity. Form without substance will result in us being easily tossed and blown about by every wind of new teaching.

To overcome this rootlessness and restlessness, you can consider joining a group of like-minded people to study, discuss, query and share ideas on how to live out your faith. When you do so, one of the first things you will learn is to correct the commonest 'thought distortion' in religion, which is 'religious piety earns you answered prayers.'

Religion becomes a trap when it is being used as a means to get what we want – personal gain and self-gratification – instead of discovering what God wants of us through the study and practice of religion. The focus of religious faiths is the transformation of the person through personal growth and spiritual development. God, therefore, often does not spare us or deliver us from undesirable antecedents, but instead uses them to grow us – starting with changing our thinking.

MORE THAN JUST CHANGING OUR FEELING

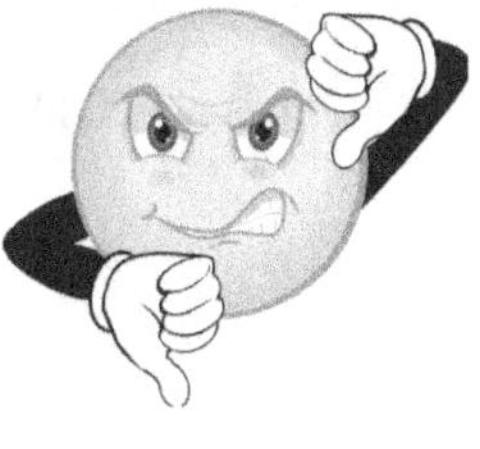

The A-B-C Model does more than just change our feeling; it changes our well-being. If our thoughts can make us sick, our thoughts can make us well too. Cognitive wellness has powerful impacts on our emotional, behavioural and physiological well-being. It goes beyond just changing our emotions. The new thoughts create a new mindset, by which we see the new world, and this opens up a whole new life of possibilities. Essentially, we become a new person. Isn't this exciting? But there is more.

We have mentioned in an earlier chapter that if there is a link between two factors, the influences usually work both ways. The same principle applies here with the links that exist amongst cognition, emotion, behaviour and physiology. Therefore, in reality, the A-B-C model is more complex and encompassing. The real-life A-B-C model looks more like this:

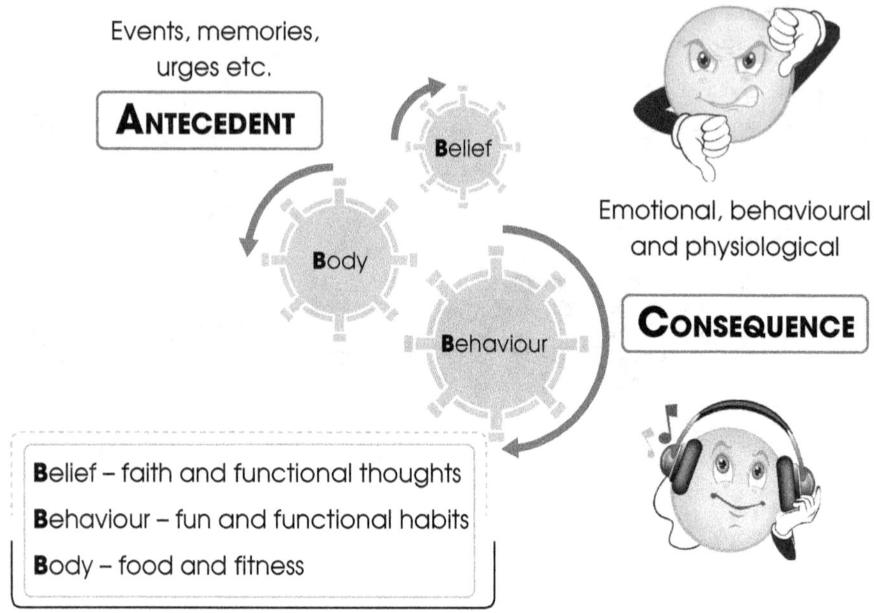

Changing the 'B' in the A-B-C Model is more than just changing the belief. 'B' can also be for modifying our **b**ehaviour and strengthening the physical **b**ody. In facing any distressing or stressful event (**A**ntecedent), a boosted three-strand cord (of belief, behaviour and body) will have a greater impact on our emotional, behavioural and physiological well-being (**C**onsequence). This is in line with what we have covered in Part I of this book: Change your **WOK** (food) and your **WALK** (fun, fitness and functional habits). That means that if you change your Wok, change your Walk, and also change your Thought (belief and thoughts), you are progressing well towards health and happiness.

It cannot be overemphasized that changing your thoughts is crucial, because when you do, changes start to turn into transformation. It is written in an ancient scripture that is almost two thousand years old, '... let God transform you into a new person by changing the way you think ...'[5]

Change your thinking. Change your life! Your thoughts create your reality. Practice positive thinking. Act the way you want to be, and soon you will be the way you act.

Les Brown

CHAPTER FIVE

CHANGING OUR TALK

I began the previous chapter by introducing you to the **A-B-C** model and ended it with a bolstered three-strand cord of **B**ody, **B**ehaviour and **B**elief to strengthen our emotional, behavioural and physiological well-being. The emphasis is placed not on averting or altering the undesirable antecedents (**A**), but on bolstering the three-strand cord to achieve holistic well-being, the desired consequence (**C**).

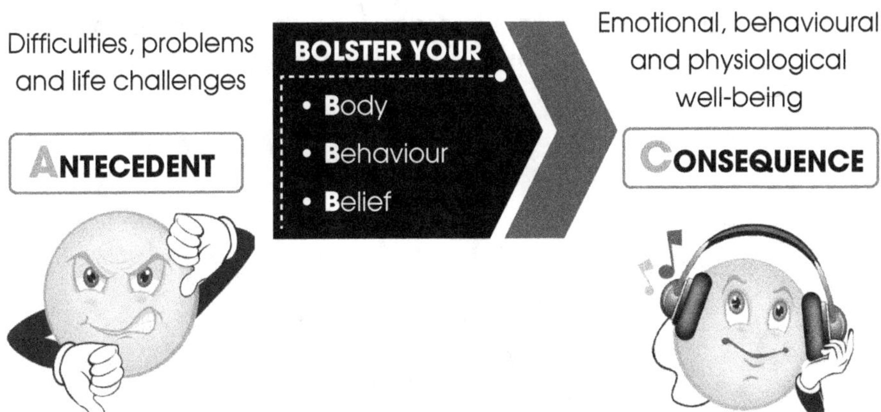

While the emphasis is not on averting or altering the antecedents, there is no need to be masochistic. If we can avoid, remove or solve a problem, let's do that! That said, there are good reasons for not placing the emphasis on changing **A**.

Many of life's toughest problems cannot be solved but only outgrown. By outgrowing, Jung had in mind a new consciousness or a new horizon. The new horizon allows the person to see a higher or wider interest through the widening view. The insoluble problem remains unsolved but loses its urgency or fades out with this new consciousness, or in the words of Derek Rydall, 'Problems aren't solved; they dissolve as you evolve.'

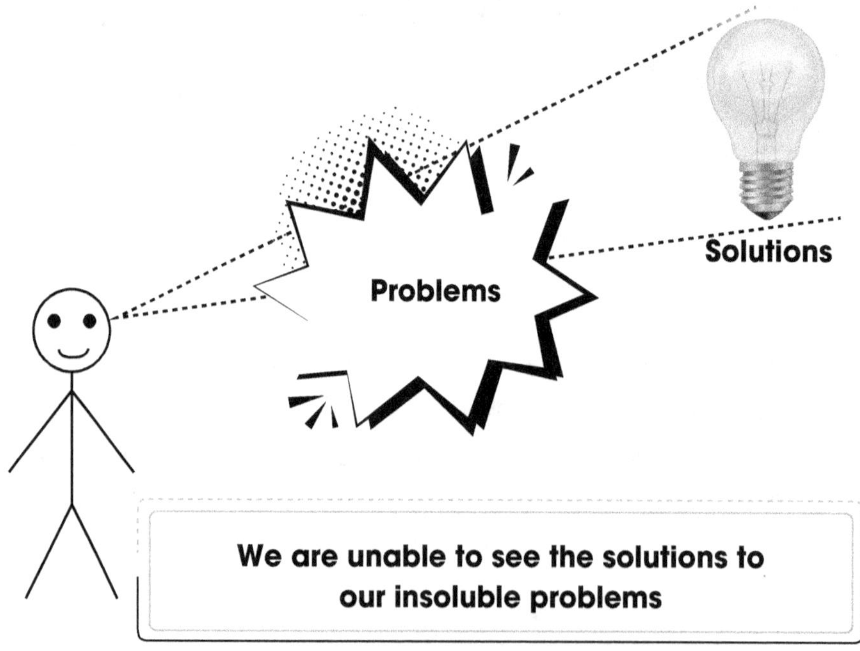

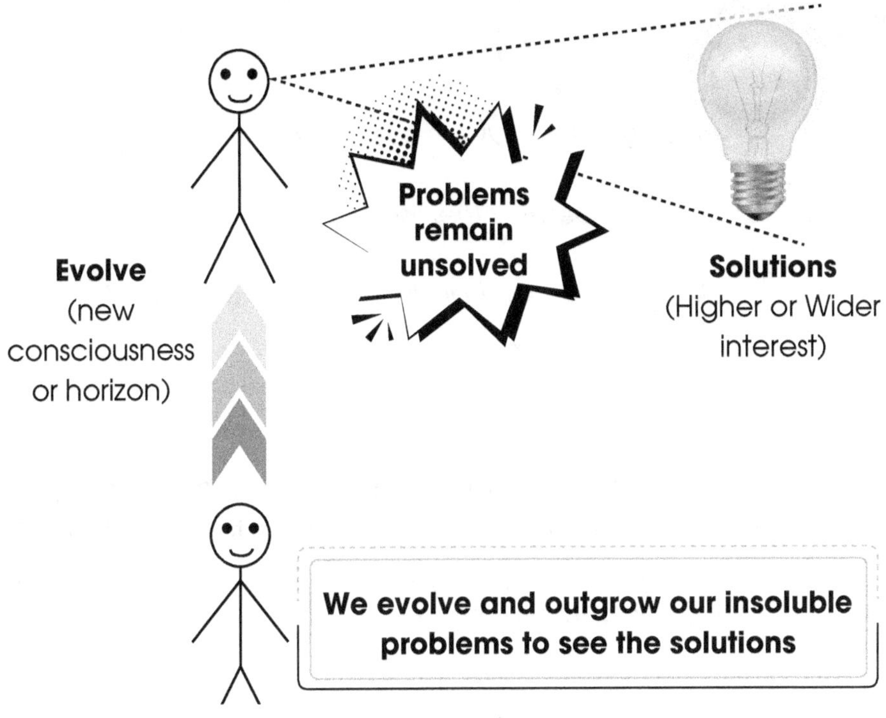

This concept, to 'outgrow' or 'evolve', brings to the fore what we have been saying about the necessity to make *changes* in our pursuit of health and happiness. Change is another name for growth.

Changes to our **WOK**, **WALK** and **WATCH** are mainly about Level 1 change (*external* change). We cross over to Level 2 change (*internalized* change) when we begin to change our **THOUGHTS** (belief). It is best not to see the two levels of change as separate pools of water, but rather two different parts of the same river. With the three-stranded cord of body, behaviour and belief, the two levels are integrated – external change is being internalized. The upstream part of the river has found its way to its midstream. The 'knowing' and 'doing' join hands with 'believing', and together, they begin the journey of 'becoming'. Transformation has begun!

An ancient Jewish scroll has this to say about a three-stranded cord:

> *'Though one may be overpowered,*
>
> *two can defend themselves.*
>
> *A cord of three strands is not quickly broken'*[1]

While a cord of three strands is not *quickly* broken, it can *still* be broken. We would have to do more to strengthen it, wouldn't we? If you are thinking what the next "B" is, don't! That is so not out-of-the-box thinking. Uh-oh, some of you are thinking, 'So, the next '**B**' is for think out of the **B**ox?'

Oh well… what really matters is that the river continues its way downstream, without impediments, so that 'becoming' makes its way to 'being'. Our destination is full transformation!

IMPEDIMENTS TO TRANSFORMATION

Life is seldom easy. When you begin to embark on transformation, you are likely to encounter impediments. Impediments to transformation can dam up the river and prevent it from flowing downstream. What is the most common impediment? Let us play a few games to find out.

Game Number 1:

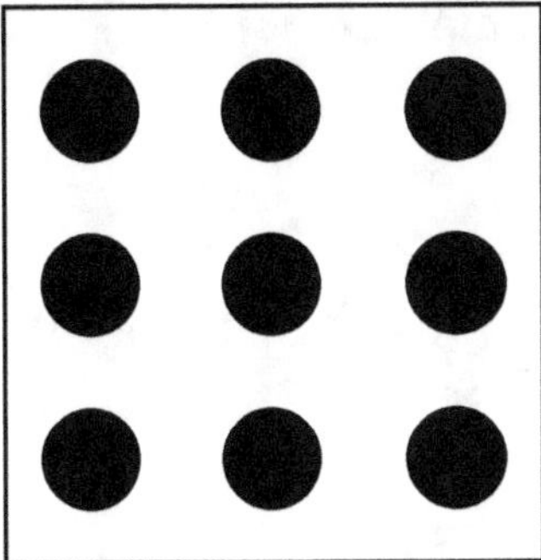

Connect the nine dots with four lines without lifting your pencil.

Were you able to complete the task?   If you cannot, you may turn to the Appendix 5 to see the answer. For those who are able to complete the task, congratulations!   Let us all go to the next game.

Game Number 2:

Connect the nine dots with **three** lines without lifting your pencil.

Were you able to do Game Number 2?

Here is the answer to Game Number 2:

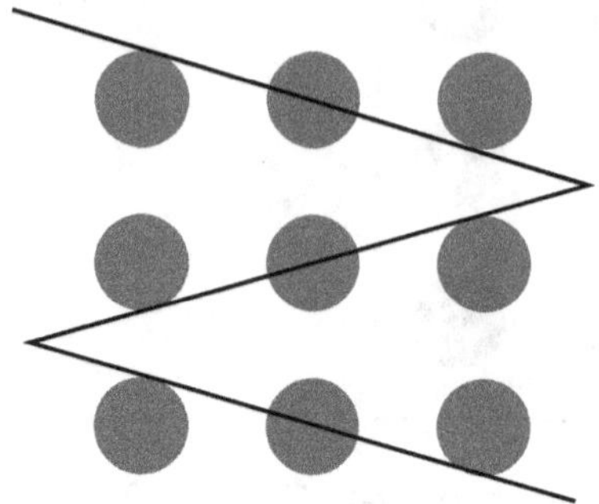

You ready for more games?

Here's Game Number 3 – first question:

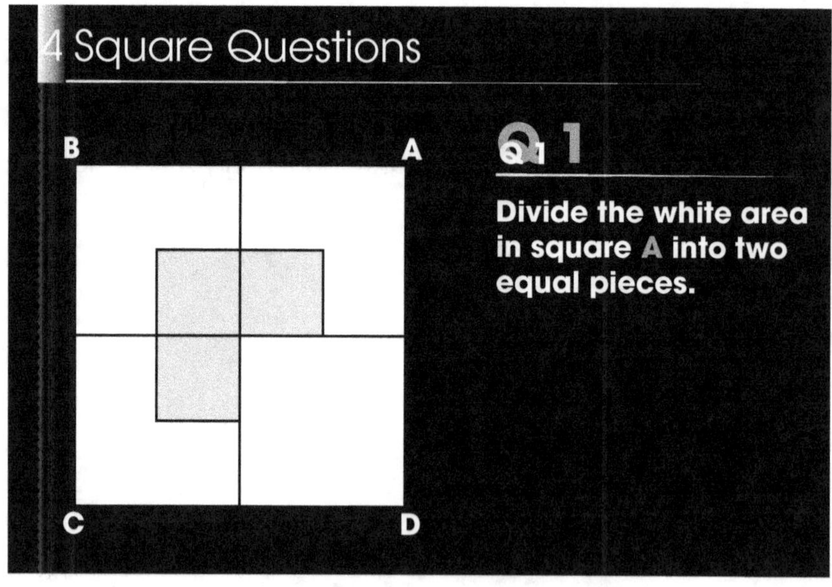

EASY? You could solve it easily, right?

Here is the answer to the first question:

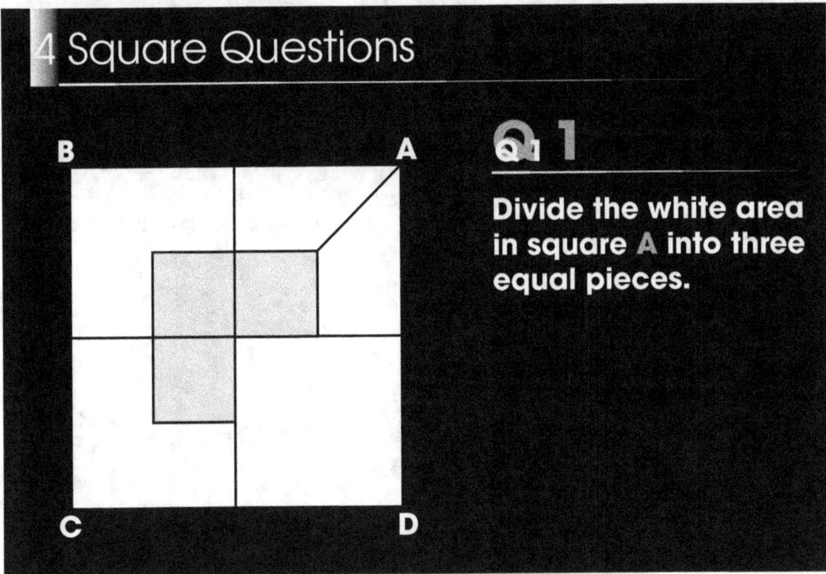

Second question to Game Number 3:

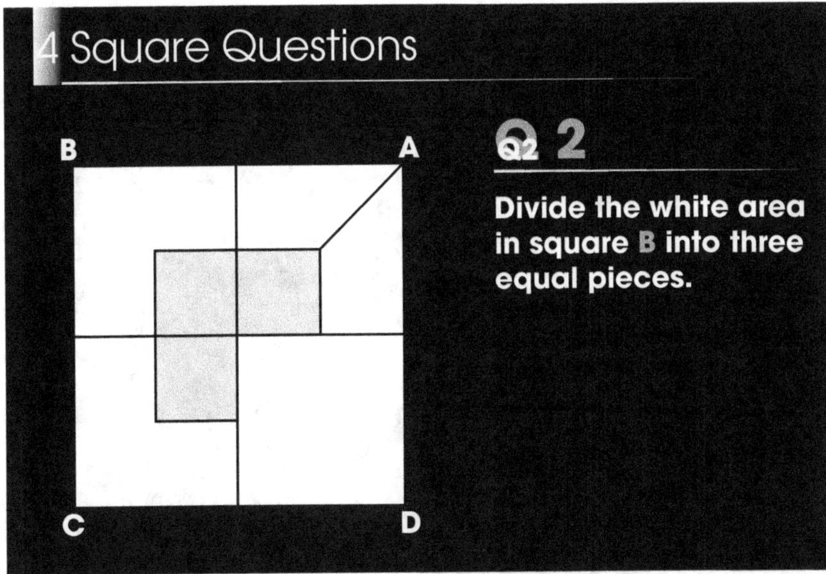

Here is the answer to the second question:

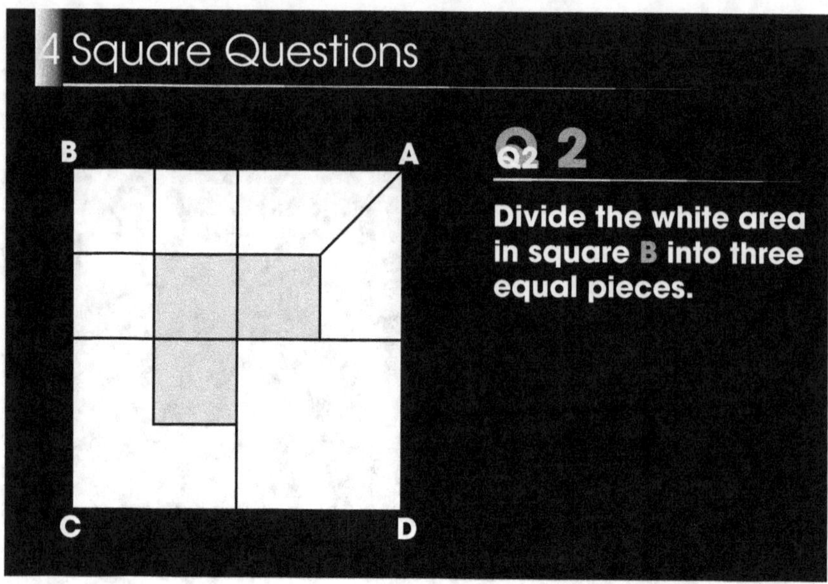

Here comes the third question.

It is going to be difficult. Take your time.

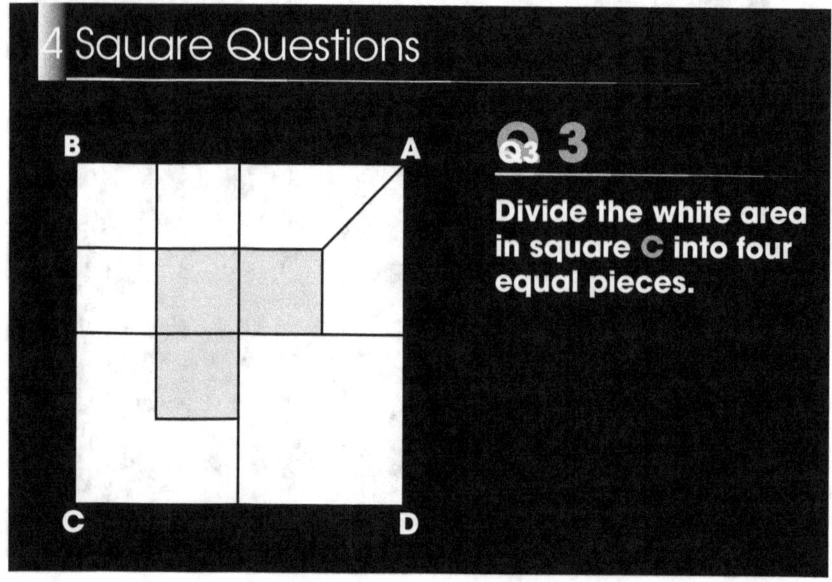

Okay, here is the answer to the third question:

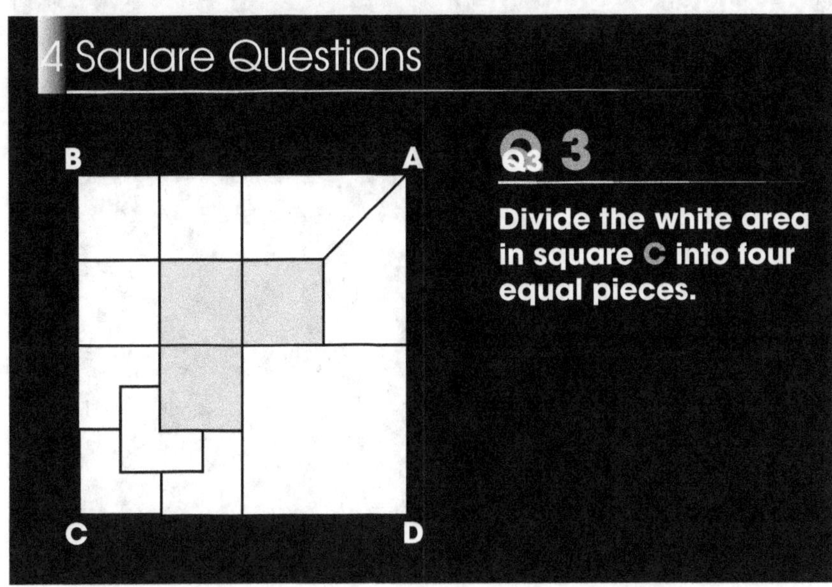

Here comes the last question. Be READY!

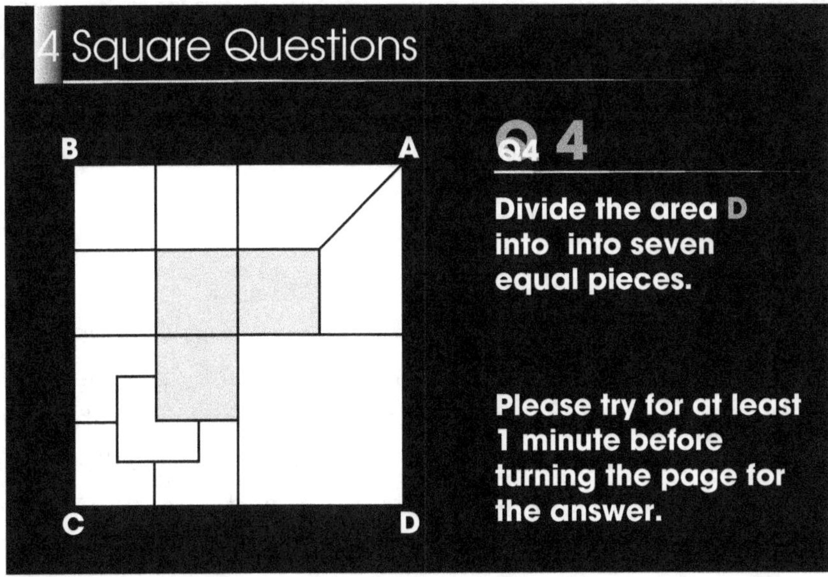

Here is the answer to the fourth question:

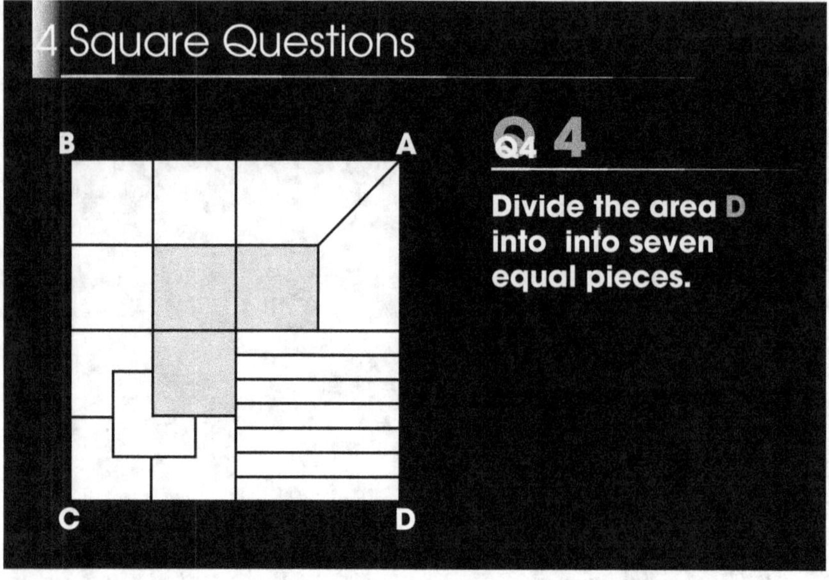

Were you able to answer the fourth question correctly, with either six horizontal or vertical lines? If you did, you are exceptional! Most people struggle to come up with an answer similar to the one in Box C. What happened? Well, these games reveal how our minds can be conditioned, making it hard for us to *think out of the box.*

The Pike Syndrome

I read about an experiment some researchers conducted on large freshwater fish called the northern pike. They put the fish in one-half of a large fish tank and put many minnows in the other half, with a glass separating them. As the pike became hungry, the visible minnows swimming freely in the other half seemed like a good dinner. The fish would make many attempts to eat the minnows, but only ended up battering its snout against the glass divider. After some time, the pike learnt that it was impossible to reach the minnows on the other side. Guess what happened when they removed the glass partition? You are right. The pike did not even try to eat the minnows even though they swam freely around the tank. The researchers called this the 'pike syndrome'.

We observe the pike syndrome in elephants too. You might have seen these huge creatures being held by only a small rope tied to their front leg – no chains or cages. The elephants could easily break away from the ropes they were tied with, but for some strange reason, they did not. The reason was that when the elephants were young and smaller, their front leg was tied with a small rope to a tree or stump which was strong enough to restrain them at that time. As they grew up, they were conditioned to believe they could not break away, so they never tried to break free. Think about that for a minute – they stopped trying.

The pike syndrome is found not just in pikes or elephants. Humans are victims of the pike syndrome too, aren't we? Our environment and experience condition us to believe assumptions or rules that make it hard to overcome our self-imposed limitations. We are being held back by an imaginary glass partition. We go through life holding on to limiting beliefs that we are incapable of certain successes, simply because we have tried but failed before. We are held tied by a small rope.

Pike syndrome prevents us from evolving to outgrow our insoluble problems. It causes us to get stuck midstream and unable to make it downstream. Pike syndrome is the most common impediment to growth.

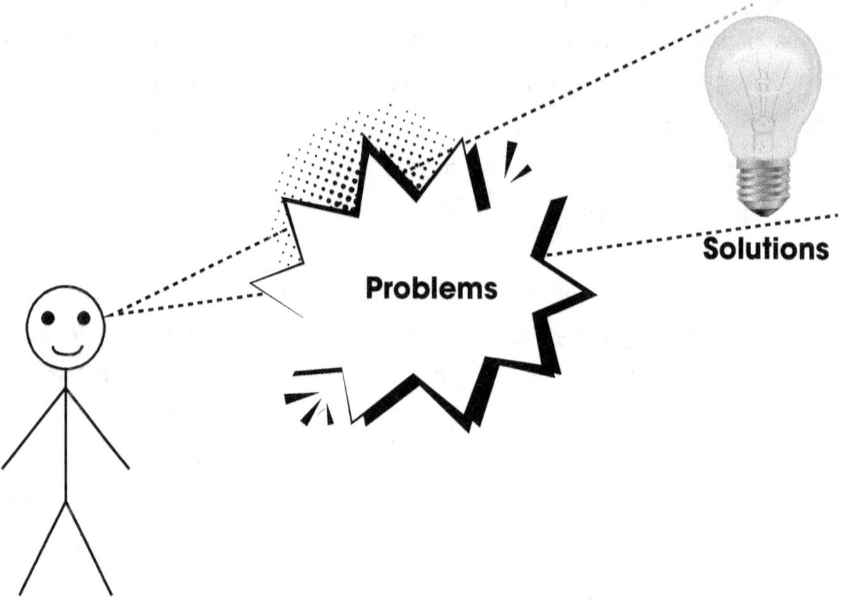

Pike syndrome prevents us from evolving and outgrowing our insoluble problems

- Problems cloud our minds

- Self-imposed assumptions and rules:

  → False beliefs and wrong assumptions

  → We automatically filter out information that does not fit into our beliefs

- Old (fixed) ways of thinking block out creative solutions, possibilities, new ideas, options, and outcomes

- Old habits weigh us down, preventing growth

We have to overcome the pike syndrome if we want to grow. 'But wouldn't changing our thoughts overcome it?' you might ask. 'What about the bolstered three-stranded cord of body, behaviour and belief? Wouldn't that help us overcome the pike syndrome?'

Yes, changing our thoughts is certainly necessary but not always sufficient. We cannot depend solely on an insight-oriented approach or changing thoughts to transform us. We need help to change the brain that has been conditioned by habits. Often our old habits will cause us to regress to our old self, and the densest element that will suck us into the black hole of our old self is surprisingly small. It is called the tongue. For example, a person may attend a weekend getaway workshop and learn the importance of positive thinking for successful living. For two days, he gains new insights and decides to change his negative thinking patterns. However, when he gets home, he falls into his old habits of talking to his family with snarky remarks, sarcasm, and cynical comments. In less than a day, his negative talk leads him back to his old negative thinking patterns.

Out of our thoughts comes our talk. This is true. No one will argue with this. However, what is perhaps less familiar is that our talk also influences our thoughts. Our talk – how we talk to ourselves, what we talk about and how we talk to others – is a habit. Habits form neural pathways in our brain. These pathways, formed by repetitions over time, are strong and hard to change. Unless they are changed, they will continue to reinforce our old thought habits, biases, and attitudes. So, unless we change our talk, it will continue to perpetuate old assumptions and thought patterns. Fortunately, our brains are malleable. But to rewire the neural pathways formed by an old habit, we need to learn a *new* habit. We therefore need to learn a new habit of talking!

Consider this excerpt taken from one of the Christian sacred texts[2], '*Consider what a great forest is set on fire by a small spark. The tongue also is a fire, a world of evil among the parts of the body. It corrupts the whole body, sets the whole course of one's life on fire...*'

Our words can poison *every part* of our body – this includes our thought patterns, mindset, attitudes, emotions, and behaviour. Just as a tiny spark can set the entire forest on fire, in the same way our words can set the whole course of our lives on fire. Sounds frightening, doesn't it?

An ancient wise Hebrew saying goes like this, '*Kind words are like honey, sweet to the soul and healthy for the body.*' We are apt to think that this saying applies to the kind words we speak to others. It certainly includes that, but is definitely not limited to that. It is crucial that we also speak kind words to ourselves, for when we do so, we nourish our soul and bring health to our body. A nourished soul and healthy body will naturally lead to growth. Only with growth can we evolve into a person with new consciousness or horizon, and outgrow life's insoluble problems. Therefore, let us learn to change the way we talk – *how* we talk to ourselves when we are alone, *what* we talk about when we are with others, and *how* we talk to others.

CHANGING THE WAY WE TALK

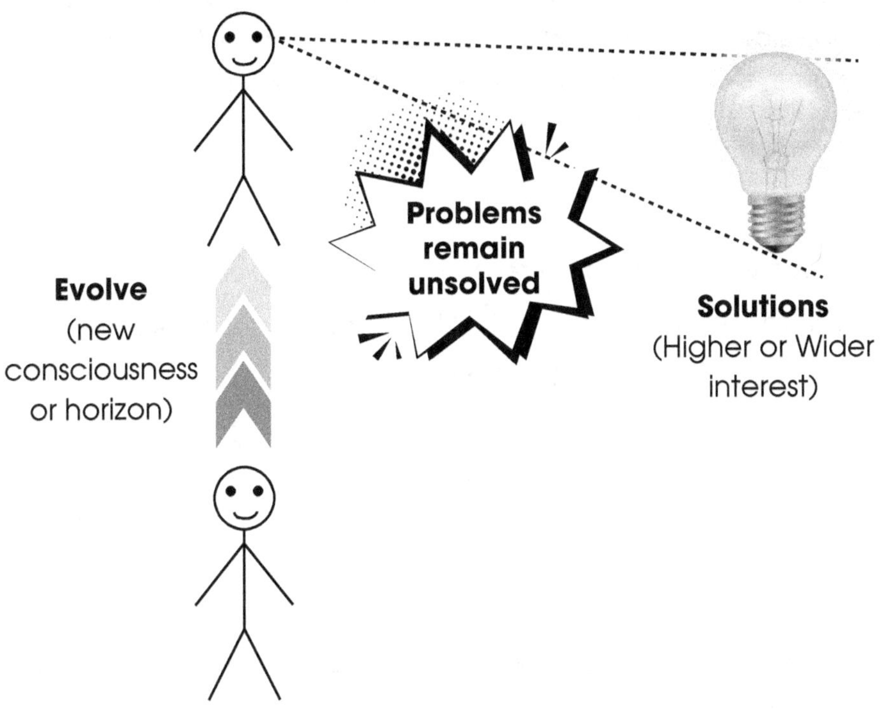

Some people prefer to talk about problems. They would talk about their most frustrating problem – what happened, how bad others were, how bad the situation was and how upset they felt. When their listeners (usually friends) try to offer a solution, they would quickly go into how it would not work, or that they had already tried that, but it didn't work. They were not seeking solutions to their problem; they were seeking for support that they were helpless victims, in order to justify their excessive blaming of others and circumstances. There is a place for venting of frustrations, but certainly not as helpless victims shirking responsibilities.

I completely understand we have the need to unload our frustrations on empathetic ears when we feel stressed by insoluble problems. However, there is a difference between talking about our feelings and complaining about our problems. In sharing our feelings with trusted friends, we seek to find strength in their empathetic response to help us confront our problems. In complaining about our problems, more often than not, we seek to justify our helplessness, passivity, fault-finding, or blame shifting.

> *Have you realized that most of your unhappiness in life is due to the fact that you are listening to yourself instead of talking to yourself?*
>
> *Martyn Lloyd-Jones*

When we engage in problem talk, rarely any solution can be generated at the end of it – nor can we evolve to outgrow our problem. Instead, we become even more convinced of how hopeless our situation is and how helpless we are; and of course, the rest are to blame.

Although we may feel momentarily better by justifying our helplessness, this is far outweighed by the negative energy produced by the problem talk. The negative energy shackles us to our old self and reinforces our helplessness. Problem talk modifies us to be like the pikes genetically.

What do we practise every day? We will get very good at what we practise every day. If we practise complaining, we will get so good at it that we will be able to find fault in everything, even when there is no fault. If we practise fault-finding, we can get so proficient at it that we will find fault in everyone – including ourselves. And if we practise problem talk, we will become an expert in magnifying problems, instead of building solutions.

While our past experiences condition our mind by imprisoning it, our complaints and problem talk complete the job by throwing away the key. To free ourselves, we need to change the way we talk. We need **OSCAR** for the prison break!

SOLUTION TALK VERSUS PROBLEM TALK

OSCAR is a framework to help you engage in solution talk rather than problem talk. It focuses on the future – your desired outcome and intended goal – instead of focusing on the past. It emphasizes your current strengths and resources and avoids deficiency language. Rather than dwelling on what is not working, it applies a detective mind to uncover what is already working in order to do more of what works. Essentially, it creates a hopeful future and energizes you by amplifying your successes, before empowering you to take the next step towards that hopeful future.

Meet OSCAR. It stands for:

Outcome

Scaling

Current strengths and resources

Action steps

Review

OUTCOME

The first stage of **OSCAR** deals with what you want for your situation. Instead of talking about what you do not want (your problem), talk about what you want (your goal). Most of my clients come to me to talk about their problems. When I succeed in getting them to tell me *what they want* instead, I would notice the change in their facial expression and body language – smiles replace furrowed brows, sparkling eyes replace dull-looking ones, and they become visibly more relaxed and energized.

Talk to your friends about what exactly life would be like if you could have what you want. Imagine your life without the problem and talk about it: What would be different if the problem did not exist? What would be the positive effects if the problem is solved? Pretending that your problem is solved, what would you be doing differently? How would that be helpful for you and others around you? Do such a good job of talking about your goal to the point that it becomes crystal clear to your friends what exactly it is that you want.

SCALING

This is the second stage of OSCAR. Problems cloud our minds when we focus or keep talking about them. We are immediately gripped by one or all of these thinking distortions: *all-or-nothing thinking, awfulising-catastrophising and negative focus.* These thinking traps lock us up in the cold dark attic, depriving us of the warm well-lit living room. While we starve in the shadowy room filled with cobwebs, our favourite foods are being served in the laughter-filled dining room. We need to come down from that filthy mould-covered attic. But to do that, we need a ladder. In our case – for solution building – we need a scale.

Ask yourself, on the scale of 1 to 10, with 10 representing the outcome or goal that you want and 1 being the opposite, where are you on the scale right now? This is not a time for false humility. It requires you to go into truthful reflection and give an honest assessment of where you are on that scale. In your conversation with a friend, it would probably go something like this, 'You know, about the goal that I've been describing to you, if that's a 10, I am probably at a 4 right now.'

Placing yourself on the scale will almost immediately free you from *all-or-nothing thinking and awfulising-catastrophising* your situation. If you struggle to come up with an answer, try asking yourself, 'Where would someone who knows me well rate me on that scale?' Scaling will save you from false binary thinking and spare you from lots of unnecessary anxiety and distress. Try it the next time you feel like a total failure.

CURRENT STRENGTHS & RESOURCES

This is the third stage of OSCAR. The scale rating obtained at the second stage can be used in two ways to help us: Performance Gap approach or Solution Building approach. Both approaches can be helpful but let's take a look at both of them, and see which is more suitable to energize us to build solution.

Performance Gap

A performance gap is the difference between intended and actual performance. It is a gap – a shortfall – between the goal and our current situation. We are expected to fill it. To do that, we usually identify the root cause behind the gap, develop the resource and put in place an action plan to bridge the gap.

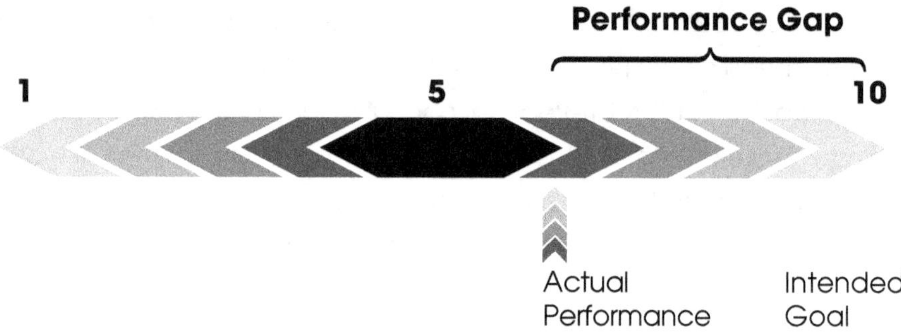

There is nothing fundamentally wrong with this approach. It is a helpful process for continuous improvement. It works very well when there is an experienced expert on hand to offer you support and advice.

However, this problem-focused approach may not be very useful in solving novel or complicated problems. Most of life's problems are complex and unique. In dealing with knotty issues such as parenting or marriage, there is no perfect blueprint, and the best experts are unable to come up with a one-size-fits-all solution.

So, while it may work well for work processes, a problem-focused approach may not work as well to solve life's problems. But for many, this is the approach they grew up with. When a child scores 70% for a mathematics test, he's likely to find that the spotlight will be on the performance gap – parents want to know why it is not 90% or full marks, and the teacher highlights the wrong answers and enters the comment

"Room for improvement".

This approach can have negative effects on one's motivation. When you are not recognized for your hard work or things done well, but instead have the spotlight shone on your shortfall, you feel undervalued and discouraged. This drains you of the energy and impetus needed to make improvements. Sadly, this is the *only* approach many of us are familiar with.

Solution Building

We need a different approach – a solution building approach. In this new approach, we identify where we are on the scale – not to spotlight the performance gap – but to examine what has already been achieved, what has already worked, or what is already working. It amplifies successes, strengths and resources instead of the shortfall. It stays away from deficient language that is distressing, discouraging and disheartening. Instead, it emphasizes strength-based language that amplifies *small* successes and *exceptions* to the problem. This energizes us and empowers us to take steps towards our desired goal.

This solution building approach uncovers possibilities instead of revealing problems. *Awfulising-catastrophising* and *negative focus* cause us to see nothing but problems. Everything we see, think or say is being coloured by the problems. By focusing and talking about our current strengths and resources, our eyes are opened to the reality that despite our problems and difficult situations, there are things that are still working! It is therefore vital that we learn to talk about our successes, strengths and resources, especially to ourselves.

In my own life as a parent, if I were to be honest, there were times I felt I had absolutely failed as a father. My thoughts would swirl around my mistakes and the utter mess I was in – what went wrong, how did the situation end up so badly and what a total failure I was. With each thought, I would sink deeper into the murky waters of *all-or-nothing thinking, negative focus, and awfulising-catastrophising*. What usually saved me from committing hara-kiri was forcing myself to solution talk to myself – repeating the goal of parenting to myself, placing myself on the parenting scale to avoid binary thinking, listing what's going on well, what's still working and what has been done well, et cetera. And of course, reminding myself of better times in the past (exceptions) always gave hope to better times in the future. All of this energized me to want to build solutions. In the end, what saved the day was changing the way I talked to myself. Indeed, how we talk to ourselves can make a huge difference!

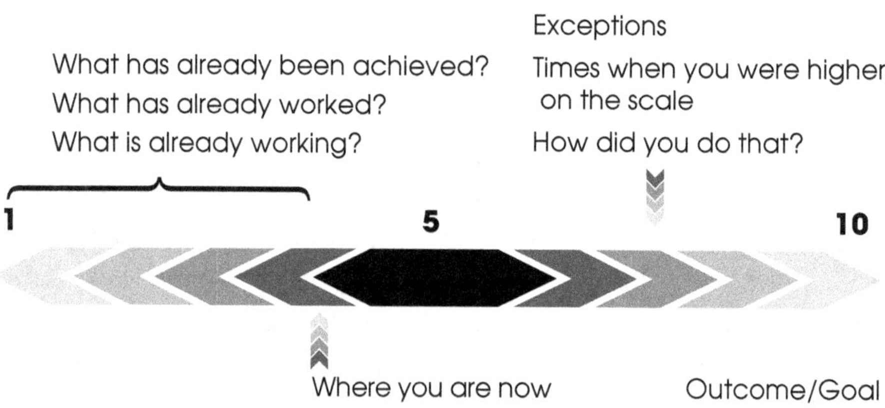

After identifying where you are on the scale, these are some things you can ask yourself to amplify your current successes, strengths and resources:

- How come you are at this point and not any lower?

- What has helped you to get this far on the scale? How have you managed to do that?

- What does that tell you about yourself? What personal qualities will help you achieve the outcome you want?

- Were there times when you were higher on that scale? How did you do that?

ACTION STEPS

This is the fourth stage of OSCAR. It is never easy to take action steps towards bridging the performance gap. We make the mistake of rushing to take action but end up finding themselves depleted of energy and motivation to work towards the goal. In OSCAR, we take action steps only *after* we are sufficiently energized and motivated by our past and current successes, and our strengths and resources.

To take the next step, visualize yourself just one or two notches higher on the scale. It is better to take small achievable steps rather than one unrealistic giant step. Make small changes and go for the ripple effect – a small change can have an enormous impact. This will prevent you from giving up or burning out in the process.

> *Life is like an ever-shifting kaleidoscope*
> *- a slight change, and all patterns alter.*
>
> *Sharon Salzberg*

Ask yourself the following questions when taking the next step:

- Where on the scale is good enough for you to be next?

- What would it take to move up to that point?

- Supposing you have reached that point, what difference would that make for you? What would you be doing differently?

Parents can use **OSCAR** as a framework to change the way they talk to their children. From my experience working with parents who send their children to me for counselling, I find that some parents have unrealistic expectations of their children. They are overly focused on the 'performance gap' and attempt to use shame, guilt, bribes and threats to bridge the gap. Through nagging, passive aggression or aggression, parents can end up damaging the relationship with their children, widening not only their children's performance gap but the gap between them and their children as well.

Expecting our children to be perfect is not a realistic goal. It not only sets you up for disappointment but creates a gulf, not a gap in performance. We must learn to set appropriate goals or **outcomes** at different developmental stages of our children's life. The use of **Scaling** prevents us from seeing our children as a *total* moral failure because of a few irresponsible behaviours. Even when we do not say it, we unconsciously communicate it through our tone or body language. No wonder many children see themselves as a total failure.

Focusing on their **current strengths** enables us to amplify and celebrate their successes (no matter how small they are) and energize them by our compliments. With wisdom and patience, we assist them to take small **action** steps towards an attainable goal.

OSCAR works best when you are able to coach your children to use the same framework for themselves. Another word: instead of setting goals for them, help them set their own goals, scale and rate themselves on the scale, and decide what action steps they would like to take.

If you would like to learn how to become a solution focused parent-coach, you can contact Egero Wellness for more information. Contact details of Egero can be found in Appendix 5.

REVIEW

This is the fifth and final stage of **OSCAR**. Have you tried walking in a straight line with your eyes closed? If you have not, try going to a park and walk for a distance with your eyes closed. You might feel you are walking straight but when you open your eyes, you will see that you have veered in a curvy circular pattern. It is the same way with our efforts to solution talk. We will tend to veer into problem talk. As such, we need to review the way we talk regularly. Use the table below to review your progress regularly.

PROBLEM TALK	SOLUTION TALK
Complain about problem	Build solution
Describe the problem	Describe life without the problem What do you want? What would be different if the problem did not exist? What would life be like without this problem?
Focus on the past What I don't want	Focus on the future: Intended goals and desired outcome What do I want instead?
Deficiency Language	Strength-based Language (Exceptions. Strengths. Resources.)
Reveal problems What's not working? Tendency to dwell on the problem	Uncover potentials and possibilities What has worked? What is working? What will work? Seek exceptions as clues to the solutions. Do more of what has already worked
Distressing Discouraging Disheartening	Creating hopeful future Energizing the person Empowering the person
Action plan to bridge the performance gap	Ripple effect – a small change can have an enormous impact

Solution Building is not 'Problem-solving'

We have now completed the discussion on all the five stages of **OSCAR**. **OSCAR** is a dynamic process that grows the person who uses it. As you engage in the solution building process, you discover your strengths and resources, and grow in awareness, insight, perspective and horizon. Your assumptions, attitudes, and mindset will also change. As a result, you could outgrow the goal that was set earlier. There is therefore a need to review your goal from time to time. Solution building is mainly about growing, not problem-solving. With growth, it enables you to outgrow the insoluble problem, and seek out a new and better goal which embarks you on a new journey to build an entirely different solution.

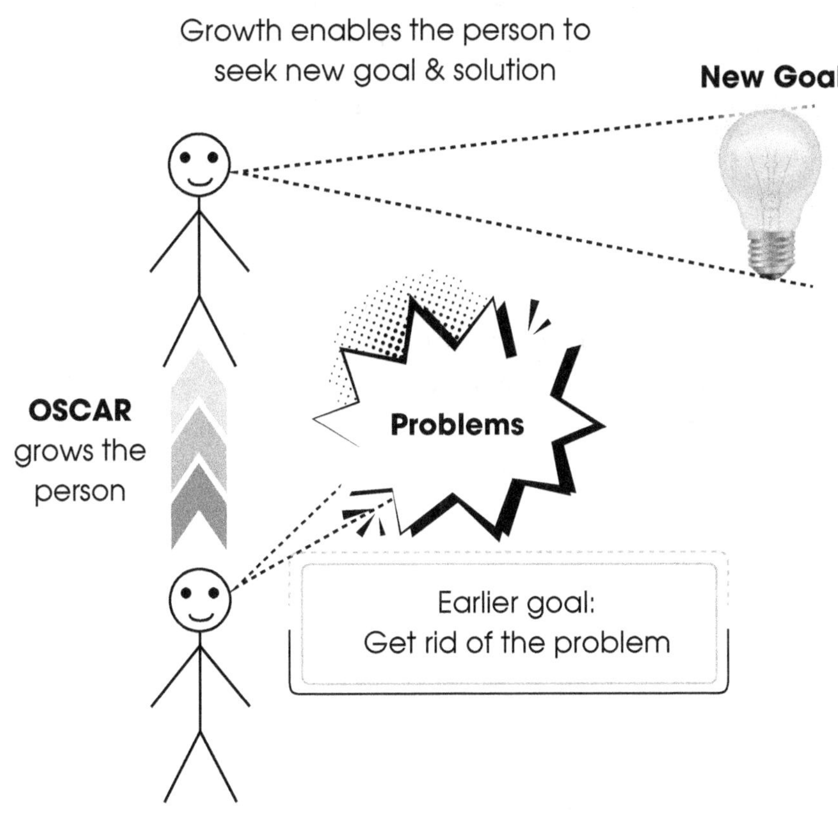

I once saw a teen whose goal was to 'change his father'. After engaging him in solution building for a few sessions, he grew as a person. He reviewed his goal and changed it to 'being able to see his father with a new pair of eyes'. Not bad for a teen. He managed to move from problem talk to solution building, and as a result, his horizon and consciousness grew. His problem was not solved (he did not change his father) but with an elevated horizon, he outgrew it by identifying a different goal – learning to see his father differently. His new goal set him on the path to build a totally different set of solutions!

> *You can only change yourself, not anyone else.*
> *Change your attitude, your behaviour and*
> *how you see your reality,*
> *then others will seem to have changed.*
>
> *create.christaherzog.com*

In life, many problems cannot be solved. Solution building is not always about solving a problem. Sometimes, it is. It elevates the person's horizon to think out of the box and solve the knotty problem. Often, solution building grows the person by growing his consciousness and behaviour to accept and outgrow the insoluble problem. At other times, solution building enables you to *cope* with the problem when you realize there is no immediate solution.

In presenting OSCAR to clients, I have been asked some very good questions. Here is one of them: *Is this approach for all issues or for mostly those where opinion or attitude is in question? Does it apply in other situations such as mundane problems experienced physically? For example, Joey's next-door HDB neighbour bangs the door and yells whenever he likes, perhaps to vent his frustration. Joey has a heart problem, and whenever the sudden loud noises come at random from her neighbour, she is startled. As a result, she does not have peace and feels anxious. The anxiety is compounded by the fact that she is living in trepidation of the next startling sound as she does not know when it will strike. She is also worried about such effects on her heart and mind. Though Joey is aware that her neighbour is a lonely single senior person and suffers from insomnia, this kind understanding is insufficient to lift her above the higher horizon to see the solutions.*

A solution building approach is certainly helpful in tackling this apparent real-life problem. That said, we need to recognize that **OSCAR** is a simple framework to help beginners shift from problem-talk to solution-talk. It is helpful in changing the way we talk. Its main aim is to help rewire the neural pathways formed by our old habit of talking by learning a new habit of talking. By changing the way we talk, over time, we hope to overcome the pike syndrome, which is a major impediment to transformation.

OSCAR is not so much a practical 5-step guide to solving a knotty real-life problem, but a framework to help us grow in our horizon and consciousness, by changing the way we talk. It is definitely worth a try to apply **OSCAR** to whatever problem you are facing. The process can help you develop the right mindset, attitude and judgment about an issue that allows you to look at a problem realistically yet creatively, then with hope and motivation, seek to build solution. However, with protracted problems, you might want to consult a solution-focused therapist or coach to help you with solution building. I have included a referral list in Appendix 5.

OVERCOMING THE IMPEDIMENTS TO TRANSFORMATION

Using OSCAR to Change the Way We Talk

OSCAR is a simple framework to help you change the way you talk – how you talk to yourself when you are alone, what you talk about when you are with others, and how you talk to others. My best hope is that **OSCAR** will help you replace an old habit by forming a new habit – solution talk instead of problem talk – and focus more on solution building rather than complaining about the problem.

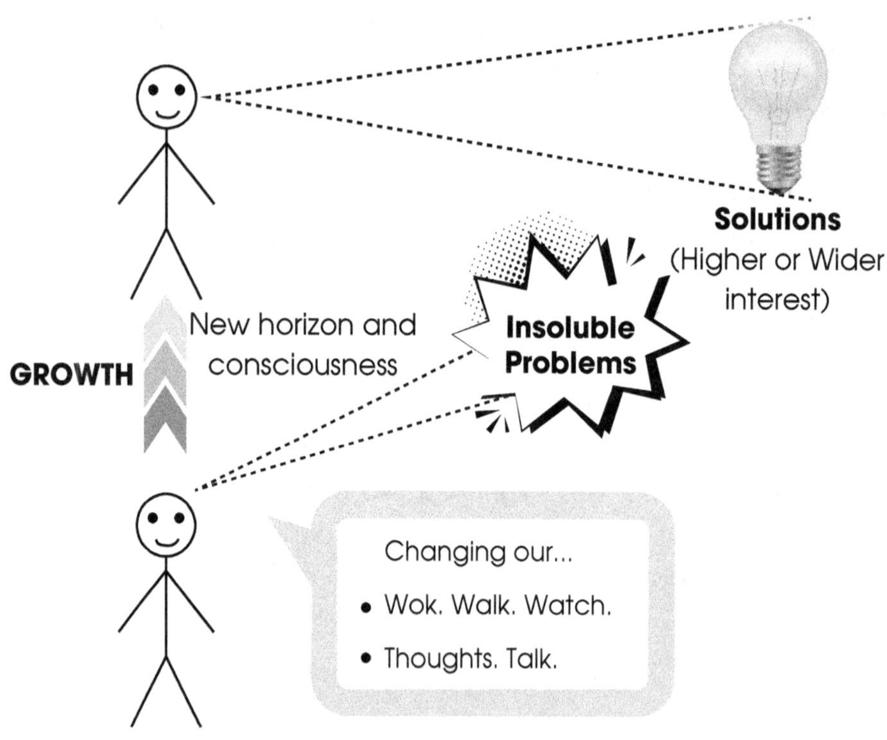

When we change the way we talk, the new habit forms new neural pathways in our brain. This neural rewiring reinforces the cognitive restructuring – the change in our talk strengthens the change in our thoughts. **OSCAR** therefore does not work alone, but together with the new effective and functional thoughts we mentioned in the previous chapter. Together, the change in thoughts and talk evolves us to develop a new horizon or consciousness. Even as our problems remain insoluble, this growth provides us with new insights, or widens our interests to outgrow the insoluble problems.

By now, it probably has become apparent to you that **OSCAR** is not about finding the solution to a particular problem. It is about becoming the person who is capable of finding solutions to every unique and complex problem that life throws at us at different junctures. The emphasis is therefore not on learning a particular skillset or thinking skill, but on becoming a transformed person, who through right eating, right action, right thought and right speech, is able to look at a problem realistically yet imaginatively, and come up with a solution for every problem – be it solving it, outgrowing it, or coping with it.

> *Transformation is who we have become,*
>
> *not just what we think, feel, believe, say or do.*

In the pursuit of health and happiness, many seek a path that would lead to the right place – a paradise – free of problems and pain, where there's perfection in everything, from people to provision to the physical environment. Unfortunately, there is no such place!

In the journey we have taken to pursue health and happiness, we advocate that we take the path of growth. Growth requires change.

Not just external or internal change, but transformational change. Instead of hoping to come to the right place, we hope to become the right person. To this endeavour, we have looked at changing our **WOK, WALK, WATCH, THOUGHT** and **TALK**. We began our journey upstream and have been making our course downstream steadily. With *changing the way we talk,* we are nearing the river mouth, but the journey is not yet done. Transformation is who we have become, not just what we think, feel, believe, say, or do. We shall therefore continue our journey of transformation that leads to health and happiness.

CHAPTER SIX

CHANGING OUR TORQUE

> *Torque? What is that?*

I posed this question to a former college teacher who once taught physics: 'How would you explain "torque" in simple layman terms?' Her answer was, 'Pulling power or rotational force, or in the Chinese language, 扭转力.' Torque refers to the amount of rotational force that an automobile engine can exert. It is the *pulling power or the oomph.*[1]

To set out in our caravan for the road trip, we need the torque of the automobile engine. Similarly, we need a pulling power for our journey to health and happiness, especially when the road becomes steep and winding. The path to a healthier and happier life is not paved with good intentions, but with *intentional changes*. Using the integrated approach of the Biopsychosocial-Spiritual (BPSS) Model, I have urged you to make changes to your **WOK, WALK, WATCH, THOUGHT** and **TALK**.

Making changes is never easy for anyone. How do you find the motivation to begin the journey of change and the incentive to continue with it, especially when the journey gets tough? What should your pulling power be? Is it more money? A bigger house? A successful career or fame? What would keep you going every day? Or simply, what is the *oomph* factor for your journey?

What you need is a **TORQUE**, a rotating force that can turn all your changes into a synergized force and propel you forward on your transformational journey to your desired destination. What is that torque?

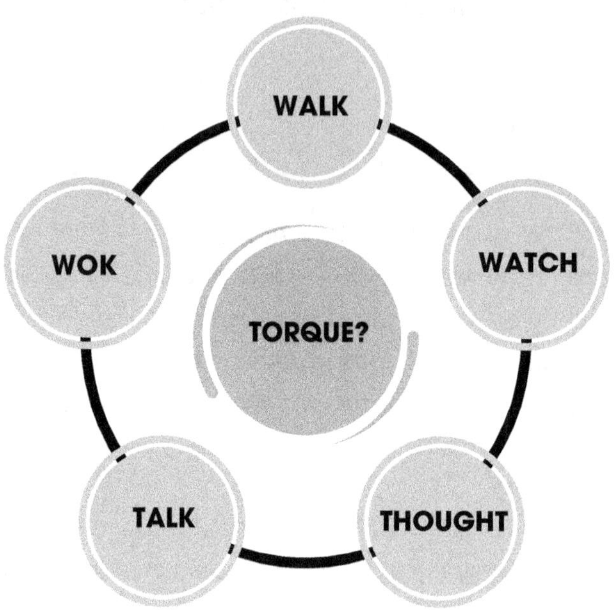

THE OOMPH FACTOR

In 1938, a team of Harvard researchers began tracking 268 of its graduates from the classes of 1939 to 1944, along with 456 young men from inner city Boston. This study is an extensive longitudinal study, and has revealed many insights. One of the most useful insights is perhaps found in the famous quote by Robert J. Waldinger, the director of the study, and it says:

> 'The clearest message that we get from this 75-year study is this:
>
> Good relationships keep us happier and healthier. Period.[2]

Below are several other helpful quotes from Professor Waldinger:[3]

> *'The surprising finding is that our relationships*
> *and how happy we are in our relationships*
> *has a powerful influence on our health.'*
>
> *'Good relationships don't just protect our bodies;*
> *they protect our brains.'*
>
> *'Loneliness kills.*
> *It's as powerful as smoking or alcoholism.'*

Professor Waldinger, convinced of the study findings himself, practises what he preaches. He invests time and energy in his relationships. 'It's easy to get isolated, to get caught up in work and not remembering, "Oh, I haven't seen these friends in a long time." So, I try to pay more attention to my relationships than I used to,' said the professor.

Having good relationships with our family and friends is fundamental to keeping us happy and enabling us to live longer. It is not money, material possessions, fame or success. The Harvard study has provided evidence that it is meaningful relationships that 'protect people from life's discontents, help to delay mental and physical decline, and are better predictors of long and happy lives than social class, IQ, or even genes.'[3]

The quality of your closest relationships is the number one key to your happiness. It is important to note that what really matters is the quality and the depth of your personal relationships – not how many friends you have. Having hundreds of superficial relationships on social media will not make you feel less lonely. On the contrary, superficiality of relationships heightens our sense of isolation and need for connection. According to a 2019 survey by YouGov, the social media generation is the one that feels the most alone.

We need good family relationships and strong friendships. They provide us with the pulling power we need in life. If you have spent most of your time and energy pursuing money, success, or hobbies, you need to change that. Change your **TORQUE** by reprioritizing and channelling your resources to invest in relationships. Devote your time and energy to cultivate deep close relationships with those around you.

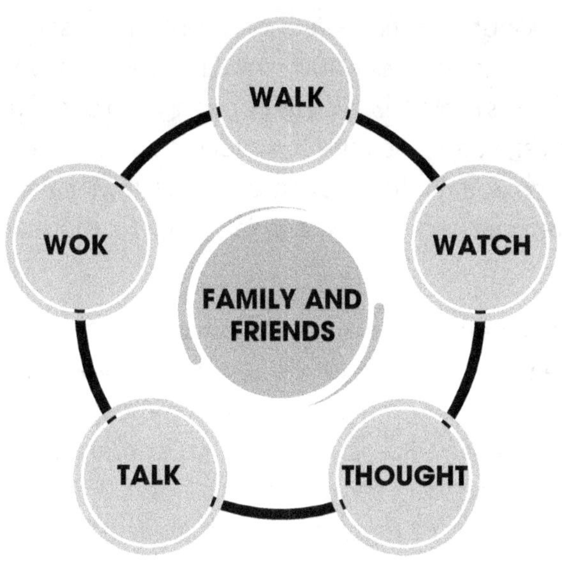

Yet, as with many changes, changing our torque is not as easy as it sounds. It takes more than just a choice in a moment of enlightenment or good intentions. Indeed, it will take commitment, hard work and discipline to learn how to build good and strong relationships. The process involves both unlearning and learning – letting go of old ways and adopting new habits. The natural question to ask next is, **"Why is relationship building so hard?"**

BROKENNESS AND CONNECTION

Humans are wired to connect with one another. Relationships are about connecting with one another socially and emotionally. However, some people are unable to form these connections. Why? What causes them difficulty in forming connections with others? In addition, we also note that when people lack these connections, they tend to replace them with video gaming, alcohol, sex or other forms of addiction. Why is that so?

I read about a series of experiments that some researchers conducted on rats in the early 20th century. This was what it entailed: 'The experiment is simple. Put a rat in a cage, alone, with two water bottles. One is just water. The other is water laced with heroin or cocaine. Almost every time you run this experiment, the rat will become obsessed with the drugged water, and keep coming back for more and more, until it kills itself.'[4]

The experiments were done to establish the theory that there are strong chemical hooks in drugs. And so, if you take them for a while, your body will become dependent on those hooks – this is how you become addicted. Based on these experiments, people thought they had understood addiction. Then in the 1970s, Professor Bruce Alexander, a professor of psychology, noticed something odd about the experiments. They were putting only a lone rat in an empty cage. It had nothing to do except do drugs.

British journalist Johann Hari reported: 'So Professor Alexander built Rat Park. It is a lush cage where the rats had coloured balls and the best rat food and tunnels to scamper down and plenty of friends: everything a rat about town could want. What, Alexander wanted to know, will happen then?'

'In Rat Park, all the rats obviously tried both water bottles, because they didn't know what was in them. But what happened next was startling.'

'The rats with good lives didn't like the drugged water. They mostly shunned it, consuming less than a quarter of the drugs the isolated rats used. None of them died. While all the rats who were alone and unhappy became heavy users, none of the rats who had a happy environment did this.'[4]

Journalist Hari went on to relate a similar 'human experiment' during the Vietnam War. Some 20 percent of U.S. soldiers became addicted to heroin in Vietnam. *Time* magazine reported that using heroin was 'as common as chewing gum' among U.S. soldiers, and the concern was that they would continue their addiction when they returned to the U.S.

Strangely but thankfully, some 95 percent of the addicted soldiers simply stopped taking heroin when they returned to the U.S. 'Very few had rehab. They shifted from a terrifying cage back to a pleasant one, so didn't want the drug anymore,' Mr Hari reported. He also highlighted another group of 'drug users' – the medical users. Medical patients use heroin for pain relief, but they simply stop using heroin altogether when they no longer need it as their painkiller. Interesting, right? Despite months of use, medical users do not end up as addicts.

All this led Professor Alexander to think there might be a different story to addiction: What if addiction is not about your chemical hooks? What if addiction is about your cage? What if addiction is an adaptation to your environment?

Professor Peter Cohen, Director of the Centre for Drug Research in Amsterdam, thinks we should not even call it addiction. He thinks perhaps we should call it bonding. Human beings have a natural and innate need to bond. We are wired for bonding and connection, and when we are happy and healthy, we will bond and connect with one another.

However, there are some of us who struggle to bond and connect with others. Why is that so? Professor Cohen thinks it is because of our brokenness – trauma, isolation or being beaten down by life. Now, when we cannot bond with one another, we will bond and connect with something that gives us some sense of relief. What is that something?Well, it might be computer gaming, alcohol or even pornography.

> *Our brains are wired for connection,*
> *but trauma rewires them for protection.*
> *That's why healthy relationships*
> *are difficult for wounded people.*
>
> *Ryan North*

All of us experience brokenness. There is no exception. The difference is that some seek and receive healing for their brokenness, while others continue in their state of brokenness. Unhealed brokenness will disconnect us from people and connect us to things. Moreover, the inability to form meaningful relationships will negatively affect our health and happiness. It is therefore crucial that we seek healing for our brokenness.

COMMON BROKENNESS

To begin the journey of healing for our brokenness, we will look at three common types of brokenness that thwart relationship building: **Conflict**, **Shame** and **Alienation**.

CONFLICT

Conflicts stress us. They can also lead to brokenness in relationships with others or to brokenness of self. We do not desire or seek conflicts, but somehow, they always manage to find their way to us. Since they are dreadful yet unavoidable, we may as well develop a deeper understanding of conflicts in order to better manage them.

A main cause of conflict is the adversarial nature of man. Our natural inclination towards distrust, self-centredness and intolerance often causes friction with those around us. On top of it, we avoid confrontation of all kinds to talk over matters because of fear, emotional pain or other possible negative consequence that may arise with any confrontation. So, we suppress our anger or unhappiness, but unfortunately this often leads to passive aggression or aggressive behaviour. In the end, we condemn, instead of caringly confronting the other person. This leads to conflicts. Conflicts not only sour relationships in the present, but also deprive us of any blessings that relationships may bring in the future.

To save valuable relationships, let us learn to employ the three-fold solution to human conflicts, as outlined below:

- First, do not avoid confrontation at all costs. If you avoid confrontation, you may lose or stunt the relationship. Learn the skills to engage in a healthy confrontation. You may refer to Appendix 6 for a simple model for *Confrontation Skills*.[5]

- Second, be the right person in any conflict instead of expecting the other party to be the right person. Right attracts right. Fight attracts fight. If you want the other person to be patient, kind and understanding, be patient, kind and understanding yourself first.

- Third, learn to communicate better. Here, I propose a simple framework, whose acronym is the same as TALK in our earlier chapter. To differentiate, this acronym will be hyphenated, denoting communication. Hence, to communicate better, adopt **T-A-L-K:**

  - **T**alk to each other, not about each other.

  - **A**ccept other people's differences. Agree to disagree, and disagree without being disagreeable. Keep reminding yourself – 'People are not difficult. They are just different.'

  - **L**isten – practise active listening.

  - **K**ind – be kind to each other.

When you confront another person, bear in mind this formula for handling people by General George Marshall, *Bits and Pieces* (1991):

1. Listen to the other person's story.

2. Listen to the other person's full story.

3. Listen to the other person's full story first.

Parent-Child Conflict

A particular area of concern for many parents is the seemingly adversarial relationship with their own children. As kids grow up to become teens, they confide less in their parents. This is natural as the child seeks independence and yearns for personal space to forge his or her own identity. However, the lack of communication could also be an indication of an adversarial relationship.

If you want to know the reason why your children are talking to you less, whether it be due to a developmental stage or a sign of an adversarial relationship, try this litmus test: Ask yourself, 'If I talk to my colleagues and friends the same way I talk to my children, would I still have any friends?'

Imagine this: You arrive late at the office and let out a string of gripes about the public transport breaking down for the third time in a week. One colleague cuts you off mid-sentence and starts to lecture you on why you should not complain but count your blessings instead and strongly suggests that you leave the house earlier in future. You probably would not count this colleague as a friend, would you?

As parents, we tend to be overly instructive with our children. The intention is good but it often puts our kids off. There is a time to be instructive with our children, but we need wisdom to discern the teaching moment. We also need to bear in mind that the teaching moment needs to be preceded and well lubricated by plenty of active listening. To improve your communication with your children, learn to T-A-L-K better, as well as change the way you talk to them by using **OSCAR** (Outcome, Scaling, Current strengths and resources, Action steps, Review. Ref: chapter on Talk).

Beyond Communication Skills

While we can improve communication by learning to T-A-L-K better, communication skills alone are insufficient to solve the problem of conflicts, unless underlying issues are also identified, understood and addressed. Thus far in this book, we have covered how to deal with our underlying issues. Let us now briefly recap the steps.

First, I would like you to recall the negative emotions which you experienced from a recent conflict. Use the Feeling Wheel (ref: chapter on Thought) to accurately identify your emotions, and understand them in the context of your self-esteem (ref: chapter on Watch). Consider how you could process your emotions with better thoughts and talk (ref: chapters on Thought and Talk). How can all these reflections change your walk (ref: chapter on Walk)?

Make the effort and time to do this exercise, because doing it will help you retain better what you have learnt. In fact, in learning anything, you need to practise and do – not just once but several times – after you have read, listened or watched. So, please complete the exercise and write down your reflections in the following table:

Identify my EMOTIONS:

(ref: Feeling Wheel in chapter on Thought)

Understand my emotions in the context of my SELF-ESTEEM:

(ref: chapter on Watch)

Process my emotions with Better THOUGHT and TALK:

(ref: chapters on Thought and Talk)

Changing my WALK:

(ref: chapter on Walk)

To be honest, I'd have to say that in almost every conflict, 50 percent of my focus is on what the other person said or did wrong, and the other 50 percent is on the hurt the wrong has caused me. Anger and pain invariably cloud my mind and emotion, making it very difficult for me to **T-A-L-K** better in resolving a conflict. This Reflection exercise helps to put a brake on my escalating emotions and provides clarity for both thoughts and emotions, which allow me to take the appropriate steps in conflict resolution. However, the greatest benefit of this Reflection exercise is that it helps me to grow as a person – self-awareness, thinking and deeds.

> *The measure of a healthy family*
>
> *is not the absence of conflict,*
>
> *but the abundance of forgiveness.*

Conflict does not have to end in brokenness. It can end in forgiveness. When conflicts end in forgiveness and reconciliation, human connections are restored and strengthened. As mentioned earlier, our adversarial nature makes conflicts inevitable. A healthy relationship is therefore not the absence of conflicts, but an abundance of understanding, compassion and forgiveness. Forgiveness is the oil of relationships, like oil is to machinery helping it to run smoothly.

Even then, let us not for a moment imagine or pretend that it is easy to forgive a person who has hurt us deeply. However, holding on to anger, grudges or resentment is like drinking poison, and hoping that the other person will die. Difficult as it is, for the sake of our own health and happiness, we have to learn to forgive.

Essentially, to forgive is 'to set free' or 'to send away'. When we forgive someone, we set the guilty person free or send away his debt or the wrongs done to us. But the greater reality is this – in forgiveness, we also set ourselves free from hatred and bitterness, and send away our own pain and hurt.

> *Resentment is like drinking poison,*
> *and then hoping it will kill your enemies.*
>
> *Nelson Mandela*

In summary, healthy confrontation, effective communication, continual reflection, and forgiveness will keep conflicts at bay and pave the way towards rewarding relationships.

SHAME

From my counselling work with young people who sought help for addiction-related issues, I realized that many of them experienced brokenness. Often, the chief reason for this brokenness is shame.

What is shame? Guilt and shame often intertwine, and some people use these two words as though they refer to the same thing. However, they are not the same. Guilt arises when we become aware of our wrong action, which has hurt others. Shame gnaws at how we feel about ourselves because of our action. Guilt relates to others, shame to self. Guilt focuses on our behaviour, shame on our feeling. Brene Brown, author of *Daring Greatly*, puts it this way: 'Shame is "I am bad." Guilt is "I did something bad." Guilt: I'm sorry. I made a mistake. Shame: I'm sorry. I am a mistake.'

But of course, guilt and shame are closely related to each other. Like two close cousins, they usually show up together. A person may experience guilt when he realizes his action has brought pain to others. A healthy dose of guilt is necessary and good. It can lead the person to self-reflect, grow in empathy and motivate them to change their behaviour. The person may also feel ashamed of himself in that he is the sort of person whose selfishness has caused pain to others. This feeling of shame is also not bad in itself. It is what we do with shame that determines whether it is good or bad. Just like guilt, a healthy dose of shame, too, can cause a person to grow.

However, when a person experiences an inordinate amount of shame, this excessive shame can cause brokenness in that person.

Many young people, instead of seeking healing for their unbearable shame, turn to computer gaming, pornography or masturbation to escape their pain. This escapism provides temporary relief, but also produces even more shame, resulting in a vicious cycle of shame, making their brokenness worse.

At times, the shame comes not from the young person's action but that of another person. This can complicate things even more, especially if it is a case of abuse by a trusted significant adult, like one's parent or an older relative.

Sadly, in some cultures, shame is commonly used by parents to correct their children's behaviour or to 'motivate' them to better their performance. For example, they might shame their 'underperforming' children by comparing them with their cousins with 'I feel awkward when my relatives ask me about you at family reunions. Your cousins are doing so much better than you.' Or the shaming can be direct, such as 'How could you be so stupid?' or 'You ought to feel ashamed of yourself.'

Children who grow up with an unhealthy dose or a source of shame usually carry the brokenness into their adulthood, and continue to have difficulties bonding or connecting with others. They often also struggle with self-worth and addiction issues.

Dr Nathanson thinks shame is a critical regulator of human social behaviour and developed the Compass of Shame in 1992 to illustrate the different ways a person may react when they feel shame. I append below an adapted version of the Compass of Shame by Ted Wachtel.[6]

The Compass of Shame

Adapted form D.L. Nathanson, Shame and Pride, 1992

The four different poles of behaviour in which a person may react when they feel shame are:

- **Withdrawal** – isolating oneself, running and hiding

- **Attack self** – put-down self, masochism

- **Avoidance** – denial, abusing drugs, distraction through thrill seeking

- **Attack others** – 'turning the tables', lashing out verbally or physically, blaming others

When a person reacts to feeling shame in any of these four manners, difficulties in relationship will arise in the areas of intimacy, authenticity, communication, trust or forgiveness. And relationship difficulties will undermine the efforts we have invested in changing our **Wok, Walk, Watch, Thought** and **Talk**. We need the **TORQUE** of good and healthy relationships to provide the pulling power for our journey to health and happiness.

What then shall we do with shame? Besides those four manners of reacting to shame, what other ways are there? We are seeking ways that lead to healing rather than hiding, connecting rather than isolating, and mending rather than running.

> *Shame dies when stories are told*
> *in safe places.*
>
> *Ann Voskamp*

Ann Voskamp, a Canadian blogger and author, thinks that shame acquires unspeakable power only if it's unspeakable. 'Shame dies when stories are told in safe places'[7]. In dealing with our scars, Ann calls for courage instead of hiding in shame. She sounds out the reminder that 'scars are proof that you're a kind of bulletproof – because living through the hardest battles proves you can live through any battle.' So, rather than feeling shame, she invites us to trace our scars and let them feed our courage that comes from the wars we have successfully lived through.

Do you have safe places where you can show your scars and tell their stories? I do not recommend that you tell the stories of your scars indiscriminately, but tell them in safe places – to people who treasure your stories in their hearts and not retell them with their mouths. Tell the stories of your scars to people who see battle scars as medals of honour, and whose responses will feed your courage, not your shame.

I have the habit of taking long walks. On one such walk, I felt strange after greeting several people along the way. I felt I had been 'looked over'. Instinctively, I glanced down at my T-shirt and realized that I had worn it inside out! Immediately, I felt embarrassed and a bit tense – do I pretend nothing is wrong, continue my walk and risk being looked over by more people, or do I remove my T-shirt, put it back on correctly but risk my naked body being seen by some more passers-by? What would you have done if you were in my shoes?

After a brief moment of internal struggle, I looked for a safe corner to remove my T-shirt and put it back on correctly. The few seconds of risk was worth taking because I was able to enjoy the remainder of my walk. And I was able to greet others with smiles, not look away in shame.

Are you struggling with a shame that is crippling you? If you are, what are you waiting for? Look for a safe place to let your shame die. Some safe places you can consider are a mature friend, a trusted teacher, a pastor or priest, a counsellor, or your parents. When you do so, you not only rid yourself of shame, but you also get to connect with a person. This first connection can spark a new beginning to many other healthy connections.

Wait no longer. Make an appointment with that person who can provide you with a safe place to tell the story of your scar.   Let your shame die and bury it there.

ALIENATION

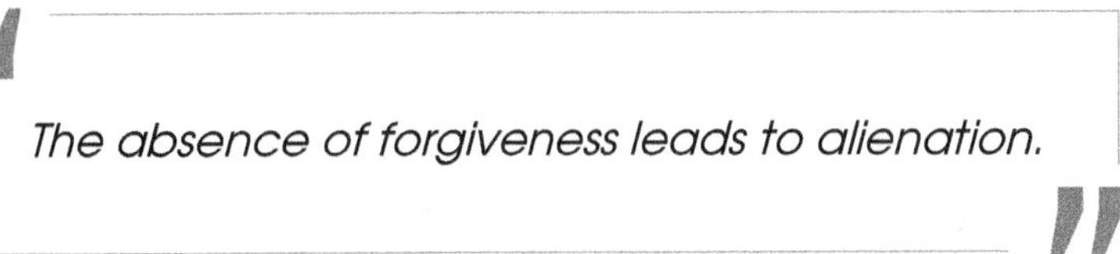

All of us make mistakes. There is no exception. As such, we all need forgiveness. When forgiveness is missing, our wrongs often produce in us guilt, shame, regret, anger or denial of our wrongs. Whether it is our reluctance to ask for forgiveness, the failure to obtain forgiveness or our inability to forgive ourselves – whenever there is the absence of forgiveness, this causes alienation. Alienation is a form of brokenness that disables us from bonding and connecting with people.

BRIDGES OR BARRIERS

We are natural expert builders – alas, not of bridges – but of walls! From a very young age, we learn to build walls to protect ourselves from being hurt by others. We might have been treated unjustly, betrayed or maligned, so we built walls of distrust, cynicism and emotional distance.

Or we might have experienced the pain of losing a relationship to death or breakup, so we built walls to prevent further heartbreak. While walls protect us from the hurt or trauma of loss and rejection, they also keep out people, happiness and love.

It turns out that walls protect but also imprison us. Walls separate people. It is a form of alienation. Rather than being proficient in building walls, we could learn to build bridges instead – bridges of forgiveness, bridges of hope and bridges to new beginnings. If we desire the torque that comes from good and supportive relationships, let us build bridges, not walls.

> *To forgive is to set a prisoner free*
> *and discover that the prisoner was you.*
>
> *Lewis B. Smedes*

Collaborative or Competitive Spirit

Our educational institutions cultivate in us a competitive spirit more than a collaborative spirit. Do not get me wrong, I am not against a healthy competitive spirit that drives us to do our best, that takes pride in our hard work and that derives satisfaction from evidence of our own progress. A healthy competitive spirit is when we are constantly competing against ourselves rather than comparing with others. Such a healthy competitive spirit can coexist with a collaborative spirit. There is no conflict.

However, there is a type of competitive spirit that is unhealthy – one that causes us to be selfish, disrespectful and constantly comparing ourselves with others. When outdoing others becomes more important than friendships, such a competitive spirit alienates us from people. It does not promote collaboration but causes conflict.

I have young people telling me that their educational experiences have produced in them a competitive spirit more than a collaborative spirit. They also find the workplace full of people who only know how to compete, but not collaborate. A common lament is how hard it is to find a true friend in the workplace. Often, the spirit of competition drives a wedge between people and causes alienation.

> *We might impress people with our strengths,*
> *but we connect with people through our weaknesses.*
>
> Craig Groeschel

Whether it is due to the absence of forgiveness, our protective but imprisoning walls, or an overly competitive spirit, alienation creates distance between people. The issues of alienation and our adversarial nature give rise to a lot of relationship problems, for which we suffer the consequences. Because of the deep and extensive effects, the root cause of our alienation condition and adversarial nature has got to be more than just simply our human nature. Indeed, there is something very much deeper that fundamentally causes these issues, and it goes beyond our relationship with people.

Our Adversarial Nature

I would like you to consider that perhaps the root cause of our alienation condition and adversarial nature is, in fact, a spiritual one – it is a result of our separation from God, spiritually. If God created humans who are meant to have an intimate bonding with Him, but because of our brokenness we are unable to bond with God, it makes sense that this disconnectedness will also affect our bonding and connections with other people.

Regardless of what our understanding of God is, or who God is, intuitively we understand God to be the *first cause* and the creator of the world we see. How we see ourselves in our relationship with the first cause would inevitably affect how we perceive the world – either a safe or dangerous place. If we perceive our relationship with God to be an adversarial one, the world becomes a dangerous place. Such an outlook will cause us to be prejudiced and adopt negative stereotypes towards the people around us. We imagine the worst in others or magnify their faults, and interact with them with our defences on high alert, which often leads to argument and resentment. Therefore, an adversarial relationship with God can easily end up with an adversarial outlook and approach to life.

There once lived a famous person who was very good with people all his life. His name is Prophet Abraham. Prophet Abraham is a notable and interesting character, who remains a unifying personality till today. He is one of the few historical figures that the Jews, Muslims and Christians have in common, and his stories are found in all their holy books. Let us take a look at his life of success with people.

During his days on earth, Abraham was a man of peace who settled disputes and conflicts with peaceful deals. His life stories tell of a man who built bridges instead of walls and collaborated rather than competed. As a generous soul who gave and forgave, Abraham died in peace at the ripe old age of 175.

How did Abraham learn to live in peace with others, and hence end up with a heritage that still connects the Jews, Muslims and Christians?

To begin with, Abraham was a friend of God (he was called

God's friend three times in the Bible). He believed God's offer of peace and promise, and lived as God's friend on earth peaceably. His life demonstrated the importance of having a friendship with God in order to be a friend to people. Seeing himself as a friend of God and believing God to be on his side, Abraham lived peaceably with God. And being a recipient of God's mercy, forgiveness and generosity, Abraham became a secure person as a result, and he learned to extend the same mercy, forgiveness and generosity to others. Abraham lived peaceably with people, because he lived peaceably with God.

Abraham's life is a good example of how alienation from God will alienate us from people, and how being a friend of God will make us a friend of people. Spiritual alienation leads to social alienation. We need to address spiritual alienation first in order to overcome social isolation.

THE HEALING OF
CONFLICT, SHAME AND ALIENATION

The brokenness that results from conflict, shame or alienation can be healed by having a spiritual relationship with the Divine. Instead of seeing our relationship with God to be an adversarial one, we need to start believing we can become a friend of God. Like Prophet Abraham, we have got to see God for who He really is – that He is love, and that He wants to be our friend who reaches towards us and longs for us to reciprocate.

God wants to be on the same side as us and He continually extends His hand of peace to us. He yearns for us to be at-one with Him and offers atonement for our wrongs to initiate the reconciliation. More will be covered on this atonement when we discuss spiritual health; suffice it to say now that a good and healthy relationship with God is vital if we desire good and healthy relationships with people.

Friendship with God resolves our adversarial outlook and approach in life. When we accept God's offer of the olive branch to us, we receive His forgiveness and promise to be on the same side as us. As God's friend, we are at peace with God and possess the peace of God, and this enables us to be at peace with ourselves. Being at peace with God and ourselves, we naturally live peaceably with others – giving, forgiving and building bridges of peace.

> *First keep the peace within yourself,*
> *then you can bring peace to others.*
>
> Thomas à Kempis

In order for our relationships to become the new torque in our life, a good relationship with the Divine is first needed to ignite this new engine. Once it is turned on, the new engine will provide the pulling power that we need. It will give us the oomph factor in life. We can then get on our caravan and continue our road trip to health and happiness.

Let us now move on to the last part of our book – **COMPLETING THE JOURNEY** – where we will look at the importance of spiritual health in our pursuit of health and happiness, and how we can develop a good relationship with the Divine.

> *Every time a man knocks on a brothel*
> *door, he is really searching for God.*
>
> G.K. Chesterton

PART III

COMPLETING THE JOURNEY

COMPLETING THE JOURNEY

We have finally reached downstream of the river. This is where you find civilization, communities of people and human activities. For some, the journey is completed. This is where the pursuit of health and happiness ends.

To others, in reaching the river's downstream, they know they have also arrived at the mouth of the river. This is where the port and ocean liners are located. For them, the journey has not ended. They would like to get on an ocean liner to see the vast wild ocean. They want to continue with their pursuit of health and happiness – the kind that is beyond this life. If you desire health and happiness that are beyond this world, turn the page to complete the journey.

TURNING EVERY STONE

Turning Every Stone

The pursuit of health and happiness is an important quest. We therefore need to make sure our ladder is leaning against the right wall. Too many people waste their lives climbing up the ladder of life only to discover that their ladder had been leaning against the wrong wall. Author Stephen Covey put it this way: 'If the ladder is not leaning against the right wall, every step we take just gets us to the wrong place faster.' So, let us leave no stone unturned to make sure that our ladder is leaning against the right wall, for without close scrutiny and constant reflection, we will never know whether our ladder is leaning against the wrong wall.

In our journey towards health and happiness, we have already come a long way. Congratulations to you who have made the progress! Now, let us recall this journey. The first step is our taking an interest in what we eat, and then we move on to say it is not just about what we are eating; it is also about what we are thinking and saying. We discuss the importance of how we value our inner worth, and also emphasize the value of actions. We explore ways to turn negative emotions into positive energy, and insist that these ways must end in transforming the person. Self-identity is given the spotlight as well as relationships with family and friends. So where does all this leave us?

Health needs to be holistic, including the physical, mental, social and spiritual aspects. When it is so, we will find happiness when we find health. This is mainly the reason why we have been focusing most of our attention on pursuing holistic health. As stated earlier in this book, health and happiness are not twin peaks to be scaled separately, but a twin-pack that is bundled closely together. The pursuit of health and happiness, therefore, is a single journey.

To guide us in this endeavour, we have been using the Biopsychosocial–Spiritual (BPSS) Model to make positive changes to our **Wok, Walk, Watch, Thought, Talk** and **Torque**. Let us see where they fit into the BPSS Model below:

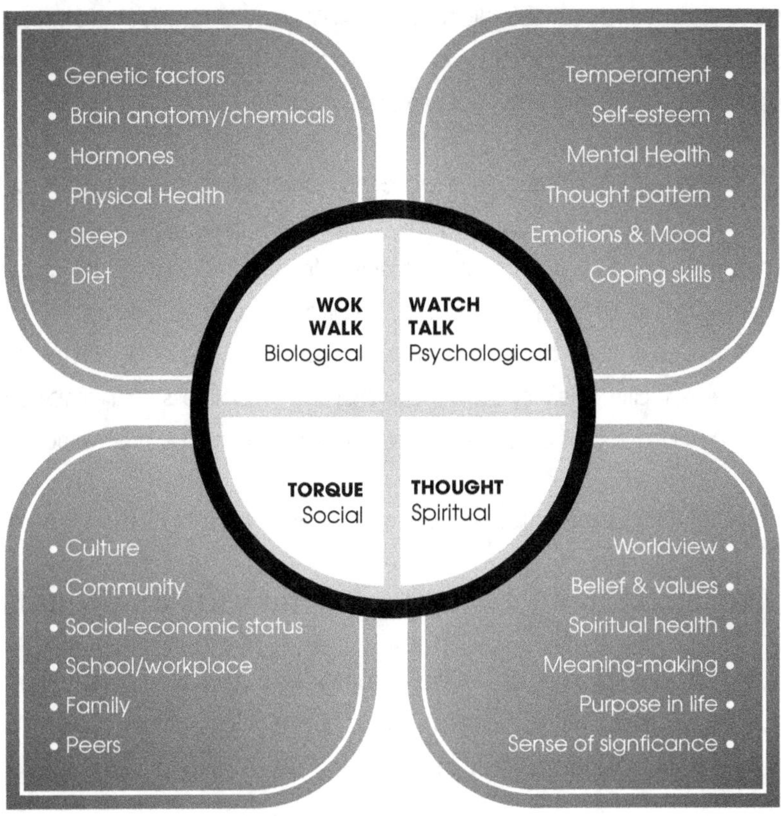

Most readers who have made it this far in this book would have a fair number of questions. Some would be wondering whether we should delink happiness from physical health? The reason being that otherwise, what would be left for a person who is born with or develops medical conditions that leave them with chronic diseases, lifelong illnesses or permanent disabilities? If happiness depends on holistic health which includes physical health, how then could this group attain happiness? Surely, happiness is within reach for people who suffer from varying forms and degrees of physical ailments. And if that is so, how is happiness attained for them?

What about people who get by with less? There are people who may not be exactly starving but they are unable to change their **WOK** as suggested by this book. Are they destined for an unhappy life until they can improve their dietary intake? Anecdotally, it seems that poorer people are capable of being happy, if not happier than their richer counterparts. How do you explain that?

Conceivably there could be other questions. I imagine most of them are likely to revolve around this *core* question – do I have to have everything in place in order to be happy? In other words, must I possess all of the physical, mental and social health in order to be happy? The questions that revolve around this core question are thoughtful ones, because essentially, they are asking whether happiness is an impossible feat for some groups of people. Here is a sample of such questions:

'What if old age strips me of my physical health?'

'What about people who suffer from mental health illnesses?'

'What about people who are locked away in isolation for political reasons? Their social health will inevitably suffer. Can they still experience happiness?'

These are valid and good questions. I like it that Facebook has *'It's Complicated'* as one of its options for listing relationship status. If relationship status can be complicated, I think it is reasonable to expect the pursuit of happiness to be complicated as well.

Models such as BPSS simplify reality and break the complex whole down into parts, in order to help us have a handle on the real-life complexity. However, models explain but do not replace reality. No *single* model can therefore fully explain the complexity of reality. To answer those good questions aimed at grappling with the complexity of happiness, I would like to offer two models: The **Table** model and the **Straight Lines** model.

The TABLE Model

Let us use the top of the table to represent our capacity to contain happiness, and the table legs our abilities to support it. Many people support their happiness with table legs such as money, material possessions, fame or success. You are free to use whatever materials you want. However, the materials of your choice need to be sturdy and durable, for when you use materials that either give way easily or are unable to withstand the test of time, your happiness will be short-lived. I recommend that you choose materials that are both strong and long-lasting.

But truth be told, even the sturdiest table legs are susceptible to the unpredictability and uncertainties of life. When the harsh realities of life strike, a person may end up losing a table leg, causing their happiness to wobble. And usually, it never rains but pours. Many people find themselves losing a second table leg right after losing that first one. It is hard to support a tabletop with just two table legs. No wonder happiness can be elusive for some people.

However, from my counselling experience, I have learnt that most people, despite having problems and difficulties, have great adaptability, and have attained and are capable of maintaining an equilibrium in their life that supports a certain level of happiness. They run into trouble only when life hacks off one or two of their table legs.

I recall a young Nicholas who had a persistent problem with procrastination but was always able to rely on the 'productivity of the last minute' to pull him through. This way of coping had never failed him before. It would have worked again when he faced several deadlines, had his girlfriend not chosen to break up with him at that time, thereby hacking off a leg of his table.

Though difficult, Nicholas might have had a chance to manage both the deadlines and the breakup if not for some criticisms from a few friends. It triggered his latent but deep-seated sense of worthlessness. Chop! Another leg of his table was axed. With two of his table legs gone, Nicholas' table began to topple, and that was what brought Nicholas to seek help.

What is the solution to the problem of losing our table legs to life's misadventures? Well, the most straightforward and common-sense solution is to have more table legs! Though it sounds simple, remember that wisdom often resides in simplicity. The solution is valid and doable. When our table is fitted with more legs, all of them made of sturdy and durable material, it will increase our chances of weathering the storms of life. With more legs, even when life brings down two or three of the table legs, our table will still have adequate support.

I would like to recommend eight legs for your table.

Eight? Does that sound like a lot to you? You probably want to know where you can find so many table legs! Well, actually we have covered six of them in Part I and II of this book. I will use different terms to represent them here. Let us see whether you are able to recognize them by their different names.

THE EIGHT LEGS TO SUPPORT YOUR TABLE

1. **F**ood

2. **F**itness

3. **F**un

4. **F**riend/Family

5. **F**unctional Thoughts

6. **F**unctional Habits

7. **F**uture

8. **F**aith

Life does not have to be perfect to be wonderful.

Annette Funicello

The **Table** model is helpful in explaining why it is still possible to experience happiness even when we are missing one or two of the table legs. As long as there are enough table legs to support our capacity to enjoy happiness, we are capable of still experiencing some forms of happiness. Life does not have to be perfect to be wonderful.

Suppose a person met with a serious car accident and broke three of his ribs, both his legs and one of his arms. His physical health is shattered, and he is likely to spend a very long time hooked up in a hospital bed, with broken legs and arm in casts, not to mention the high financial costs. Now try putting yourself in his shoes, and then let us just suppose that the person is you. In such a situation, several of your table legs would be knocked out – **fitness, fun** and possibly **functional habits**. These are really painful to lose, and I understand how you would feel initially. Nonetheless, you can still continue to enjoy happiness if the other five table legs are firmly in place – the love and support of your **family** and **friends, functional thoughts** and your focus on the **future** (knowing that you will eventually heal). And if you have a religious **faith**, it would help tremendously in situations like this.

Life is not perfect under such circumstances, but it can continue to be wonderful. This is because there are sufficient table legs to support a certain form and level of happiness.

However, a couple of questions might spring up in the mind of some, such as 'Won't my happiness be shaky then?' and 'Will the *quality* of my happiness be compromised?' To answer these questions, let us now turn our attention to the **Straight Lines** model.

The STRAIGHT LINES Model

A straight line is the shortest distance between two points. I do not intend to go into the details of this mathematical definition, as I am only interested in using straight lines to make my points. There are two points which I would like to make about happiness, and I will use a **Straight Line** and a set of **Parallel Lines** to make them.

One Straight Line

It is best not to see happiness in binary terms. For when you do, you create a situation where you are either happy or unhappy, with nothing in between. It is better to see happiness existing along a straight line, or a continuum.

The Range of Happiness

We do not have to always feel overjoyed to qualify as being happy! Happiness can range from being content to being in seventh heaven. All the different shades of happiness are equally valid experiences, arising to meet us at different but fitting moments of our life. We need to savour and appreciate the precious value of every single one of them – the calming contentedness of a morning walk, pleasure with a good dinner, gladness in a meaningful conversation or discourse, elation with a piece of good news or feeling overjoyed at our first snow experience.

When we picture happiness along a line spectrum, we learn to recognize happiness by its different names and welcome each of them without prejudice. As a hospitable host who entertains the entire range of happiness, we grow in our capacity for happiness. We worry less about whether our happiness is compromised because we are missing a table leg or two, for we are too busy entertaining the different happiness guests in our life.

The **Straight-Line** model immediately helps us realize that we can be happy, even if we are not feeling ecstatic or exuberant every single moment. In fact, it would be tormenting, if not strange, if all of life was an unending orgasm!

Two Parallel Lines

Human beings have an inclination to make sense of things by their antithesis, that is, understanding things from their opposite. For example, we contrast good and evil to help us understand better what good is. Admittedly, this can be helpful but sometimes, it can also plant the seed of confusion. Let me explain.

What is the opposite of happiness? A dictionary or thesaurus will tell you the opposite of happiness is sadness, sorrow, affliction, grief, suffering, et cetera. Fundamentally, there is nothing wrong with contrasting these emotions with happiness. Our problem begins when we place them on the opposite ends of a straight line and start to think that as opposites, they therefore have an inverse relationship, meaning the more of one, the less of the other.

Happiness

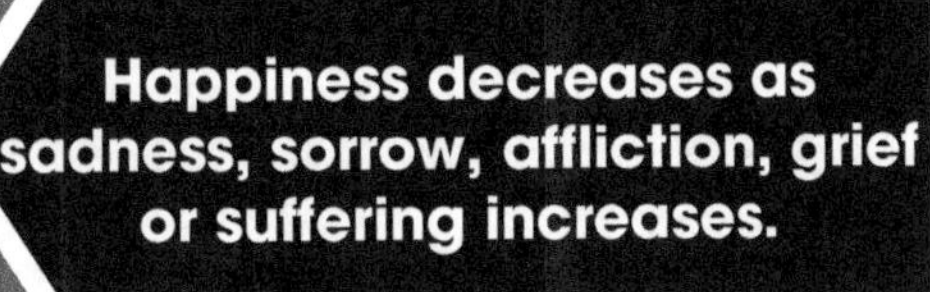

If this is how we view happiness, then we will invariably be averse to sadness, grief and all other forms of suffering and pain, and will therefore relentlessly and incessantly work very hard to eliminate all of them. When we can't – and of course we can't – we fall into the trap of thinking we can never be happy because of our failure to rid life of pain.

Our minds have been conditioned by popular culture to believe that suffering should not coexist with happiness. We therefore pursue a mythical happiness that has the absence of pain. The truth is, happiness is not the absence of pain. In fact, life is pain and to be alive is to suffer. The reason for this is that we live in a fallen world. The only path to happiness is learning to be happy despite our circumstances – our stormy emotions, unfulfilled desires, unmet expectations, failures, chronic illnesses, tragedy of death, et cetera.

Life does not have to be perfect to be wonderful, and we do not need to rid life of all its problems and pain before we can be happy. The sooner we learn to accept that pain can coexist with happiness, but on a different parallel line, the sooner we will learn to be happy despite our circumstances. For example, you can be 6/10 on the scale of happiness while being 8/10 on the scale of pain and suffering.

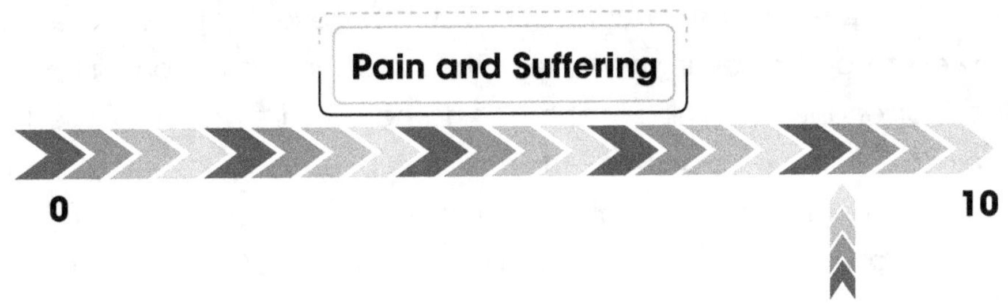

The **Parallel Lines** model immediately helps you see that it is possible to be happy in your pain and suffering, and that happiness is not the absence of pain and suffering, but in spite of them.

Many religions support and encourage the **Parallel Lines** concept of happiness, and help their followers to 'rejoice in sufferings'[1] and teach them that they can be 'sorrowful, yet always rejoicing'[2]. You probably have read about or might personally know a religious person or spiritual leader who is 9/10 on the happiness scale while at an 8 or 9 on the scale of suffering and pain. The truth is, the only way happiness can be a reality is for it to exist alongside the parallel reality of pain.

Finding Joy in Grief

The **Parallel Lines** model can be particularly helpful for the bereaved. It helps them understand that they are *allowed* to experience happiness while grieving. When a person loses a loved one, especially to an untimely death caused by an accident or sickness, it is understandable that the person will experience deep sorrow. Grief is a natural response to a loss. Though it becomes less intense over time, grief can last a lifetime. Some parents never get over the loss of their child, and the loss of a spouse can be equally devastating. For many, grief never ends. It just goes through changes over the passage of time.

There is nothing wrong with grief. Dr Colin Murray Parkes, a British psychiatrist, said, 'Grief is the price we pay for love.' When we love deeply, we grieve deeply. Grief is often how we express our ongoing love for the person who died.

However, some people mistakenly believe that they are not allowed to be happy in their grief. They see that as dishonouring the dead, or erroneously think that by being happy, they have ceased to love or respect the deceased. This could be a result of placing grief and happiness on the same straight line. Once you change your paradigm by placing them on two separate parallel lines, you'll begin to realize that while you continue to express your love through grief, you can also continue to receive love and experience happiness. The two of them are not contradictory.

Grief, I've learned, is really just love. It's all the love you want to give, but cannot. All that unspent love gathers up in the corners of your eyes, the lump in your throat, and in that hollow part of your chest. Grief is just love with no place to go.

Jamie Anderson

There will be moments, parts of the day or special dates when memory is your only way of holding on to the person you never want to lose, and your grief is the love you want to give, but cannot. However, there will also be times when you relish the love shown by your family, delight in the company of your friends, laugh at a good joke, enjoy a good movie, take pleasure in a good workout, make and savour a satisfying meal, take a blissful walk or are grateful you can continue daily functions – caring for yourself and your children, working, paying the bills, et cetera.

Remember, although you may not erupt into many joyful moments, you can certainly continue to entertain the other guests of happiness. And who knows? When the moment comes, be ready to be surprised by joy again.

INCLUSIVENESS OF HAPPINESS

The pursuit of holistic health is important for when we have a healthy mind, body and spirit, we radiate happiness from the inside out. However, the **Table** and **Straight Lines** models help us understand that happiness is not exclusive to those with perfect physical and mental health. People who have physical and mental health problems are also capable of experiencing happiness.

Physical and mental illnesses are often episodic, and people who suffer from them can enjoy periods of remission. And while a cure may not always be possible, physical and mental illnesses can be treated effectively with medication and lifestyle adjustments. The patients are still able to enjoy a certain level of health, even if it is less than perfect. The preference for perfect health is understandable, but preference needs to be tempered with reality.

Thankfully, the **Table** model helps to shift our paradigm to see that life does not have to be perfect to be wonderful, and the **Straight Lines** model teaches us to celebrate the different shades of happiness despite our difficult and challenging circumstances. Yes, indeed life does not need to be perfect to be wonderful or liveable, and we can certainly continue to find happiness in the midst of our pain and suffering.

Interestingly, the **Table** model also raises the question: 'Is there a minimum number of table legs that are needed to support happiness, and if there is, what should these legs be?' Personally, I think these are excellent questions. Wisdom and experience teach us that misfortunes or time will eventually strip us of most of our table legs. And before that day draws near, we want to invest time and energy in preserving, enhancing and strengthening the essential legs that we can't do without.

The physical world and physics perhaps have given us clues to the minimum number of table legs that are required. In the three-dimensional world in which we live, we need at least three legs to support a stable table.

The important question is: 'What should these three essential legs be?' If you were to choose from among the 8 Fs, which three would you pick as absolutely necessary for happiness? Circle the three you pick below:

Food	Fitness	Fun	Family/Friends
Functional Habits	Functional Thoughts	Future	Faith

THE ESSENTIALS FOR HAPPINESS

Most people struggle with this previous activity: picking the three absolute essential table legs for happiness. But I have good news for your struggle – in real life, you do not have to limit yourself to just three legs. The activity is to help you identify the three essentials which ought to *always* be in place. But once you have taken care of these essentials, by all means, pursue the others. Why limit yourself to three legs unnecessarily? The whole idea about identifying those three essential legs is this: **These you ought to have, without neglecting the others.**

I am curious about what you picked for your three essential legs. Intuitively, many people will include in their list things that will last, such as functional thoughts, future and faith. Are these your pick for the essentials too? Here is a piece of priceless advice by a spiritual leader who lived almost two thousand years ago: 'We don't look for things that can be seen but for things that can't be seen. Things that can be seen are only temporary. But things that can't be seen last forever.'[3]

The body needs air, water and food.
The soul needs purpose, truth and love.

Human beings are more than just body and mind; we have a soul too. The soul needs nourishment that comes from a good mind, but it also needs spiritual sustenance. Paul Tournier was a Swiss physician who in his midlife left medical practice for pastoral counselling. Peterson (2018) says this of Tournier, 'For the rest of his life he used words – listened to and spoken – in a setting of personal relationship as the primary means for carrying out his healing vocation. He left a way of medical practice that was primarily focused on the body and embraced a medical practice that dealt primarily with the whole person, an integrated being of body, soul, and spirit.'[4]

The **BPSS** has guided our understanding of holistic health and happiness. The **Table** and **Straight Lines** models help shift our paradigm of happiness. Growth in understanding and the paradigm shift are important first steps in shaping the reality of our health and happiness, but how can we bring that new reality into our life?

I believe in order to bring that reality into our life, we need to embrace the same approach that Dr Tournier took. We have to learn how to view and deal with the whole person as an integrated being of body, mind and spirit. The physical body, mind and spirit are too intricately connected for us to take them apart and deal with the health of each of them separately. We need a unifying paradigm to consider the person – body, mind and spirit – as a whole.

Up to this point, we have not directed much of our attention to the spiritual factor of the **BPSS** Model. In Part III, we will look at the role of ***spiritual health*** in the pursuit of health and happiness, as well as it being the unifying force that integrates the body, mind and spirit as one.

In bringing in spiritual health, we would inevitably discuss what spirituality is. Although there is no universal agreement on what spirituality is, there is sufficient common ground to discuss the importance of spiritual health in the pursuit of health and happiness. As I am a Christian, I will present the Christian perspective on spirituality and spiritual health. I understand some of my readers may belong to other faiths or religions and would have different views on spirituality and spiritual health. I respect your religious faith and views on spirituality and understand if you prefer to skip the last section of this book. I offer the final section of the book as an invitation for you to take a peek at the Christian perspective on spirituality and spiritual health.

CHAPTER SEVEN

UNDERSTANDING SPIRITUAL HEALTH

Introduction

Modern **societies** are fragmented into different spheres: public and private; economic, social and political; secular and religious, et cetera. You might not agree with such fragmentation, but this is the current reality thrust upon us.

The **person** is not spared from similar fragmentation. We are so used to dividing the whole person into body, mind and soul, to the point we sometimes think they are separate entities. Conceptually they may be different parts of a person, but they are not distinct entities. In identifying these different parts of a person, we need to remember they are interconnected and are different parts of the *whole*.

I think the fragmentation is worse when it comes to **health**. It has become common to divide health into physical health, mental health, social health and spiritual health. While it is helpful to know that holistic health comprises all of these different areas, we do ourselves a great disservice when we forget how interconnected they are and fail to integrate them into the whole.

I hope that when you finish reading this chapter, you will have a better appreciation and clearer understanding of how crucial it is to have a holistic and integrated approach to the whole person and to health – in particular, *spiritual* health.

What is Spiritual Health?

We are familiar with physical health. As physical beings, our first and foremost concern is our physical health. We are familiar with hospitals, clinics, doctors, nurses and laboratory technicians, whose primary interest is our physical well-being. We also deal frequently with the multibillion-dollar health industry that is both hailed and hated.

We are *less* familiar with mental health. Dr Jamie Chiu, a clinical psychologist in Hong Kong, told the story of a young man whose mental health deteriorated as a result of school demands, escalating family conflicts and persistent insomnia. At a loss as to what to do and on the verge of a breakdown, the young man sought help from his teacher. Dr Chiu related, 'The teacher just looked at him, patted him on the shoulder and was like, "Ka yao ah ("keep going" in Cantonese). Work harder, and you'll be fine. Just study more."' The psychologist concluded, 'That really sums up how people think of mental health issues in Hong Kong.'

Are we any better in Singapore? For too long, people with mental health difficulties have suffered in silence because of the stigma and shame. Thankfully, there are signs that things are changing, going by the increasing exhibitions, campaigns and voices from different quarters. These may be an indication that Singaporeans are tired of being silent about mental health difficulties and are ready to cry out for help.

We are *least* familiar with spiritual health. We do not usually talk about it, even in religious settings. It is also rarely taught in schools or homes, if at all. Generally, people have an incomplete or hazy understanding of what spiritual health is; there are many reasons for this lack of understanding.

In the discussion of spiritual health, one of the first things you will notice is there is not a universal definition of spiritual health. It really depends on the milieu you are in. For many people, their religion defines their spirituality, thereby determining what spiritual health is for them. However, religious people do not have a corner on spiritual health. People without a religion can perceive themselves as deeply spiritual, and can cultivate and enjoy good spiritual health too.

So, what is spiritual health? If you recall the Biopsychosocial-Spiritual (**BPSS**) Model, the biological, the psychological, the social and the spiritual are four different dimensions of the person.

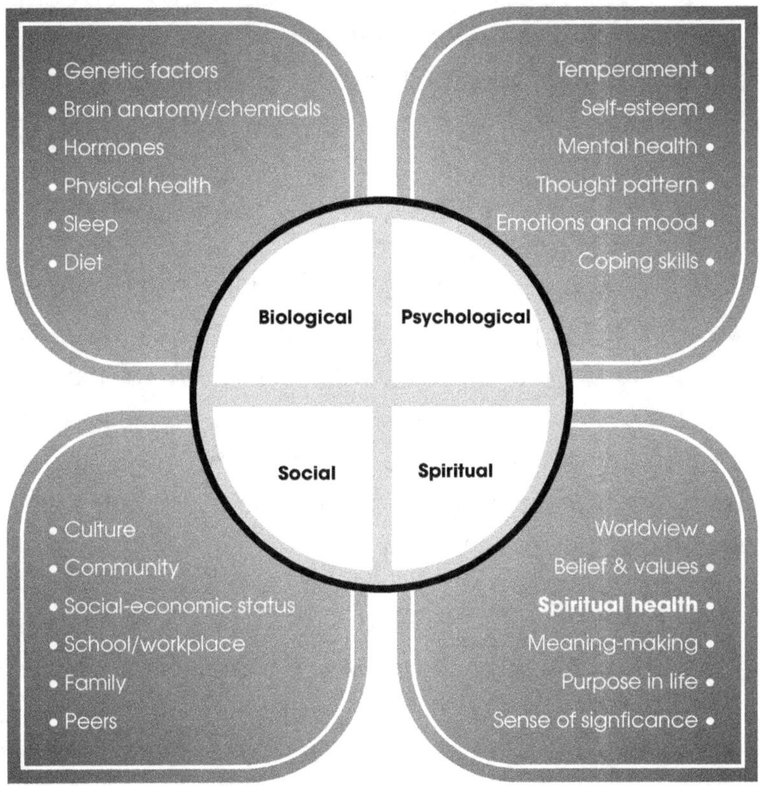

In the **BPSS** model, the spiritual dimension has to do with a person's worldview, belief, values, spiritual health, meaning-making, purpose in life, sense of significance, et cetera. But what exactly is a person's *spiritual* health?

Spiritual health is often associated with having a clear sense of one's purpose in life and being meaningfully engaged in pursuing this purpose, which in turn leads to happiness, fulfilment and peace of mind. But what is the purpose of life?

The Dalai Lama opined that 'the very purpose of life is to be happy which is sustained by hope.' Before you jump on him as being hedonistic, you need to know that the Dalai Lama believes that 'the more we care for the happiness of others, the greater is our own sense of well-being.' He also teaches that love is the principal source of success in life: 'If love is defined as a wish that others be happy, and compassion as the wish that they be free from suffering, and you cultivate love and compassion within yourself, it will ensure happiness, good health and peace of mind.'

While there is nothing implicitly wrong with seeking happiness – for ourselves and for others – it depends on how we define happiness. Do we *limit* happiness to just a feeling, a sense of pleasure or gratification? Or do we *expand* happiness to include the wellness of our body, mind and soul? It seems that the Dalai Lama has in mind a happiness that is broader, for he wrote elsewhere, 'We must acknowledge that there can be no hope of gratifying the senses permanently. At best, the happiness we derive from eating a good meal can only last until the next time we are hungry.'

It seems that where properly understood, love and happiness can be referring to the same thing. When you seek loving others as the purpose of your life, you reap happiness as its by-product. And in seeking happiness for others, you are in fact loving them. With regard to the importance of love, the famous Christian apostle Saint Paul put it this way, 'For the whole law can be summed up in this one command: "Love your neighbour as yourself."'[1]

*The purpose of human life is to serve,
and to show compassion and the will
to help others.*

Albert Schweitzer

There are still others who prefer pursuing something bigger than themselves as their purpose. That 'something bigger' could be environmental or humanitarian causes such as relieving poverty or social injustice, or it could be religious movements, or a relationship with the Divine. People who seek to connect with something bigger than themselves see this as *spirituality*.

For religious devotees, spirituality is being rooted in their relationship with the Divine and living out that relationship in ordinary everyday life – loving others, giving their best in whatever way they work on, caring for the environment and looking forward to the completeness of their relationship with God in the restored world, or in simpler terms, living together with God in the new heaven and the new earth.

Despite there being no universal understanding of spirituality, spirituality is an important part of our spiritual health. It is a devotion to a belief or conviction that gives people focus, strength, vigour, oomph and happiness.

Most people will agree that spiritual health involves having a purpose in life, someone to love, something meaningful to do and something awesome to look forward to. All of these can be wonderful spiritual experiences which lead to happiness, hope and peace of mind that give them spiritual health.

However, if our discussion on spiritual health ends here, we are making the mistake which I mentioned earlier – the belief that since the spirit is not part of the body or mind, it is unaffected by them. Fortunately, people are increasingly beginning to realize that their spiritual health contributes to the well-being of their body and mind.

In my experience, that which is still often overlooked is this – the body and mind can *also* affect the spirit. Since the body, mind and spirit are interconnected, each of them will have effects on the other two. We must therefore not cultivate spiritual health while neglecting our physical or mental health.

The Jews are familiar with the interconnection among the physical, mental and spiritual dimensions of our lives. They get this understanding from their ancient Scriptures. Take for example, this song[2] from their prayer book:

> The instructions of the Lord are perfect,
> reviving the soul.
>
> The decrees of the Lord are trustworthy,
> making wise the simple.
>
> The commandments of the Lord are right,
> bringing joy to the heart.
>
> The commands of the Lord are clear,
> giving insight for living.

From this song, we could see the Jews believe that spiritual health (that is, devotion to God's instructions) would bring about mental and emotional health – *reviving the soul, making wise the simple, having joy* in *the heart and having insight for living.*

At the same time, the Jews also understand the effects that physical sustenance can have on one's emotional and spiritual wellness. Take a look at another song[3] from the same prayer book:

> *He makes grass grow for the cattle,*
> *and plants for people to cultivate –*
> *bringing forth food from the earth:*
> *wine that gladdens human hearts,*
> *oil to make their faces shine,*
> *and bread that sustains their hearts.*

The Jews understand food, wine, oil and bread not only give them physical sustenance, but can also give them spiritual nourishment – gladden *human hearts, make their faces shine* (being cheerful), *and sustain their hearts.* For these ancient Scriptures, dating back more than 3,000 years, this understanding was rather ground-breaking. But of course, to the Jews, these ancient Scriptures are Holy Scriptures, reverently God-breathed and given to them by their God for their holistic living.

The Jews have been taught from very early on by their Scriptures to understand that the body, mind and soul are all interconnected. For them, of course, spiritual well-being will result in the wellness of their physical and mental lives, but they also know that the reverse is true as well. Jesus, the great spiritual leader, was a Jew and naturally was familiar with the same Holy Scriptures. He believed, practised and taught the same truths.

Too many people live as though the spirit is a separate entity of our being and is therefore only affected by our spiritual experiences. In reality, the spirit is closely connected to all the other aspects of our being. So, instead of a fragmented approach, we need to take an integrated approach to our understanding of spiritual health. This will allow us to take into consideration various contributing factors to our spiritual well-being.

Factors Contributing to Spiritual Health

The biological, the psychological, the social and the spiritual are different dimensions of the person, yet they are so intricately interconnected with one another that no one aspect can be separated from another or disaggregated from the whole. Each aspect interacts with and affects all other aspects of the person.

To illustrate that a person has four different aspects, we have been using the following diagram to portray the **BPSS** Model.

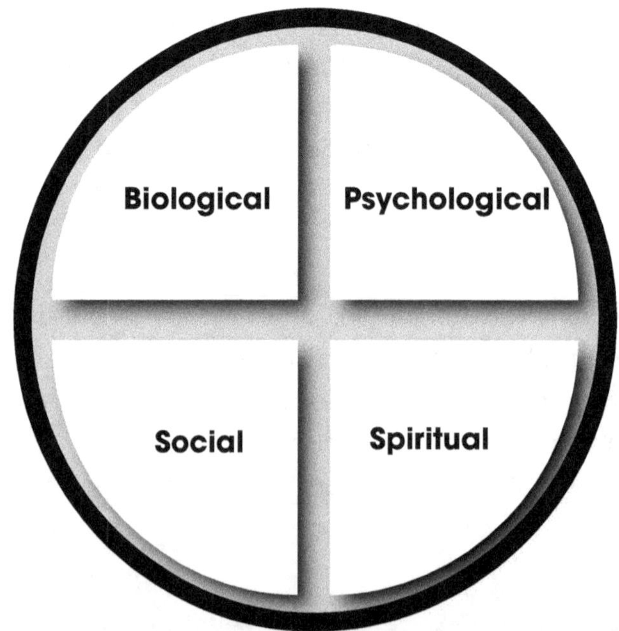

The **BPSS** model helps to clearly illustrate the four different dimensions of a person. However, in reality, these dimensions are not distinct or disconnected from one another, as depicted by the diagram (which serves to facilitate the initial understanding of the concepts). A better and more precise illustration would be this:

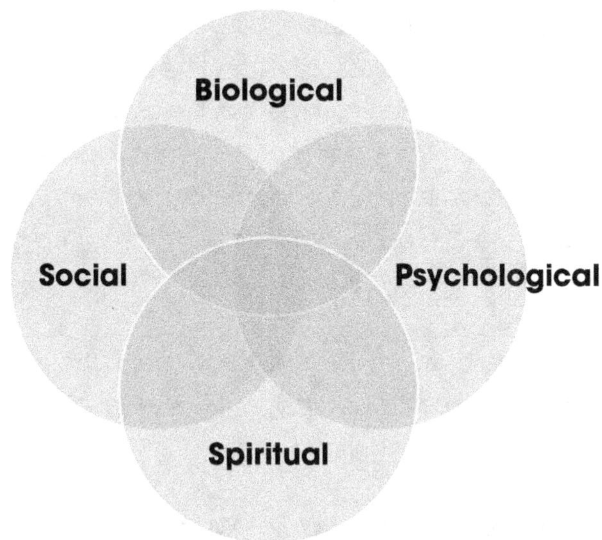

The illustration above helps us see that though conceptually distinct, the four aspects are interconnected and affect one another in reality. Hopefully, this added clarity will help us reject the false dichotomy between the spiritual and the material as well as the distinct separation between the sacred and the secular.

Another common mistake is to set spirituality above all the other aspects of our life, and to view it as the *only* aspect that really matters. We need to guard against such over-spiritualization. This is especially true for certain groups of religious people, who tend to overemphasize spirituality over all other areas of life. This can lead to a form of pseudo-spirituality, for example, parents who withhold medical care from their children for religious reasons, or religious sects who refuse medical treatment, adhering strictly to spiritual healing. Over-spiritualization can also cause a person to believe that every case of psychiatric illness is demonic possession, requiring spiritual deliverance rather than clinical evaluation and treatment.

Of course, these are rather extreme examples. Usually, over-spiritualization cascades down to most of us in milder, albeit still lethal forms, in persuasion or advice such as 'Don't be stressed but instead focus on how you've been blessed', 'Don't be sad because everything happens for a reason', 'When you feel troubled by stress, pain or failure, the best antidote is to pray – nothing more, nothing less', 'Do not fear any infection in the community, but come, worship with us and lay your claim on the promise of God's word that *no harm will come to you and no sickness will come near your house.*'

When we set spirituality *apart* and *above* all the other aspects of life, we engage in a false dichotomy, or in over-spiritualization, both of which are unhealthy for our spiritual health.

However, some might argue, 'What's wrong with prioritizing spiritual matters over physical matters?' There is absolutely nothing wrong with it. Personally, I prioritize my spiritual life over all the other aspects of my life. However, to prioritize spirituality over the material world is not setting it *apart* and *above* it, or thinking that only it *alone* matters. Prioritizing is setting it first *among* the other aspects of life. Spirituality has to be practised in the material world and among things, matters and people. There is a better and clearer way of understanding how prioritizing spirituality can look like in our life. I will share that at the end of the chapter.

The greatest threat to spiritual health, however, is to think that we cultivate spiritual health by attending *only* to the 'spiritual aspects' of our life, such as religious piety or spiritual practices. In reality, the state of our spiritual health is also affected by other aspects of our life. Let us take a look at three of these aspects: Physical health, mental health and emotional health.

Physical Health

Physical health is not spiritual health. Nonetheless, it contributes to the well-being of our spiritual health. It is so closely interconnected with our spiritual health that we ignore it at our own peril.

Spiritual teachers often use literary devices such as similes, metaphors, personification and hyperbole in their teachings. Take for example these metaphors: *the bread of life, the living water, the fountain of life, the tree of life, God is a sun and shield.* Why do spiritual teachers use metaphors? Why use the language of the material world to explain or illuminate the spiritual world? The purpose is to take something we know (physical) and use it to better understand the lesser known (spiritual). But if you ponder over the use of metaphors, they are also evidence that the physical world intersects the spiritual world in some ways. Otherwise, metaphors make little sense. If you are, like me, one who believes in the end of times, when heaven and earth come together as one, aren't you curious whether there will still be the use of metaphors in the new language of the age to come? More about this new heaven and new earth later. Let us not get distracted!

We sometimes miss the points of the great spiritual leaders because we trip over such metaphorical language. However, even when the spiritual leaders speak plainly, we sometimes still miss their points. Why? There are many reasons for this. One of the chief reasons is selective listening. Often, we listen selectively because we like to over-spiritualize the teachings of the sages.

For example, when Jesus said, 'Man shall not live on bread alone, but on every word that comes from the mouth of God', he did not say man shall not live on bread **at all**. Unfortunately, that is what some people hear Jesus said. Jesus did not teach us to neglect our physical needs, but what he taught us was not to pursue material things **alone**. *Materialism* is the problem, not material things. Spiritual (inner) development is vital, but as physical beings, physical (external) sustenance is also essential.

• Physical Sustenance

At the peak of his career, Jesus was arrested, mistreated and killed. Among his twelve closest disciples, the treasurer betrayed him, his commander-in-chief by the name of Peter denied him, and everyone else abandoned him. When his dead physical body made a comeback in glorified form, Jesus sought out his disciples to reinstate them. According to the resurrection accounts told by His disciples, on one such occasion, Jesus cooked breakfast for them!

Going by the tendency to over-spiritualize, a number of Christians in Jesus' situation would probably have chosen a spiritual retreat to restore the disciples, preferably one that began with a three-day fast. Instead, the great spiritual leader Jesus reached out to the fear-stricken and directionless disciples by cooking breakfast for them. Imagine this: The supreme spiritual teacher had supernaturally victoriously conquered and returned from the dead, but what he did for his disciples was amazingly down to earth – filling their bellies with food he cooked – before he went on to fill their minds with truth and their souls with love. The great spiritual leader did not set spirituality apart from and above physical needs. This account shows that spiritual health does not exclude physical health, but instead, often begins with it.

It is worth noting that in the historical accounts of Jesus' resurrection, many of them involve eating. One example is the story about Jesus joining two men on a journey and travelling with them to the village of Emmaus: *'When he was at the table with them, he took bread, gave thanks, broke it and began to give it to them. Then their eyes were opened, and they recognized him.'*[4]

In Jesus' first appearance to his disciples (The Eleven), *'he asked them, "Do you have anything here to eat?" They gave him a piece of broiled fish, and he took it and ate it in their presence... Then he opened their minds so they could understand the Scriptures.* [5]

Isn't it interesting that spiritual nourishment took place alongside physical sustenance in those resurrection accounts? And that spiritual awakening or growth *(eyes were opened, recognized him, opened their minds, could understand)* often took place at the dining table.

On another important resurrection appearance, Jesus repeated his promise to give the gift of the Holy Spirit to his disciples. Would you like to guess what Jesus was doing when he did so? Well, it took place *while he was eating with them.*[6]

Meeting the needs of our physical body is never the problem. The problem is thinking that it alone is enough. In the words of the Dalai Lama, '... it is the underlying assumption that full satisfaction can arise from gratifying the senses alone.'

The material world is not bad in and of itself. Things and matters are not evil to be rejected or obliterated. But what needs to be eradicated are the beliefs that money, materials or machines could solve all human miseries, and the failure to recognize that we are spiritual beings who also need spiritual nourishment. As physical and spiritual beings, we need both physical bread and spiritual bread to sustain us. It is never one or the other. We become blind guides when we teach otherwise.

> *Everything God created is good,*
> *we should not reject any of it but receive it with thanks.*
>
> *Saint Paul*

• What About Fasting?

'What about fasting?' some of you may ask. 'Do people not abstain from food for spiritual purposes? Isn't fasting a common religious practice to seek God for spiritual strength, guidance or for the sole purpose of drawing near to God himself?'

Yes, most religious or spiritual seekers engage in some kind of fasting. Personally, I fast too during Lent, the period of 40 days before Resurrection Sunday, as I recognize that fasting is a powerful spiritual discipline. I encourage regular, meaningful and purposeful fasting for spiritual reasons. Yet, let us bear in mind that fasting is abstinence for a season, and that abstinence is not ascetic.

> *(The demon Screwtape writes:) (God, the 'Enemy', is) a hedonist at heart. All those fasts and vigils and stakes and crosses are only a facade. Or only like foam on the seashore. Out at sea, out in His sea, there is pleasure, and more pleasure. He makes no secret of it; at His right hand are 'pleasures for evermore.'*
>
> *C.S. Lewis*

Fasting is giving up food voluntarily in order to seek God. You cannot give up what you do not have. Therefore, fasting and eating are not mutually exclusive. Instead of being contradictory, they are complementary. There is a time to eat, and there is a time to fast. Whether fasting or eating, both can be powerful spiritual exercises, and can bring about spiritual wellness. What we want to avoid are extremes – extreme ascetical fasting and self-indulgent gluttony.

- **Physical Rest**

Besides physical sustenance, having regular and adequate rest for our physical body is also important to our spiritual health. *'Remember the Sabbath day, to keep it holy'* is the fourth Commandment in the Ten Commandments. The instruction given to the Jews in their Torah is *'Six days you shall labour, and do all your work, but the seventh day is a Sabbath to the LORD your God. On it you shall not do any work.'* The English word 'Sabbath' or 'Shabbat' in Hebrew means 'to rest from labour', or the day of rest.

The interconnection between physical rest and spiritual health is not foreign to the Jews, as there are two parts to their 4th Commandment: (1) Remember the Sabbath, and (2) To keep it holy. Sabbath is the day of rest **and** worship. To 'Shabbat' is to rest from our work in order to focus on God's worth. Surely, this must count for a key path to spirituality – pausing in order to pursue meaningful connection with something bigger than ourselves.

The 4th Commandment is more than a command – it contains one of the greatest secrets to spiritual health. A careful reading of this commandment will reveal a further and deeper connection between physical rest and spiritual health. The Sabbath commandment ends with *'For in six days the Lord made heaven and earth, the sea, and all that is in them, and rested the seventh day. Therefore, the Lord blessed the Sabbath day and hallowed it.'* The Lord **blessed** the Sabbath day and **hallowed** it. Whoa! Pause for a moment and drink deeply from this mystery.

God wants us to rest our physical body. In our rest, we receive God's blessing as we focus on God's holiness – His worth and work in creation. Unfortunately, most of us neglect physical rest. We may take a break from our work, but we do not rest. We are too busy shopping, video gaming, binge watching Netflix, et cetera. We therefore miss out on the blessing that comes from rest, and passing over the opportunity to care for our spiritual well-being.

Religious people do not usually fare very well in having regular and adequate rest. They may busily engage in religious activities on their holy day but there are hardly any 'hallowed' moments in those activities. It is hard to gaze on God's holiness unless you slow down, hit the pause button and rest. As a result, they too, miss out on the blessed and hallowed rest. It is not until we are convinced of the connection between physical health and spiritual health, that we will then take seriously the 4th Commandment: 'Remember the Sabbath day, to keep it holy'.

If you are a Christian, take some time to read through the four gospels. Take note of the parts that record Jesus as eating or drinking, seeking or taking a rest, and sleeping. Why did the early disciples record these parts of Jesus' life if they were unimportant? Why let these segments take up precious space in the gospel accounts? Why do many Christians seek to emulate Jesus' teachings, healings and miracles, but not His attention to self-care? Jesus said of Himself, 'The Son of Man came eating and drinking.' Given the low view on eating and drinking among us, how likely are we to cast our lots with the critics of Jesus in disparaging Him, 'Here is a glutton and a drunkard'?[7]

For many of us who are seeking to improve our spiritual health, I imagine the first things Jesus might say to us are 'Now come and have some breakfast!' or 'Let's go off by ourselves to a quiet place and rest awhile.'[8]

Mental Health

Besides physical health, mental wellness is another important aspect that influences our spiritual health. The Hebrew Bible tells the interesting story of Prophet Elijah[9] who fell into depression, most likely due to a combination of fatigue, fear and discouragement. It got so bad that Elijah exclaimed to God, 'I've had enough! God, take my life.' What was God's response? Struck him dead with lightning? Told him to snap out of his depression? Sign him up for a Bible lectureship or Hillsong conference?

No. God sent an angel to take care of Elijah's physical needs – allowing him to sleep and rest, cooking for him, and waking him up at intervals to feed him with food and water. When Elijah gained sufficient physical strength, he continued his journey to the mountain of God, where he had an encounter with God.

I like the author of *Girls' Club*, Joy Clarkson's post, on Facebook about this story: 'This is your gentle reminder that one time in the Bible, Elijah was like "God, I'm so mad! I wish I were dead!" So, God said, "Here's some food. Why don't you have a nap?" So, Elijah slept, ate and decided things weren't so bad. Never underestimate the spiritual power of a nap and a snack.'

> *I've learnt that sometimes*
>
> *the most spiritual thing a person can do*
>
> *is to take a nap.*

The story of Elijah brings out the interconnectedness of our physical and spiritual health beautifully, and how important physical sustenance and rest are to our spiritual wellness. In addition, Elijah's bout with depression also highlights mental health as another important contributing factor to our spiritual health.

Mental health refers to our cognitive, emotional and behavioural well-being. Mental illnesses such as depression affect how we think, feel and behave. In practical terms, depression can affect our performance, daily functioning, physical health, ability to cope with adversity, and relationships, et cetera.

In Elijah's case, his depression affected his perception of reality, energy level, ability to cope with his problem, emotional stability and his *spiritual* health. In restoring Elijah to health, God showed Himself to be the Great Therapist – patient, empathetic, skilful and timely. He sent an angel to provide Elijah with physical care, which included food, drink and touch, and also to nudge him into action. When Elijah arrived at a quiet cave at Mount Sinai, God reached out to him and asked him a reflective probing question and listened patiently without judgment to Elijah's complaints.

After preceding a terrifying windstorm, an earthquake and a fire, with a gentle whisper, God gently led Elijah out of the cave, where Elijah had a spiritual encounter with the Divine. Once again, God probed him with the same reflective question. And once again, Elijah repeated the same complaint. But one thing was different this time round – Elijah was ready for God to change his perception of reality and he was ready to launch forth into action once again.

The story ended with Elijah enjoying holistic wellness. Through restoring his physical and mental health, God reinstated Elijah's spiritual health. Not only was he healed emotionally of his depression, but he was also healed spiritually – for, once again, Elijah could hear God's voice and see God's reality, and he boldly launched out once more with a clear purpose from God.

It is God's prerogative who He will heal, and when and **how** He will heal. I have no doubt God can heal miraculously. The Divine is sovereign over matter, space and time. There are occasions when God chooses to infuse physical, mental and spiritual healing into a single moment. But God also heals by developing in us good habits, sound minds and healthy relationships, all of them leading to physical, mental and spiritual wellness.

> *People need healing for their mental illness. But even if they receive healing, miraculously or medically, it won't really work unless they develop better habits, sounder minds and healthier relationships as well.*

It must be noted that even when a person receives miraculous healing for his mental illness, if he does not go on to develop and maintain habits that support a healthy body, mind and soul, and cultivate healthy relationships, his mental health will eventually suffer a relapse, and so will his spiritual health.

I often hear this complaint from Christians who have struggled with mental health problems: 'It is not helpful seeking help from other Christians. All they do is tell me to have faith and pray. It's hurtful because they are implying the problem lies in my lack of faith and prayer life.' It is interesting, isn't it? When we have a fall and break our arm, we immediately admit ourselves to a hospital, while praying softly all the way to the A&E. But when our friends come to us with a mental health problem, all we do is ask them to believe and pray?

There are many possible causes of mental health illnesses, such as depression. The BPSS Model comes in handy in understanding the various factors causing depression. You could have the wrong biology, psychology (thoughts, emotions, self-worth, coping ways et cetera), social environment (abuse, neglect, trauma, dysfunctional relationships et cetera) or spirituality. Depression could be caused by one or a combination of these factors. However, all these factors are influential – but not determinative. With the right ploys, you can bring yourself to joy again.

It is normal to feel sad from time to time, but when you find yourself wrestling with emotions such as hopelessness and despair for two weeks or more, and they interfere with your ability to work, study, eat, sleep, pray or play, it is time to consult a mental health professional.

Emotional Health

I like this piece of advice by Values-based Education Resources: 'Sit with your emotions as they arise, feel them, listen to them, appreciate them, but never run from them, because they'll track you down and haunt you until you are courageous enough to face them and ultimately learn the lessons that they hold.'[10]

This advice serves as a good reminder of our earlier section on negative emotions. We should not deny, avoid or suppress our negative emotions, but allow ourselves to feel each of our genuine emotions. It is when we feel our genuine emotion that we are able to name it correctly, process it and grow from it. Let us not spiritually short-circuit our negative emotions. 'It's impossible to be spiritually mature while remaining emotionally immature'[11], wrote Peter Scazzero, the author of *Emotionally Healthy Spirituality*. Get hold of a copy of this book to find out the importance of emotional health, and learn to mature emotionally in order to mature spiritually.

Once I waited over three hours for a Christian friend, yet on arriving, she admonished me, 'Don't be angry. Christians are not supposed to be angry.' As I recall her advice, what is really troubling was that she was supposedly a mature Christian giving advice to a younger Christian. She was not alone in her view of what being 'spiritually mature' was. I grew up surrounded by 'mature' Christians who denied, suppressed or spiritualized away anger, fear or grief. These emotions were seen as signs of weakness in faith, or of spiritual immaturity. The prevailing belief was, and probably still is – Christians who are mature spiritually do not feel anxious, sad or upset.

How far from the truth is this brand of spirituality! But it was only when I started to read and pray the Psalms daily that I began to realize God wants us to be honest with our emotions, and welcomes us to express our anger, fear and grief to Him honestly. Reading and praying the Psalms more than blessed my emotional and spiritual health, and out of this growth came the book, *Praying the Psalms for the Half-full Soul*[2], which I wrote to bless others.

Psalms is a collection of prayers, composed into sacred songs meant to be sung in worship. It begins the *Writings* (Hebrew Ketuvim), the third and final section of the Hebrew Bible. It is often called the prayer book of the Jews and was used in the temple and synagogues during the time of Jesus. This makes *Psalms* the prayer book of Jesus. The great spiritual teacher was familiar with the *Psalms* and prayed the Psalms!

Eugene Peterson, the author of *Answering* God – *The Psalms as Tools for Prayer,* wrote, 'The Psalms are the best prayer tools available for helping us to being and becoming; 150 carefully crafted prayers to attend to all parts of our lives, at various times and in different ways – rebellious and trusting, hurting and praising, lamenting and thanksgiving, crying and singing.'

Some authors observe that about 40 percent of the *Psalms* are laments. Eugene Peterson puts it at 70 percent. But what are laments? Laments are anguished prayers coming out of heartfelt pain, expressing deep sorrow and crying out to God over our despair, anger, protest and doubt. Why is it that so much of the Jewish prayer book is centred on laments or complaints?

God wants us to be in touch with our emotions, be honest with how we feel, and to bring them before Him openly, in order for us to work through them with God. As God, He is able to handle our emotional outbursts, tantrums and complaints. And as our Creator, He knows how important this is for our emotional health, and how necessary this is for nurturing our spiritual health.

While the end goal of our negative emotions is positive energy and spiritual maturity, the process cannot be short-circuited, fast-forwarded, or hurried. Wounded souls and doubting minds need time and space to grow in faith. If we take a fast-food approach to churning out spirituality, is it any wonder we end up with a spirituality that is hollow instead of hallowed?

People who are having a difficult time can experience feeling the absence of God, struggle with uncontrollable thoughts and feel intense pain in their hearts. It is normal for them to cry out in desperation. *Psalms* help by giving us words to pray our despair, anger, protests and doubts. Some examples are *'How long, O Lord, will you utterly forget me?'*[13], *'Why, O Lord, do you stand aloof? Why hide in times of distress?'*[14], and *'I am as good as dead and completely helpless.'*[15] In His agony on the cross, Jesus Himself prayed the words of the 22nd Psalm, *"My God, my God, why have you forsaken me?"*

Instead of denying or suppressing our emotions, *Psalms* normalizes and validates our fears, anxieties and anger, and encourages us to express them to the Lord in prayer. A wounded soul needs an empathetic listener. By giving *Psalms* to us as our prayer book, God is allowing us to question and lament. And when we do, the empathetic God listens attentively, patiently and compassionately. How loving is our God!

When people are allowed to pour out their laments and bare their souls, they feel understood and in time will become ready to hope again. Pain soothed and attended to by empathy becomes a fertile ground for faith and hope to grow. Laments will turn to praise. However, there are no short cuts. Give people the space of time. Healing often begins with crying.

I have seen this circulating on social media: 'Never trust your tongue when your heart is bitter. Hush until you heal.' I think there are truths in 'never trust your tongue when your heart is bitter', but I am not too sure about 'hush until you heal'. Often, healing only begins when we empty out our bitterness in words. But, not just any words. Try praying the words of *Psalms* to pour out bitter words and begin the road that leads to healing.

You probably have heard of this or a similar piece of advice: 'Don't complain. No one cares. No one wants to hear your complaints. No one wants to be near a complainer.' From my experience, this is probably true. Complaints can wear a person out – both the complainer and the ones who listen. I do not encourage you or anyone to complain mindlessly or indiscriminately. The weight of your complaints is often too heavy to bear for the listeners, especially if they are of the emotional type, for they may be dragged down as well. It is better to seek out and complain to a trained helper, like a counsellor or psychotherapist, a priest or pastor.

Of course, the best person to go to with your complaints is still God. God is an empathetic Counsellor who listens to your pain and your fears patiently. Go to Him with your questions, complaints and pleas.

Complaints can be healing or harming. Pray the *Psalms* daily so that your complaints are spruced up to bring healing to your emotional and spiritual selves. Furthermore, praying all the 150 psalms, one psalm a day, will help you not to focus on any single aspect of your life, but rather on all parts of your life, 'at various times and in different ways – rebellious and trusting, hurting and praising, lamenting and thanksgiving, crying and singing.'

Emotional health and spiritual health are so closely connected that you cannot have one without the other. I have seen religious people who are deeply committed to their faith but suffer from poor emotional health. Though pious and devoted, their spirituality smells of decay and death because of their poor emotional health. In many cases, their spouses and children suffer the brunt of their poor emotional and spiritual health, and are often victims of emotional or spiritual abuse. In my counselling work with teenagers, many of them turned away from God because they saw contradictions in the religious devotion and the emotional immaturity of their parents. From a young age, they were not allowed to display anxiety, fear, anger or sadness. When they did, they were 'spiritually bullied' to feel guilty by their parents, who cited religious teachings or alluded to God's disapproval. Yet, they witnessed and experienced their parents' own emotional insecurities, outbursts, constant nagging, or cold shoulder.

Our poor emotional health not only affects our own spiritual health, but it can also negatively impact the emotional and spiritual health of those around us, especially those closest to us. For their sake and for ours, let us seriously look into the state of our emotional health. It may be helpful for some readers to re-visit the chapter on **Turning Negative Emotions into Positive Energy.**

Prioritize your spiritual world over the material world by all means. However, do not set your spiritual needs *apart* from your physical, mental and emotional needs, or pursue spirituality as though it *alone* matters. Pursue and practice your spirituality *among* all the other aspects of your life. You have a body, mind and spirit, and they are interconnected. Take care of your physical, mental and emotional health, as you care for your spiritual health.

A HOLISTIC APPROACH TO
WHOLESOME SPIRITUAL HEALTH

We have said many things about spiritual health. But what are we really saying? Essentially, we are saying, 'Don't box up spirituality.' Our body, mind and soul are interconnected. Each aspect of the Self interacts with the other aspects, affects and is being affected by them. You cannot cultivate any single aspect of your life while neglecting the other aspects, and still hope to attain holistic health. This is particularly true for our spiritual health. For too long and for too many people, there has been the pursuit of a spirituality that focuses only on the soul, and there is hardly a trace of any care for the body or mind. I am calling for a holistic approach to wholesome spiritual health – that also includes caring for the body and mind.

A spiritually healthy person does not set spirituality *apart* and *above* the physical, mental, emotional or social aspects of his life, or thinks that only spirituality *alone* matters. Spirituality has to be lived out in the material world. Though spiritual beings, we are also physical beings living in a physical world, among other beings, animals, matters and things. We cannot attend only to our spiritual world while ignoring the physical one. This will result in poor spiritual health.

Often, religious people have the biggest problem with this integrated approach to spiritual health, mainly due to over-spiritualization that is continually reinforced by selective hearing or reading.

We have earlier used the example of Jesus quoting the Hebrew

Bible, *"Man shall not live on bread alone, but on every word that comes from the mouth of God."* This has its context in the well-known temptations of Jesus, after His baptism and before He began his public ministry. This was Jesus' response to His first temptation. Let us take a look at the second temptation, shall we?

Then Satan took him to Jerusalem to the roof of the Temple. "Jump off," he said, "and prove you are the Son of God; for the Scriptures declare, 'God will send his angels to keep you from harm, ... they will prevent you from smashing on the rocks below.'" Jesus retorted, "It also says not to put the Lord your God to a foolish test!"' [16]

There are many things to learn from the second temptation of Jesus. Chief among them, in my opinion, is not to blackmail God by misusing trust in God. This is pseudo faith that attempts to twist God's arm into serving our own purposes by invoking our faith in God. Whether we are people of faith or not, we are subject to the law of gravity. So, if we jump off from the 30th storey, without a parachute or without God telling us to do so, we will most likely die. It has nothing to do with faith in God, but everything to do with misusing faith to serve our own purposes.

We see signs, wonders and miracles, and quickly recognize them as clear evidence of the Divine Presence and Work in the physical realm – the invasion of the spiritual realm into the physical realm. The supernatural are encounters with the spiritual realm, and they can be immensely rich spiritual experiences that help us grow spiritually. But surely the natural must also count as equally valid spiritual experiences, and not just the supernatural?

Both natural and supernatural experiences can be equally valid spiritual experiences. What do I mean? Well, the God to whom the supernatural events point to is also the God who created the natural world, and set in place its natural laws. We must not forget that the nature we see reflects the nature of the Creator we seek, and that natural laws reveal the character of God who put them in place. The nature – its design, laws, order, beauty and strength – are the fingerprints and footprints of its Creator.

As much as is the supernatural, nature and its natural laws, are also from God. They too reflect God's glory[17], and are clear evidence of the Divine Presence and Work, as much as the supernatural. If we see the supernatural as the invasion of the spiritual realm into our physical realm, then nature and the natural laws are imprints of the spiritual realm on the physical realm. While encounters with the supernatural can be immensely rich spiritual experiences, ordinary daily experiences in the natural world are the foundational spiritual experiences that provide our daily spiritual nourishment.

Let us not despise our daily bread in our greed for spiritual bread. And let us not ditch the natural laws and throw ourselves off the pinnacle of the temple of our pride, to arm-twist God into performing the supernatural for our own gratification.

One story tells of a mega storm that was brewing, and the police sent out an emergency warning that a flood was impending. An order was given for everyone to evacuate immediately. A man heard the warning and decided to stay, saying to himself, 'I trust God to deliver me.'

His uncle came by his house and said, 'We're leaving and there is room for you in our car, come with us!' The man declined and declared, 'I have faith that God will save me.' As the man stood on his porch watching the water cover the steps, a neighbour paddled by in a canoe and called out to him, 'Come into my canoe, the waters are rising quickly!' But the man said, 'No thanks, God will save me.'

The floodwaters poured into his living room and the man went up to the second floor. A police motorboat came by and saw him at the window. 'Come with us!' they shouted. But the man refused, waving them off and proclaiming, 'God will save me!' The flood waters rose higher and the man had to climb up to his rooftop. A helicopter spotted him and dropped a rope ladder. A rescue officer came down the ladder and yelled, 'Grab my hand!' But the man still refused and insisted, 'No thank you. God will save me!'

Shortly after, the floodwaters swept away the house and the man drowned. When in Heaven, the man stood before God and asked, 'I put all of my faith in you. Why didn't you save me?' God said, 'Son, I sent you a warning. I sent you a car. I sent you a canoe. I sent you a motorboat. I sent you a helicopter. What more were you looking for?'

SHOULDN'T GOD COME FIRST?

'But shouldn't we put God first?' I imagine this would be the commonest and strongest objection to what I have said about not setting spirituality apart and above everything else in life, and not to seek it alone. To answer this objection, I am quite ready to move on to the third temptation of Jesus. Are you ready?

'Again, the devil took him to a very high mountain and showed him all the kingdoms of the world and their splendour. "All this I will give you," he said, "if you will bow down and worship me." Jesus said to him, "Away from me, Satan! For it is written: 'Worship the Lord your God, and serve him only.'"' [18]

I am not sure what your understanding is of Jesus' response to the devil's third temptation. I understand this as He is saying that we should worship and serve **GOD** only, not kingdoms and their splendour. If we are not careful, we will do exactly what Jesus says *not to do*. But of course, we can creatively justify that our own 'little kingdoms' are parts of God's kingdom. These 'little kingdoms' could be our particular brand of theology, doctrines or religious practices, including our over-spiritualization.

It is exactly because we worship and serve God only, that we do not set spirituality *apart* and *above* everything else in life, or seek spirituality *alone*. The 'alone' is reserved for God – worship and serve God *only*. There is only one '*only*' in our life, and that's God. Spirituality is *not* God. God alone is above everything else, not spirituality.

When we seek God above all things, spirituality can no longer remain a part of our life, but permeates every part of our life – physical, mental and relational. A better and clearer way of understanding how spirituality should look like in our life is therefore this:

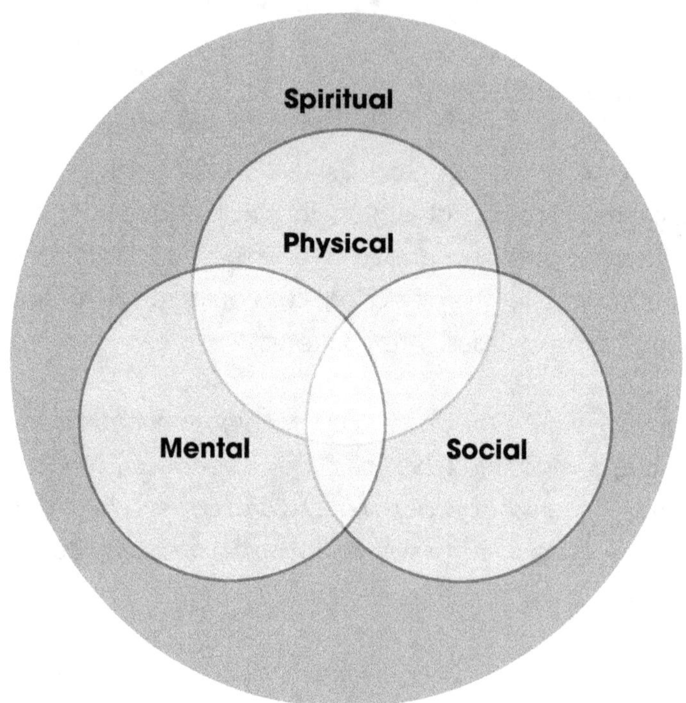

When God is above all things, spirituality is brought into every area of our life, and is being practised in the physical and social world, among all things, matters, minds and emotions, as well as our relationships. Such spirituality leads to wellness of our spiritual health.

WHOLESOME SPIRITUAL HEALTH

As discussed, conceptually, it is useful to fragment the broad notion of health into physical, mental, social and spiritual health in order to understand and find ways to improve health in each area. Yet the person as body, mind and soul cannot be taken apart. It is therefore crucial that we see the person as a whole being and adopt an integrated approach to holistic health.

True spirituality must bring that 'something bigger than ourselves' into the ordinary of everyday living. In this chapter, I have proposed a model of spirituality that can be the universal and unifying dimension of the whole person. Such spirituality provides meaning, purpose, reasons and values in our life and our relationships with others. We seek a spirituality that integrates and unifies our physical, mental and social life. This form of spirituality brings about spiritual health, and consequently supports and reinforces holistic health and happiness.

Now that we have a better understanding of spiritual health, let us find out how we can begin our journey to spiritual health.

CHAPTER EIGHT

BEGINNING THE JOURNEY OF SPIRITUAL HEALTH

One with Everything

In 2011, Karl Stefanovic, an Australian television presenter, had a chance to interview the Dalai Lama. Karl tried telling him a joke, 'So the Dalai Lama walks into a pizza shop, and says, "Can you make me one with everything?"' The joke by the Australian anchor failed badly, as it was only met with an empty gaze from the Buddhist leader. Using hand gestures, Karl repeated the punchline, 'Can you make me one with everything?' But this was only met with even more blank stares.

I hope what I have been trying to say about spiritual health or spirituality, it being the unifying dimension that is supposed to make us 'one with everything', hasn't been a bad joke to the readers.

In the previous chapter, we learnt that **Spiritual health** is the universal dimension that unifies the whole person – body, mind and soul – as one. It involves having a purpose that is larger than self, someone to love, something to do and something to look forward to. To attain and maintain this spiritual health, we need to practise a spirituality that brings that larger-than-self purpose into ordinary, everyday living. We also looked at this model of **spirituality** that unifies the whole person – their physical (biological), mental (psychological) and social life.

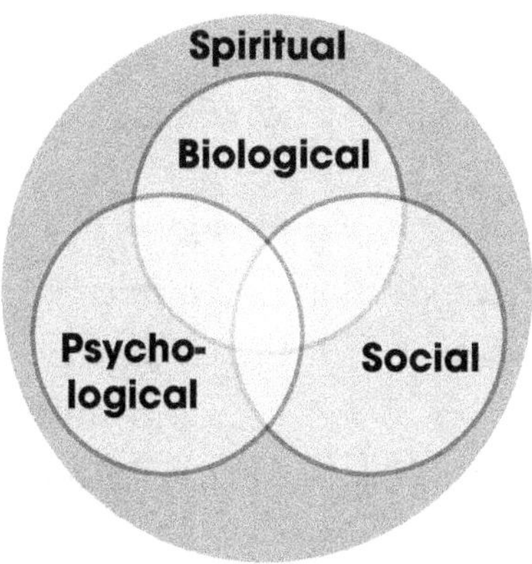

This form of spirituality not only provides meaning, purpose, reasons for living, and values in our life, but it also integrates these into every aspect of our ordinary life: our food, habits, thoughts, speech, behaviour and our connectedness with others. This integrated approach to spirituality results in wholesome spiritual health where love, faith and hope blossom. Consequently, this spiritual wellness brings about the holistic health and happiness that we have been seeking.

Spiritual health that *makes us one with everything* – yes, that is what we want. But where do we begin?

WHERE DO WE BEGIN?

There are many definitions and perspectives of what spirituality is. Where we begin the journey of spiritual health depends on our beliefs and worldviews. I will here share my own spiritual journey as a follower of Jesus, offering it as a guide for those who seek to chart their own paths. For those of you who have already begun your own journey, I share my experiences so that you may compare your notes with mine.

Grace

It might surprise many that grace is where we begin. What is grace? It has often been said that mercy is not receiving what you deserve, and grace is getting what you do not merit.

Sometimes, when I listen to people tell me their problems, while my heart swells with compassion and empathy, my mind often wonders, 'How come it's not worse than this?' Listening to the poor choices or bad decisions that some people make, or the entangled situations that they get themselves into, I cannot help but be awed by the divine grace and mercy in their lives.

I am a believer of 'a person reaps what he sows', but I am even more convinced that if we *always* receive the consequences of our actions, we would probably all be dead by now! The fact that we are still alive and continuing to enjoy our blessings is clear evidence of unmerited favour from the Divine.

Jesus said this of His Father in heaven, 'He causes His sun to rise on the evil and the good, and sends rain on the righteous and the unrighteous.'[1] Many of our blessings are sheer divine grace, and have nothing to do with our right conduct or behaviour, but have everything to do with the God who 'is kind to the ungrateful and the evil.'[2]

In seeking spiritual health, let us begin with grace. For even though we do not have all the answers in life, or have our life all together, God is kind and continues to cause His sun to rise and send rain on us. When we begin to recognize that we are freely blessed with the necessities for living and the beauty of creation, we instinctively become thankful, and if we ponder deeper, our hearts will point us to a loving God who willingly grants all these blessings to all people on earth. Like Prophet Abraham, we have to see God for who He really is – a kind and loving God who bestows His common grace on all mankind. This is God's **universal grace** for everyone – the good and the evil.

When we perceive God as a kind and loving God, our need for safety and security are being met. While our path may be strewn with problems and obstacles, we trust in the kind and loving God to help us overcome them. We begin to see the world as a difficult, but safe place. This outlook causes us to have a positive view of life and of the people around us. It influences us to be at peace with ourselves and to live peaceably with others. The peace within and without is an important *first* step towards improving our spiritual health.

Enabling Grace

It is hard to recognize grace without knowing justice. Justice is fairness in how people are dealt with – the administering of deserved punishment or reward. Mercy is not receiving what we deserve, but we would not appreciate mercy unless the threat of the deserved punishment is real. Grace is getting what we do not merit, but we would not value grace until we know that we – who we are and what we have done – do not merit the goodness from God.

If you were raised in a family where wrongdoings are never taken to task, you would not know what grace is. You would expect to be excused each time you commit a wrong. It is the way things have always been and should be. For the times when you are not excused, you would cry out, 'That's not right!' You probably would not even know that you have done wrong. Children who grow up in such an environment are unable to recognize what grace is, for they do not know what justice is.

Grace and justice are two sides of the same coin. A coin with the same face on both sides is usually used for deception or trickery. Reject any form of spirituality that separates justice from grace, or has extremes in either grace or justice.

> *Grace and justice form the pair of chopsticks that God uses to lift us to holiness.*

True grace is grounded in justice. Justice helps us to be cognizant of our having to bear the undesirable consequences arising from our badness. But here comes grace, so that we do not have to bear those consequences, but instead receive the goodness we do not merit. When such is the case, grace becomes the *enabling* gift that helps us grow - out of the appreciation for the grace we receive and gratitude to God for His goodness.

In my counselling work, I have learnt how important it is for justice and righteousness to be right there, together with grace and mercy. Otherwise, instead of enabling grace, we end up with an entitlement mentality that is inhibiting and not conducive for growth. In filling us with optimism, universal grace wants to continue leading us to enabling grace that nudges us to grow.

Why is it that for some people, universal grace becomes enabling grace, whereas for others, it becomes an entitlement mentality that is inhibiting growth? This is not an easy question to answer. There are likely to be multiple reasons for this.

> **"**
>
> *The same sun that melts the butter hardens the clay.*
>
> *Billy Graham*
>
> **"**

Psychologist Carl Rogers, founder of the Person-Centred Counselling approach, believes **six** necessary conditions are needed for clients to engage in meaningful self-exploration that leads to their growth process. Out of these **six necessary** conditions, much attention has been focused on the **three core** conditions to be created by the therapist, namely:

1.   the therapist is genuine with the client;

2.   the therapist provides the client with unconditional positive regard and acceptance; and

3.   the therapist shows empathy to the client.

In creating these core conditions for the client, the therapist is in effect extending *enabling grace* to the client. Jeanne Watson (2002) sums it up this way: 'Therapists need to be able to be responsively attuned to their clients and to understand them emotionally as well as cognitively. When empathy is operating on all three levels – interpersonal, cognitive, and affective – it is one of the most powerful tools therapists have at their disposal.'[3]

However, you need to know that the **first** of the six necessary conditions is this: The client is in a state of incongruence (being vulnerable or anxious), perceives his incongruence and seeks therapeutic intervention.

When a person does not think he is in trouble or that he is in need of help, it is hard for the therapist to provide him with the core conditions, for he might not even want to meet with the therapist. Even when he is compelled to meet the therapist against his will, the meeting is quite unlikely to be effective. For you see, the **second** necessary condition requires a relationship to exist between the client and the therapist, one in which each person's perception of the other is important. If the client is resistant to change or refuses a relationship with the therapist, the provision of the core conditions by the therapist may only simply amount to a pleasant conversation with the client. Such an encounter rarely leads to growth. Works are needed to help the client overcome his resistance first.

In the same way, in order for universal grace to become enabling grace that leads a person to the growth process, the person needs to perceive or agree that he has a problem and is in need of help. He cries out, 'What must I do?' What would cause a person to cry out, 'Help me! What must I do?' Here are some common experiences that bring a person to his knees to seek help: problem, illness, pain, suffering, brokenness, cognitive dissonance, et cetera.

I know many of us do not like to hear this, but it is when our wrongs catch up with us or when our life is thrown into disarray that we cry out for help. Problems often spark the growth process. The pain produced by the bitter consequences of our actions often leads to a broken spirit, humility and submission.

A broken spirit creates space for grace. Humility replaces arrogance and pride. Submission sets in place readiness for growth and change. It takes the justice of God to purge us of our self-sufficiency, self-interest and self-righteousness.

> *The truth is that our finest moments are most likely to occur when we are feeling deeply uncomfortable, unhappy, or unfulfilled. For it is only in such moments, propelled by our discomfort, that we are likely to step out of our ruts and start searching for different ways or truer answers.*
>
> *Scott Peck*

Enabling grace is grace that is grounded in justice. Grace and justice are the works of the Divine Being to bring us closer to spiritual health. While universal grace nudges us to take the *first* step towards spiritual health, enabling grace brings us to its *door*, because it produces in us a willing attitude and appetite for change and growth. Now having arrived at the threshold, we will need the door to be opened. But who will open the door to spiritual health for us?

Regenerating Grace

It is regenerating grace that opens the door to spiritual health, allowing us to enter and enjoy spiritual health. By regeneration, I mean a new birth or a new beginning. But **what** is being born again and given a new beginning? It is our *spirit*.

Spirit, what is that?

The person is commonly understood to have three parts that are intricately interconnected – *body*, *soul* and *spirit*. For readers who are familiar with the person being **body, mind, soul** and **spirit**, this can be rather confusing. This can be resolved in two ways: You can go with either the popular understanding that the mind and soul are referring to the same thing, or that the **mind, emotion** and **will** are three parts of the soul.

The Greek word for soul is ***psyche*** (ψυχή). This is the Greek root of the word *psychology*, which means the study of the psyche or soul. In the Biopsychosocial-Spiritual (BPSS) Model that we have been using in this book, the mind, emotion and will are included in the psychological dimension.

The person is therefore a three-part whole: the body, soul and spirit. However, a better way of understanding and saying this is: 'We are a ***spirit***, have a ***soul*** and live in a ***body***.'

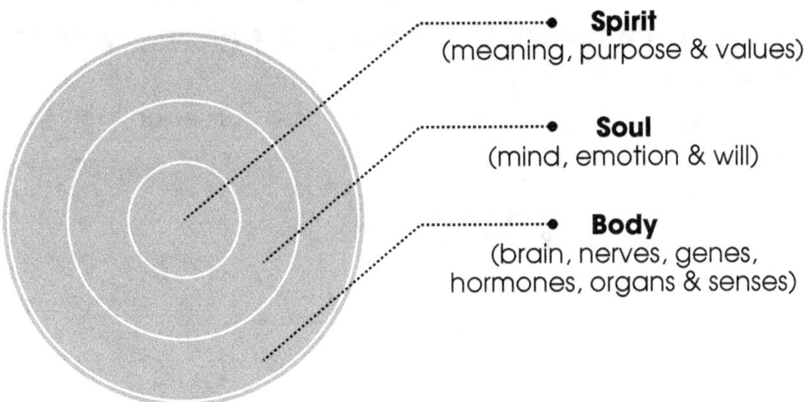

In regeneration, the spirit is born again and given a new life. While you may enjoy good physical, mental and social health, it is when you have a reason for living, true meaning in life and larger-than-self purpose that your inert spirit springs to life and undergoes a new spiritual birth. The journey of spiritual health starts when you stop living a life of mere existence and begin living a life of meaningful engagement.

Regenerating the spirit

How can we find the meaning-making larger-than-life purpose to regenerate our spirit? Admittedly, the search can be rather difficult. Some seek it through building their career or business empire, or through noble causes such as saving children, protecting the environment, and fighting against cancer, social injustice or poverty.

I have seen people trying to inject meaning and purpose into their life through a fulfilling career or a worthy cause. However, it is not as easy or straightforward as it seems. To begin with, you have to correctly identify the career or cause that is a good fit for you, a unique individual. At the same time, it has to make a difference to the world.

You could borrow the model used to identify *ikigai* or 'a reason for being' from the chapter on **Changing Your Watch**, and discover your **purpose** by identifying the sweet spot which fits '*that which you are good at*' (**proficiency**), '*that which you love*' (**passion**), '*that which the world needs*' (**practicality**) and '*would reward you for*' (**payoff**).

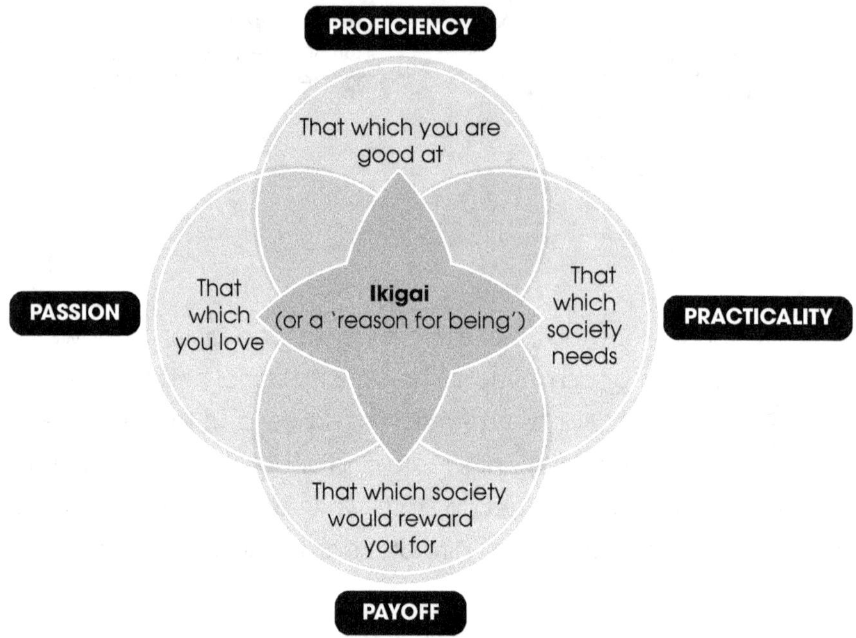

The assumption here is that 'a reason for being' will automatically give you that larger-than-life purpose. I wish it were that simple and straightforward. *Ikigai or* 'a reason for being' may work well for picking a rewarding career or noble cause, but it does not necessarily give you that larger-than-life purpose. This is because while *ikigai* can give you a purpose that makes your life on earth worthwhile, it is unfortunate that *ikigai's* purpose is not larger than life. Why? To borrow a term from insurance policies, it lacks portability. Portability? Well, have you, in the rare moments of quiet contemplation while gazing into the wide blue sky, ever thought of life after death? It may surprise some of you, but the fact is that you, the real person without your current physical body, extend beyond your life here on earth. As for *ikigai*, its purpose of life is just not portable to the afterlife. You cannot transfer the 'credits' gained here on earth to the life that is beyond our current life.

Sure, purposeful engagement offers you satisfaction and meaningful activities in this life, but it does not necessarily give you the meaning of life. In living out a meaningful life, it is important that we first figure out the meaning of life. This deliberation has to go beyond the relatively straightforward 'What should I do with my life?' to deeper probing questions of 'Who am I?', 'Where did I come from?', 'Why am I here?' and 'Where am I going?' These are fundamental questions we need to answer in our journey to spiritual health.

For those who seem content to live out a meaningful life by living out their *ikigai*, many would end up being disillusioned at some points of their life or at the end of their life. It appears that *ikigai* works well only for people who have already figured out the meaning of life in the first place. Otherwise, *ikigai* only succeeds in helping you live an occupied, but not a truly meaningful life.

In turning to a career or cause for that meaning-making larger-than-life purpose, there is something else that does not seem quite right. Life's meaning and purpose are supposed to regenerate our spirit, and thus rejuvenate our life. Simply put, they are supposed to improve our spiritual health. However, I have noticed that at some points, be it career or cause, no matter how fulfilling it is, this life would drain us of our energy, rob us of our enthusiasm and cast doubts on our commitment. Most people find it hard to summon the will to hold on to their dream all the time. Instead of guaranteeing spiritual health, a satisfying career or worthy cause often produces fatigue, burnout, disillusionment, inner turmoil, et cetera.

This does not seem quite right. It reinforces the fact that fulfilling work, or a noble cause works well as that larger-than-life purpose only if you have already figured out the meaning of life in the first place. It is the meaning of life that helps sustain our meaningful career or cause. Not the other way around. So, the right questions to ask should be: 'What is the meaning of life?' and 'How can we lay hold of it?'

Some shrewd readers might point out that we have missed out relationships from our discussion, and offer the suggestion that perhaps we could add meaningful relationships to *ikigai*, career or cause, to make it work.

Many have turned to relationships (or loving others) as that meaning-giving larger-than-self purpose. This is definitely a noble and worthy purpose.   However, as we have covered in the chapter on **Changing our Torque**, human adversarial nature gives rise to a lot of relationship problems. The root cause of this goes beyond human personalities or differences between individuals; it is a spiritual one – a result of our separation from God.

> *Spiritual health begins, only when*
>
> *our relationship with God begins.*

Humans are created to have an intimate bonding with God, but because of our brokenness we are often unable to bond or connect with God. As a result of this disconnectedness, we also have difficulties bonding and connecting with other people. Before meaningful relationships can improve our spiritual health, we need to first mend our relationship with God. Spiritual health begins only when our relationship with God begins.

But a dead spirit is incapable of a relationship with the Living Spirit. To begin our relationship with God, we need a new birth, one in which our spirit is made alive by God's Spirit and is given a new life.

Regenerating Grace

Our experience with the current reality points to this truth: a new birth is required before we can live out a new life. In turning to a career, cause or relationship to regenerate our spirit, we are trying to force upon ourselves a new birth by living out a new life. The sequence is wrong. Nature will not have it. Neither will the spiritual realm. We need to be born again *first* before we can start living the new life.

The Chinese idiom for rebirth is 脱胎换骨, which literally means to *shed one's mortal body and replace one's bones*. For transformation to be thorough and complete, we need more than a change in habits, thoughts and words – we need a spiritual experience – one that gives birth to a new spirit, and for the new spirit to gradually permeate into every crevice of our body and soul. For all these to happen, we need a spiritual rebirth, or in the words of the Chinese idiom, we need to undergo 脱胎换骨.

Rebirth of our spirit? But how can it be done? Will spirituality or religion suffice to regenerate the spirit?

An unregenerate spirit can with his *mind* understand spiritual health, with his *emotions* taste spirituality, and with his *will* reach out to the Divine Spirit, but his *soul* is unable to drink deeply from the Eternal Living Spirit who is the wellspring of spirituality. This is because the unregenerate spirit is separated from God.

By His grace and mercy, God showers His spiritual blessings on all mankind. But the unregenerate spirit needs more than general blessings or a sporadic shower of spirituality – he needs the baptism of the Holy Spirit for his regeneration!

I have read great spiritual writings from people who have profound understanding of spirituality. Yet, though they themselves are spiritual teachers, they experience deep brokenness in their soul and suffer breakdowns in their relationship with others. Their incongruence comes not from the lack of spiritual knowledge or wisdom, but from their inability to live out their spirituality. It is most unfortunate. Their misery is best expressed in these words, '*I want to do what is right, but I can't. I want to do what is good, but I don't. I don't want to do what is wrong, but I do it anyway.*'[4]

The root of this spiritual incongruence stems from an unregenerate spirit. A sick man needs healing before he can enjoy physical health. An unregenerate spirit needs to come alive before it can experience spiritual health. But a spirituality that sputters and struggles to come alive will not do. We need to be baptized into the Eternal Living Spirit for our spirit to come alive.

What about religion or religious practices? Surely, the practice of spiritual discipline can bring about the baptism of the Spirit and connect us to God, can't it?

Unfortunately, no amount of religion or religious piety can give life to the spirit of the unregenerate man. Nicodemus, a religious leader of standing and learning during the time of Jesus, found out that he could not rely on his religious devotion, learning or understanding to bring about this new spiritual birth. As a Professor of Theology, Nicodemus fasted twice a week and gave 10% of all his income. Yet none of this is enough. Jesus told him plainly that he needed to be born again spiritually, for only God's Spirit can give this new lease of life to the human spirit. 'Men can only reproduce human life, but the Holy Spirit gives new life from heaven'.[5]

Saint Paul, an apostle of Jesus, experienced this spiritual rebirth first-hand and spent the rest of his life telling others the secret to this spiritual regeneration. He wrote, 'At one time we too were foolish, disobedient, deceived and enslaved by all kinds of passions and pleasures. We lived in malice and envy, being hated and hating one another. But when the kindness and love of God our Saviour appeared, he saved us, not because of righteous things we had done, but because of his mercy. He saved us through the washing of rebirth and renewal by the Holy Spirit, whom he poured out on us generously through Jesus Christ our Saviour, so that, having been justified by his grace, we might become heirs having the hope of eternal life.'[6]

Two things are clear about this spiritual regeneration:

1. It is the work of the Holy Spirit.

    'The Holy Spirit gives new life from heaven'. It is 'through the washing of rebirth and renewal by the Holy Spirit.'

2. This grace is given to us freely.

    It is 'the kindness and love of God … *not because of righteous things we had done, but because of his mercy'.*

As with our physical birth, we cannot bring about our new spiritual birth by our own effort. It is entirely God's regenerating grace. The Giver and all recipients of this new birth are in complete agreement that it is through the power of God's Divine Spirit that our spirit is born again.

However, being a gentle Being, God does not impose His Spirit or His gift on us forcefully. Lovingly and patiently, through enabling grace, He leads us into His Holy Presence and offers us this regenerating grace. To be born again, we have to open our hands and heart to receive His precious gift of a new life.

Jesus told Nicodemus, 'For God loved the world so much that He gave his only Son so that anyone who believes in him shall not perish but have eternal life.'[7] Saint Paul said that God pours out His Holy Spirit on us generously *through* Jesus Christ. The promise is free as it is real. To receive this new spiritual birth through God's Spirit taking up residence in us, we just have to believe in Jesus and what He did for us. It is that simple. That is why it is called regenerating **grace**.

No one can come to this faith except by the grace of God. It is *enabling* grace that leads you to the undeniable truth that God loves you so much that He gave Jesus, his Son, for you. Jesus came to earth as a man, died for your sins so that you can be connected to God, and He conquered death by His resurrection. When you declare with your mouth, 'Jesus is Lord', and believe in your heart that God raised Him from the dead, you receive Jesus into your life. And at this point, though you cannot see anything new physically because it is spiritual, something mysterious and truly momentous happens: Through your faith, your dead spirit is made alive by God's Spirit. For through Jesus, God pours his Spirit generously into you – body, soul and spirit – and you are given rebirth and renewal by the Spirit. Such is the *regenerating* grace of God.

'So simple? How can it be? There must be more that I need to know or do. How can the new spiritual birth be so easy?' many of you will ask.

My response is two-fold. First, perhaps you need more of God's enabling grace to believe and accept this truth. His enabling grace will eventually lead you to this truth. Continue to pay attention to what God is doing in your life. Second, while you can know or even believe with your mind what Jesus did for you, you will never *completely* understand this spiritual truth before your spiritual rebirth. For you see, the person without the Spirit does not accept the things that come from the Spirit of God but considers them foolishness, and cannot understand them because they are discerned *only* through the Spirit.[8]

In a person's state of brokenness, his spirit is separated from God's Spirit. Just as the body is dead when the spirit leaves it, so a person is spiritually dead because his spirit is separated from God's Spirit. The spirit of the unregenerate human therefore needs 'the spark of regeneration' before he can understand the things of God.

> *You must have a capacity to receive, or even omnipotence can't give.*
>
> C.S. Lewis

When we surrender our own will and accept by faith, the truth revealed to us by God's Spirit, the life-giving Spirit comes and takes up residence in our spirit. A spiritual regeneration – a mystery only fully known to God – takes place when our spirit is joined with God's Spirit. We come alive and are given a new life. With the rebirth and renewal of the spirit, our spiritual nature is transformed by God's Spirit. We now stand ready to understand the things of God, and are thus ready to begin our journey of spiritual health.

In bringing us to spiritual health, God works mysteriously and relentlessly. Through His *universal* grace, God starts us off on our journey to spiritual health; and by His *enabling* grace He brings us right to the entrance of its gate. And with *regenerating* grace, God throws the gate wide open and ushers us into His Kingdom, the true home of spiritual health.

If you are ready to receive God's regenerating grace to be reborn to live a new life of spiritual health, now with your whole heart, pray aloud the following prayer to Jesus:

Dear Lord Jesus,

Thank you for loving me in spite of my brokenness. I have tried so many ways to fix my brokenness but failed. I am not only broken by the sins of others, but my own spirit is also broken by my own sins. I am turning to You now for help and healing.

Lord Jesus Christ, Son of God, have mercy on me, a sinner. Please forgive my sins and heal my brokenness.

I receive You as my Saviour and Lord of my life. Please pour out your Spirit into my life so that my spirit can be made alive by Your Spirit. Please help me live my new life by the power of Your Spirit.

Thank you, Jesus, for hearing and answering my prayer. Amen.

Your Journey of Spiritual Health has Begun!

If in faith, you pray this prayer to receive Jesus into your life, you have been born again! Congratulations! The promised Holy Spirit comes and quickens your dead spirit. He takes up residence in you, and you are marked spiritually with a seal[9] by His Presence in you. You have become a brand-new person inside. You are not the same anymore. A new life has begun![10]

With the rebirth of your spirit, your spiritual nature is renewed by God's Spirit. You now stand ready to understand the things of God through the Spirit Who lives in you, and hence you have begun the journey of your spiritual health.

Now that you have begun, you need to continue to nurture your spiritual growth and nourish your spiritual wellness. To do that, turn the page to embark on **Improving Our Spiritual Health.**

CHAPTER NINE

IMPROVING OUR SPIRITUAL HEALTH

The Regenerated Life

A person who accepts God's regenerating grace is spiritually reborn and receives a new life. Where before his spirit was dead unto God, now his spirit is made alive by the Spirit of God and begins everything new. Most of all, this new life signifies the beginning of his spiritual health.

The new life not only gives a person a meaning-making, larger-than-life purpose, it also renders a new way of living that helps him live out a spirituality that is *one with everything* - his **WOK, WALK, WATCH, THOUGHT, TALK** and **TORQUE**. This is the spirituality that we have been seeking - one that unifies the whole person and integrates the larger-than-life purpose into ordinary everyday living. There is also congruence in this regenerated life when the Eternal Living Spirit who raises the dead spirit also empowers the renewed spirit to walk in newness of **L-I-F-E.**

When we put our faith in Jesus as our Lord and Saviour, we are born again by the Holy Spirit. The mighty power of the Spirit enables us to live the new spiritual **L-I-F-E** that is characterized by **L**ove - **I**dentity - **F**reedom - **E**nthusiasm.

Let us take a brief look at each of these four aspects of the new **L-I-F-E:**

LOVE

The new life is conceived and brought forth in love. It is therefore lived out in love. Having tasted the kindness of God, we extend kindness to others. And having received the grace and mercy of God, we offer grace and mercy to those around us. Our spiritual birth continually reminds us of God's love, grace and mercy. '*For God so loved the world*' becomes the anthem of our new life. '*Love God*' and '*Love your neighbour as yourself*' are the refrains of our new song, by which we now live out our new life.

We love because God first loved us.[1] Yes, loving others is a natural response to God's love for us. Yet, our love goes beyond gratitude, indebtedness or 'paying it forward', it is rooted in the very nature of God. Apostle John, one of the three who formed the inner circle of Jesus' disciples, said this of God after spending three years following Jesus, 'God is love.'

Love is God's signature character trait. Love is also God's eternal nature. Before He created the universe and everything in it, God is love. It has been said that God is love but He has no one to love, so He created man as object of His love, in order that He could love man. This is so wrong!

God is a Triune God - One God in Three Divine Persons. Love exists within the Holy Commune from eternity. It is God's signature character trait and nature from before time began. God is love and is complete in love from eternity - before the creation. It is definitely not the case that God has nobody to love so He had to create man! But rather, as an expression and extension of the love that exists among the three Persons of the Trinitarian God, God said, 'Let us make mankind in our image, in our likeness.' Out of love and in love, God created man in His image and loved him as He would His own offspring.

God is One in Three Persons - the Father, the Son and the Holy Spirit – all three of them are co-equal, co-eternal and consubstantial. The mystery of the Triune God can never be fully explained in human words. However, the truth of the Holy Trinity is explicitly and emphatically expressed by Jesus and the Holy Scriptures. In the Jewish Bible, you read of the Triune God right at the beginning - in the creation account – 'In the beginning God created the heavens and the earth... And the

Spirit of God was hovering over the surface of the waters. Then God said, "Let there be light," and there was light.'2   God brought forth the creation by speaking it into existence, or by His *Word* God created everything.

All Three Persons of the Triune God - the Father, the Son and the Holy Spirit – were involved and active in the creation story. Jesus is the Word of God in the creation story. Apostle John said this of Jesus, 'In the beginning the Word already existed. The Word was with God, and the Word was God. He existed in the beginning with God. God created everything through him. The Word became human and made his home among us. He was full of unfailing love.'3

About this unfailing love, John went on to say, 'God showed how much He loved us by sending His one and only Son into the world so that we might have eternal life through Him. This is real love - not that we loved God, but that He loved us and sent His Son as a sacrifice to take away our sins.'4

The plot of God's love story just got thicker - we were created in love, and we are currently being re-created in love! In the first creation, we were created in the image of God. Being the bearers of God's image, we were supposed to have dominion over the earth and care for it on His behalf. Unfortunately, we missed the *mark or the target* of being God's image bearers. Essentially, that is what sin is - ἁμαρτία (in Greek), missing the mark, target or bullseye.

In the second creation, having been regenerated by the Spirit, we are currently being re-created into the image of God by the same Spirit. God loved us so much that He sent His one and only Son as a sacrifice to take away our sin - our missing the mark of bearing God's image - and in Christ, God is now transforming us into His image through His Spirit who lives in us[5].

The Triune God - the Father, the Son and the Holy Spirit - is present and active in both the creation and second creation.

Amazing? There is more...

IDENTITY

When the Holy Spirit regenerates us, He also gives us a new identity. We now belong to Christ and are called children of God.[6] Our new identity will always serve as a constant reminder that our relationship with God has been reconnected. Not just reconnected, but we have been adopted as children of God.[7]

Our identity as children of God not only reminds us of 'who we are' but also 'whose we are'. We are no longer mere mortals but children of God. And as His children, we are God's heirs. We will inherit the glory of God when God reveals who His children really are at the regeneration of the creation. Yes, between our regeneration and the regeneration of the whole creation, we suffer and share in Christ's suffering, but our suffering now is nothing in comparison to the glory that God will reveal to us later. Even as we join the creation in painful groaning, longing for our physical bodies to be set free from sin and suffering, we wait with eager hope for the day when God will give us our full rights as His adopted children, including the new bodies promised to us.[8]

What we will become is not completely clear yet. Who knows how we will end up! But we know that when Christ returns, we will see Him - and in seeing Him, become like Him.[9] C.S. Lewis wrote in *Mere Christianity*, 'The Son of God became a man to enable men to become sons of God.'

Remember what we said earlier about the true pillar of self-esteem? The true pillar of self-esteem is the intrinsic worth of the person. Man is created in the image of God. All of us missed the mark, but God continues to love us. The second Person of the Holy Trinity - the Son of God -became man to take away our missing-the-mark, that we might become sons of God again, and bear God's image once more. The third Person of the Holy Trinity - the Holy Spirit - takes up residence in us, to make sure what Jesus has begun in us, He will carry on to completion until the day of Christ Jesus. How is that for self-esteem and self-worth?

In our spiritual re-birth, we are born of God and become a new creation, created in Christ Jesus to become partakers of the Divine nature through the Holy Spirit who takes up residence in us.[10] Our new identity not only gives us our sense of self-esteem and self-worth, but also the meaning to our life. We now have a meaning-making, larger-than-life purpose that serves as the guiding compass for our new life - becoming like Christ, or **the imitation of Christ**.

Imitation of Christ is the practice of spiritual disciplines to become like Jesus in our life. The first Christian book I read was the *Imitation of Christ* by Thomas à Kempis. It is a devotional book on living a spiritual life that practises following the example of Jesus. I strongly recommend that you get hold of a copy and read it if you have not.

Imitation of Christ is the fundamental goal of our spiritual life, because essentially, spiritual maturity is becoming like Jesus.[11] Christ is the image of the invisible God.[12] The more we become like Christ, the more we become like God. And as God is the well-spring of health, we enjoy increasing spiritual health as we draw closer to being like Jesus, the exact representation of God.

Essentially, spiritual maturity is becoming like Jesus.

Humans are not cosmic accidents or products of evolution that drift aimlessly in a meaningless universe or sail through cosmic space in random fashion. God has called us to His purpose. Our life, though seemingly haphazard at times, is moving towards God's purpose. His purpose for us is to become partakers of His Divine nature. This is written clearly into the Catechism of the Catholic Church, 'For this is why the Word became man, and the Son of God became the Son of man: so that man, by entering into communion with the Word and thus receiving divine sonship, might become a son of God.'

How is that for the meaning of life? The larger-than-life purpose?

Christlikeness is God's purpose for us. And that is why we can be so sure that when we love God, everything that happens to us happens for this reason - to shape us into the image of His Son.[13] Every person who has been regenerated reflects the image of God. And Christ our Lord - who is the Spirit - works actively in our life to make us more and more like God as we are being changed into Christ's glorious image.[14] When Christ comes again, we shall see Him just as He is, and we will be just like Him.

Of course, we do not actually become God, that is ontologically become equal with God or merge with God to become one in essence. Instead, we would share in the divine life with God as His children, and become true image-bearers of God.

> *When I understand that everything happening to me is to make me more Christlike, it resolves a great deal of anxiety.*
>
> *A.W. Tozer*

God became man so that man may become God, or as the Bible puts it, that we may 'be partakers of the divine nature'. Upon our regeneration, God puts His Spirit in our hearts as a deposit, guaranteeing the promise that is to come.[15] When Christ comes again, we will receive the promise in full. We will become just as our identity says we are - the children of God.

Amazing? There is more...

FREEDOM

Picture yourself having a family dinner out at the best restaurant in town. You have fine wine, great food, good service and excellent ambience. Everybody is having a wonderful time enjoying the sumptuous meal and delightful service. All is good. But wait! Food and service at an expensive restaurant is costly, who is going to foot the bill? Dad?

So far, up to this point of our new life in Christ, everything we mentioned has been good - new life, spiritual health, love, new identity, hope of divinization, et cetera. All this, despite our shortcomings and unworthiness. We messed up but someone cleaned up our mess. We failed but were given the reward of somebody else's success. We found ourselves helpless in a hopeless mistake, but another person bore the brunt of our mistake. We got away scot-free from our mess, failure and mistake. Instead of paying the price of our sins, we receive the prize of divinization. All is good. But who foots the bill?

Jesus paid for the costly bill. He personally carried our sins in His body on the cross and died for our sins in order that we might live. By His wounds, we were healed.[16]   Eugene Peterson, the author of *The Message,* puts it this way, 'Because of the sacrifice of the Messiah, His blood poured out on the altar of the Cross, we're a free people - free of penalties and punishments chalked up by all our misdeeds. And not just barely free, either. Abundantly free!'[17]

Freedom is the third characteristic of our new life. We are a free people! Not just barely free, but abundantly free. We are set free from the penalties and punishments of our misdeeds. Consequently, we are also set free from the guilt and shame of our wrongdoings, as well as free from the fear of death and the unknown future. This freedom comes to us freely, but it is not without cost. It comes with a hefty price tag. It costs the life of Jesus. Jesus died for our sins to set us free us from sin and its power. He paid for the penalties and punishments of our sin by the blood He poured out on the cross. He also took our shame and bore it on the cross. And by His resurrection, he overcame death and firmly secured our future!

Someone might ask, 'Why must Christ die for our sin? Why can't God just snap His finger and erase all our sin? Isn't God supposed to be omnipotent?'

The short answer to this question is: No. God cannot.

God is loving and merciful. He is also just.[18] It would be against God's nature to act unjustly and leave sin unpunished. God's character requires justice be served. It is impossible for God to be inconsistent by ignoring or excusing sins. This has nothing to do with His omnipotence. It has to do with God's nature and character. God cannot lie. God cannot sin. God cannot break His promise. And God cannot just snap His finger to make sin disappear. This has nothing to do with His power. It has everything to do with His character.

> *God cannot will or do anything that will deny His character.*
> *It is not absolutely everything that God is able to do, but*
> *everything that is consistent with His character.*
>
> *Wayne Grudem*

God is perfectly loving, perfectly merciful and perfectly just. With all these character traits residing in a perfectly wise God, Jesus, the One and only Son of God - the Second Person of the Triune God - came to bear the punishment of sins Himself. In His doing so, love is poured out, grace and mercy are offered, and justice is satisfied. By dying on the cross in our place, Jesus took the condemnation of our sins upon Himself so that we might be made right with God.

Jesus died that we might live. This is the **sole** reason Christians are free people -

`For God took the sinless Christ and poured into him our sins. Then, in exchange, he poured God's goodness into us!'[19]

`Christ suffered for our sins once for all time. He never sinned, but he died for sinners to bring you safely home to God. He suffered physical death, but he was raised to life in the Spirit.'[20]

In being the sacrifice that atones for our sins[21], Jesus made atonement for us. Atonement seems like a big word. A simplified definition of atonement is 'at-one-ment' - God enables you to be **one** with Him.[22] Jesus' atoning death mends our brokenness and reconnects us back to God. When we put our faith in the death, crucifixion and resurrection of Jesus as the only solution for our missing-the-mark-brokenness-disconnectedness problem, we receive justification from God. Justification seems like another big word. A simple definition of justification would be 'just as if I'd never sinned.'

Someone might ask, 'It's great that Jesus made atonement for my sin, and enables me to be one with God again. But what if I sin again after my new birth? Will my new life be tainted and be broken again? Do I become spiritually dead again? Do I lose the promise of divinization?'

When we turn to Jesus in faith, we find full forgiveness for our sin, and are set free from sin. There are three senses (and tenses) in which we are set free - We **have been** set free from the penalty of sin, we **are**

being set free from the power of sin and we **will be** set free from the presence of sin.[23]

As forgiven people who have been set free from the penalty of sin, we desire to sin no more. However, even though we have been set free from the penalty of sin, we are not yet free from the pollution of sin. We continue to live in a world marred by sins and among sinful people (we are included in this group). At our new birth, we turned away from sin and sin no longer reigns in our life, but it remains real in our life. And though sin no longer has dominion over our life, it continues to do damage to our life.

Nonetheless, there is a huge difference between the unregenerate and regenerated life. Before, we walked in sin. Now, we wrestle with sin. Before, sin ruled our life. Now, sin ruins our peace. Before, we were ignorant of our sin. Now, we are unable to ignore our sin. Before, we sought to revel in sin. Now, we seek to repent of sin. Before, the penalty of sin awaited us. Now, the power of forgiveness awakes us. Before, we sought excuse for our sins. Now, we seek forgiveness for our sin. Before, we concealed our sin. Now, we confess our sin. And when we confess our sins, God is faithful and just and will forgive us our sins and purify us from all unrighteousness.[24] Thanks be to God! Before, sin led to death. Now, sin leads us to the faithful and just God who forgives sins.

> *Religion: I messed up. My Dad is going to kill me.*
>
> *Gospel: I messed up. I need to call my Dad.*
>
> *Source: Unknown*

We are a people of freedom who live in hope of total freedom. We look forward to the return of Jesus when we will be set free from the pollution and presence of sin completely. Upon His return, Jesus will renew all of creation and set it free from decay. He will also give us a glorified body that is free from sin and suffering. As for now, between the regeneration of men and the regeneration of creation, sin continues to exert its power and presence.

However, make no mistake. Though sin continues to exert its power and presence, it no longer has the power to disconnect us from God or cause brokenness. Let us not forget we have been set free from the penalty of sin, and God will give life to our mortal bodies because of His Spirit who lives in us. Both sin and death no longer reign in our lives because we have life in Christ.

Eugene Peterson puts it this way, 'But if God himself has taken up residence in your life, you can hardly be thinking more of yourself than of him. Anyone, of course, who has not welcomed this invisible but clearly present God, the Spirit of Christ, will not know what we're talking about. But for you who welcome him, in whom he dwells – even though you still experience all the limitations of sin – you yourself experience life on God's terms. It stands to reason, doesn't it, that if the alive-and-present God who raised Jesus from the dead moves into your life, he'll do the same thing in you that he did in Jesus, bringing you alive to Himself? When God lives and breathes in you (and he does, as surely as he did in Jesus), you are delivered from that dead life. With his Spirit living in you, your body will be as alive as Christ's!'[25]

Although we are not yet totally free from the pollution and presence of sin, let us never forget we *are being* set free from the power of sin - the loosening process began at our new birth and continues into our new spiritual life. The more we become like Jesus - or spiritually mature - the freer we are from the power of sin.

Our freedom is eventual and certain, for the power of sin has no chance of reigning over us again. This is because we no longer rely solely on our feeble human effort but are counting on the incredibly great power given to us. This is the same mighty power that raised Christ from the dead.[26] We have been given the same resurrection power of Christ to overcome sin!

In the words of the song *Same Power* by Jeremy Camp:

Greater is He that is living in me

He's conquered our enemy

No power of darkness

No weapon prevails

We stand here in victory

The same power that rose Jesus from the grave

The same power that commands the dead to wake

Lives in us, lives in us

The same power that moves mountains when He speaks

The same power that can calm a raging sea

Lives in us, lives in us

He lives in us, lives in us

Same Power! Amazing? There is more...

ENTHUSIASM

By 'enthusiasm', I am referring to the meaning of its Greek root "ἐνθεός", which means 'God within' (from en 'in' and theos 'god'). When we receive regeneration grace, we are born from above by the Spirit of God. Through the supernatural power of the Holy Spirit, our lifeless spirit springs to life. The Spirit of God takes up residence in us, and our body becomes the temple of the Holy Spirit[27]. God lives in us.

The word 'enthusiasm' comes from the Greek word "entheos" which means the God within. And the happiest, most interesting people are those who have found the secret of maintaining their enthusiasm, that God within.

Earl Nightingale

When God lives in us through His Spirit, sin has no chance. The Spirit of God within us empowers us to overcome the power of sin. People live in sin or are spiritually ill because they lack spiritual understanding or discernment. But for those who have the Spirit of God, we are able to understand the things of God which the Spirit reveals. Through Spirit-taught words and Spirit-led discernment, we are able to accept and understand spiritual realities, and make good judgments about all things.[28] And with a Spirit-filled life, we are able to overcome sin.

However, make no mistake, God did not give us His Spirit to just overcome sin. He wants us to be people of enthusiasm (God-within)! The Spirit of God quickens our dead spirit and enables us to live a life that's full of spiritual health - one that is filled with love, joy, peace, faith, goodness, hope, purpose, meaningful engagement, and power! Jesus said, 'I came that they may have life, and have it abundantly.'[29]

Remember the eight **F**s that support health and happiness? **F**ood. **F**itness. **F**un. **F**riend/**F**amily. **F**unctional Thoughts. **F**unctional Habits. **F**uture. **F**aith. A person who has enthusiasm or 'God-within' acquires all these elements with ease when the situations allow him, but when the conditions do not permit him to have some of these (for examples, food, fitness, fun or friend), the Spirit-filled person continues to experience happiness.

The Apostle Paul, an example of a God-filled man, once told his friends, '*I have learned how to get along happily whether I have much or little. I know how to live on almost nothing or with everything. I have learned the secret of contentment in every situation, whether it be a full stomach or hunger, plenty or want; for I can do everything God asks me to with the help of Christ who gives me the strength and power*'[31]

A God-within person lives an abundant life. An abundant life overflows. And when it does, blessings brim over into the lives of those around it. It is not Jesus' idea to get us out of the ICU and recuperate in the hospital ward for the rest of our life until His second coming. His idea is to get us up and out of the mortuary, and send us out as spiritually healthy people into the streets and alleys to bring in the dead, so that He can also get them up and out of the mortuary to bring in more dead spirits.

Regeneration is something that is accomplished by God. A dead man cannot raise himself from the dead.

R.C. Sproul

However, only a Spirit-filled life - a person who has God-within - can live an abundant life. Many religious or good people have tried attaining spiritual health by making changes or reforms through human understanding or wisdom. Some have tried spiritual teachings, religious instructions or practices. But in God's eyes, they failed miserably. For unless you are born of the Spirit and have the Spirit of God within you, you will not be able to understand spiritual truths, much less live them out. The person without the Spirit does not accept and cannot understand the things that come from the Spirit of God, because they are discernible only through the Spirit. If you experience difficulties understanding this chapter, I suggest you re-read the chapter on **Beginning the Journey to Spiritual Health** and let God's Spirit gently lead you to receive regenerating grace, be born again and welcome God's Spirit into your life.

A spirit-filled life is a God-filled life. When God lives within us, we are full of life, for God is the Author of life. One sure sign of life is dynamism and growth. The regenerated **L-I-F-E** is therefore - being loved and learning to love, being free and being set free, filled and being filled with God, transformed and being transformed, saved and being saved.

A TRANSFORMED L-I-F-E

We begin our journey to holistic health by making changes – changes to our **Wok**, **Walk** and **Watch**. These external changes are important, for when we make these changes, we begin our journey to health. The beginning is an important part of any work.

However, we need to go beyond making external changes, for such changes can be temporary and reversed easily. We therefore move on to making *internalised* changes - changing our ***thoughts***, ***talk*** and ***torque***. *Internalised* changes are important as they come from an informed *mind* and a reformed *heart*, thus leading us to deeper and more lasting changes. Unfortunately, even with internalized changes, we can still experience the revolt of our heart, mind and will.

We are therefore looking for *transformation* - a renewal that is radical, thorough and permanent. Only a Spirit-birthed, Spirit-filled, Spirit-led and Spirit-powered life can lead to a truly transformed life. In our earlier chapter on **Transformation**, we mentioned a few characteristics about transformational change - **R-I-C-E**: **R**elational-based, **I**dentity-driven, **C**ontinual growth and **E**nigmatic. These characteristics are revealed and explained fully in the new **L-I-F-E** regenerated by the Holy Spirit - **L**ove. **I**dentity. **F**reedom. **E**nthusiasm.

A L-I-F-E BEING TRANSFORMED

A spiritually healthy person continues to grow spiritually. Growth is a sign of health. Full spiritual maturity is when a person is fully transformed into the image and likeness of Jesus. The Spirit will continue to work in us to transform us into the image of Jesus. Full spiritual maturity is God's purpose and will for every person.

The chief enemy of spiritual health is lifelessness, stagnation, non-growth, or resting on our laurels. This could be due to pride, laziness, self-absorption or navel-gazing. One of the vows made by the Benedictine monk is *conversatio morum*, a Latin phrase often translated as 'conversion of life' or 'reformation of life'. Richard Foster, the author of *Prayer*, rendered *conversatio morum* as 'Negatively, it means death to the status quo, death to things as they have always been. Positively, it means constant change, constant conversion, constant openness to the movings of the Spirit.'

Scott Peck, the author of *Further Along the Road Less Travelled*, believes God has created human beings to be *perpetual embryos.*

What distinguishes humans most from other creatures is our dramatic relative lack of instincts or pre-formed, pre-set inherited patterns of behaviour, which give other creatures a much more fixed nature than we have. What distinguishes us as human beings is the extraordinary freedom and variability of our behaviours. We do have to grow old physically, and all of us will eventually become decrepit and die, but most of us do not have to stop growing mentally. It is this capacity for ongoing change and transformation that is the most salient feature of our human nature.[32]

> *That is why we never give up. Though our bodies are dying, our spirits are being renewed every day.*
>
> *Saint Paul*

Our spiritual regeneration *begins* at a particular moment. When we put our faith in Christ, we are born again spiritually. Our spirit which was dead unto God comes to life. This carries the idea of once *I was dead, but now I live.* However, spiritual growth still continues after spiritual regeneration. This involves the concept of continual renewal or 'new birth' through the work of the Holy Spirit and the word of God. A common word used by Christians to describe this process of continual growth is **sanctification** - which means 'the process of being made holy'. God is holy in the sense He is separate and distinct from the other. No one and nothing in the universe shares God's holiness, for God alone is God. Yet God has adopted us as His children through Christ and called us to be like Him, or to be holy as He is holy.[33]

Whichever term you prefer to use, be it *conversatio morum, perpetual embryos* or *sanctification*, God's will and purpose for you is that you **become like Jesus**. This is the secret to spiritual health. All the fullness of God lives in Jesus. When we become like Jesus, we become like God. And in being like God - the Author of life - we enjoy eternal life or live the God's life (godly life).

Hence, to improve your spiritual health, become like Christ - have the mind of Christ and follow His manner of life.

Becoming Spiritually Healthy

Our new **L-I-F-E** comes to us through the Spirit of God. And since it comes to us entirely by the works of the Spirit, it is therefore wholly through the grace of God - **universal grace, enabling grace** and **regenerating grace** that we enter life or are saved.

The Greek word $\delta\iota\alpha\sigma\dot{\omega}\zeta\omega$ for 'save' means more than rescue or escape to safety, it includes the idea of cure, heal, or make whole.

And there are three tenses of the Greek verb 'to save' in the Bible[23]. We therefore experience spiritual wellness in three senses: 'We **have been** healed'; 'We **are being** made well'; and 'We **shall be** made whole.'

In our regeneration, we have been healed. In our imitation of Christ, we are being made well. In Christ's return, we shall be made whole. The continuous spiritual development after our spiritual birth is essentially becoming more and more like Jesus. Are you not curious what kind of grace God pours on us to help us become like His Son Jesus?

Continuous spiritual development is essentially becoming more and more like Jesus.

God uses the process of sanctification to make us holy and whole, fully mature and perfect in Christ.[34]   Hence, it is through **sanctifying grace** that we are being made whole and fully mature in Christ. God seeks nothing less than a new creation that is in the fullness of His image in which we are created. Through sanctifying grace, He has freely given us His presence and power to re-create us into the likeness of His Son, Jesus Christ. But, how do we *receive* His sanctifying grace to attain perfect spiritual health?

Christ & Spiritual Health

Christians received spiritual wellness (salvation) by grace

through faith, but when it comes to improving spiritual health or spiritual development, many Christians seek to attain it through religious practices or spiritual exercises. To this group, Saint Paul would say, 'How foolish can you be? After starting your new lives in the Spirit, why are you now trying to become perfect by your own human effort?'[35]

Human effort can bring about changes or reforms but without grace, these are often superficial, temporary, and reversible. It is therefore vital that we rely on God's grace to improve our spiritual health. Yes, religious practices or spiritual exercises are required but it is best not to see them as means to achieve spiritual health but means to receive God's grace. Only grace alone can help us attain spiritual health.

> *For from His fullness we have all received, grace upon grace. No one has ever seen God. The only begotten God, who is at the Father's side, He has explained God.*
>
> *Apostle John, the disciple whom Jesus loved.*

God pours out His grace on us lavishly and freely. To receive God's abundant grace, we come to Him with vessels to contain His grace. Religious practices or spiritual exercises are merely containers or the means by which we receive God's grace. At no time should we confuse spiritual disciplines - the means to receive grace - with human effort to achieve spiritual perfection.

To avoid this confusion, we need to put Christ at the centre of all spiritual disciplines. All our religious practices must lead us to Christ, and from His fullness, receive grace upon grace. In all our spiritual disciplines, we must fix our mind on becoming like Christ, the only God who has come to explain God. Christlikeness is the goal of spiritual development and the path to spiritual health.

Spirituality and Spiritual Health

In putting Christ at the centre of our pursuit of spiritual health, we are placing Christ over all things. If Christ is over all, spirituality cannot be just a part of our life, or apart from the other parts of our life. Our spirituality - the imitation of Christ - must permeate into every part of our life - biological, psychological and relational. I have therefore illustrated the BPSS Model as follows to give a more accurate depiction of their relationships:

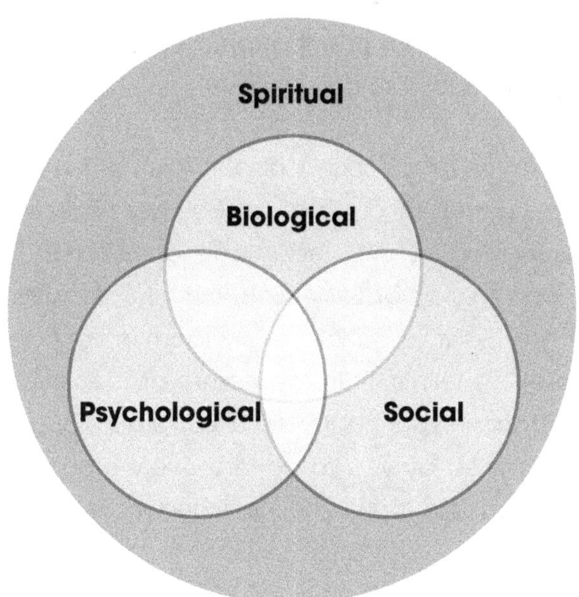

When spirituality is being practised in the biological, psychological and social realms, our body, soul and spirit flourish; for such spirituality not only improves our spiritual health, it also leads to the holistic wellness of our body, soul, and spirit.

As we live out our spirituality in every area of our life, may God Himself, the God of peace, *sanctify* us through and through. And may our whole spirit, soul and body be kept blameless at the coming of our Lord Jesus Christ.[36]

Sanctifying Grace & Spiritual Health

John Wesley, the founder of Methodism, taught that God's grace is unearned. He also taught that we are not to wait idly to experience grace but to engage in the means of grace. The means of grace are ways that God works to hasten, strengthen and confirm faith in disciples of Jesus, so that God's grace pervades in and through disciples.[37] This is the spirituality that we seek - one that permeates into every part of our life - biological, psychological and social.

The means of grace bring about spiritual health, for through practicing them, we open our lives to the Holy Spirit who works in us to sanctify us, making us into the image of Christ more and more. Paraphrasing John Wesley, Dr. Lester Spencer says 'Sanctification is when you invite the Holy Spirit to go into every room in your heart, your life - every dark closet - every spot in the corner of the attic - every single square foot of space in your heart, soul, life! It's a lifelong process where the Holy Spirit is invited by you to go into every place in your life and begin to perfect you and make you more and more like Jesus.'[38]

The Wesleyan means of grace can be divided into works of piety and the works of mercy.[37] Devote yourself to these practices in order to nourish your spiritual health. However, in living out these means of grace in your life, constantly bear in mind to put Christ at the centre, and focus on imitating the Person of Christ, not complying to a set of practices.

Means of Grace

Works of Piety

Individual Practices – reading, meditating and studying the scriptures, prayer, fasting, regularly attending worship, healthy living, and sharing our faith with others.

Communal Practices – regularly share in the sacraments, Christian conferencing (accountability to one another), and Bible study.

Works of Mercy

Individual Practices - doing good works, visiting the sick, visiting those in prison, feeding the hungry, and giving generously to the needs of others.

Communal Practices – seeking justice, ending oppression and discrimination (for instance Wesley challenged Methodists to end slavery), and addressing the needs of the poor.

Among these practices, I would like to highlight a few of them. These are not necessarily the most important, but are the ones which I feel have been ignored, neglected or misunderstood in our time, at the peril of our spiritual health.

- **The Sacraments of Baptism and Holy Communion**

Sacraments are rituals that were instituted by Jesus and are 'outward signs of inward grace'. The sacraments of baptism and holy communion are 'means of grace', through which the Holy Spirit uses the physical (water, bread and wine) to make visible the spiritual - grace, forgiveness, and the presence of Christ. Sacraments are not merely symbolism. In a real but mysterious sense that is beyond our grasp, they improve our spiritual wellness. They are the coming together of our physical and spiritual world at the highest level - a mystery to be received not explained. If you have not yet received God's grace through these two sacraments, give priority to talk to a church pastor to find out more. Participation in baptism and the holy communion are vital for our spiritual well-being.

By allowing our active participation through sight, smell, touch, and taste, ritual enables spiritual truths to be experienced at a deeper level and thereby to 'stick' in our souls.

Jeffrey Truscott

- **Healthy Living**

Give attention to healthy living and lifestyle, for they are important contributing factors to your spiritual health. Do not neglect your **Wok**, **Walk** and **Watch**. Eat a healthy diet, cultivate good, strong habits, be selective in what you watch and read. Read books and watch movies that are good for your body, soul and spirit. I suggest you re-read the chapters on **Changing your Wok, Walk** and **Watch**, and learn to live out your spirituality in ordinary everyday living.

- **Personal Altar**

Set aside daily quiet time to be alone with God - reading or listening to Scriptures, meditating, praying and worshipping. For urban dwellers whose busy schedules require us to juggle work, family, friends, volunteering, and personal downtime, this can be rather challenging. I suggest you tap into your creative imagination by approaching the Holy Spirit for help to come up with creative and lateral solutions that best fit your unique situation.

On most days, I spend more than an hour walking - combining personal downtime, physical exercise, prayer, worship and listening to Scriptures. Over time, the Holy Spirit enabled me to turn my daily walks into spiritual habits I do naturally, where He supernaturally nourishes my spiritual, mental, emotional and physical health. The Holy Spirit too can structure a workable routine for your unique situation. Ask Him for help to protect your personal altar. Our quiet time, even if it is 15 minutes, leavens the rest of the day - the holy minutes make holy the rest of the day.

Let your daily quiet time be **relational** based. It is easy to make the common mistake of focusing on *doing* quiet time, that is, on the activities we *do* during quiet time - reading and praying et cetera. Focus on the relationship with Christ instead. Christ should not be absent during your quiet time. Neither should you. It is easy to turn the quiet time into nothing more than a to-do list to be checked off, where we either do not invite Christ to join us or we are not totally present. In being fully present, we need to bring our whole person, including our emotions, to meet with Christ.

A common misunderstanding is that quiet time must always be characterized by peace and calm, joy and love. This misunderstanding has succeeded in hindering many people from bringing their genuine emotions into their quiet time. In reality, quiet time can sometimes be tumultuous in emotions, plagued with agitation and disquieting moments.

Human emotions are given by God. They are natural responses to stimuli. None of the six basic emotions - anger, sadness, happiness, surprise, fear and disgust - is wrong. None will hinder our growth as a Christian. They become wrong only when they become destructive - wrong timing, wrong place, wrong target, wrong magnitude, wrong frequency, wrong reason, or wrong expression et cetera.

Take for example, anger is an appropriate response when we witness injustice done to the helpless poor. We have the examples of Jesus getting angry in the Bible, and the Bible talks about the wrath of God. Anger becomes destructive (hence wrong) when it becomes rage (inappropriate magnitude), or aggression (wrong expression), or too frequent over inconsequential matters (wrong reason).

The Christian path is to learn the way of Jesus - be in touch with our genuine emotions but subjecting them to the law of love. We labour to become like Jesus in the expression of all our emotions. We get angry over what he would get angry over, sad over what he would grieve over, be concerned over what he is concerned with, and be happy over what he rejoices over.

Emotions do not bring us nearer or further away from God; but how far we are in our relationship with Jesus does. That is why it is crucial that we spend quiet time with Jesus every day. In our quiet time, the Living Word informs our mind, guides our emotions, directs our decisions, feeds our soul, gives health to our body, changes our behaviour and transforms our life. But unless we bring our whole being, including our emotions, to the Living Word for healing, we miss out on the chance of being made whole by the Spirit.

To learn the way of Christ in managing our emotions, learn also to meditate and develop it into a daily habit. Refer to Appendix 2 for the three stages of Christian meditation.

For your spiritual wellness and growth, discipline yourself and give effort to developing and maintaining the habit of daily quiet time with God.

> *The path of spiritual growth in the riches of Christ is not a passive one. Grace is not opposed to effort. It is opposed to earning. Earning is an attitude. Effort is an action.*
>
> *Dallas Willard*

• Happiness Habits

Through our practice of the means of grace, God sanctifies us by making us whole and holy. Happiness ensues as a by-product of the holistic wellness of our body, soul and spirit. Nothing makes this clearer than the means of grace which I call the 'happiness habits.' Those who practise the 'happiness habits' reap happiness, but for those who practise them in order to become like Christ, the blessing is doubled by the fact that they experience both material and spiritual happiness.

Essentially 'happiness habits' are functional habits that are rooted in functional thoughts and solution talk that build strong and meaningful relationships. I recommend that you re-read the chapters on **Changing your Thoughts, Talk** and **Torque**. Enough has been said about the 'happiness habits' in those chapters, well, except one - acts of kindness.

> *Every act of kindness grows the spirit and strengthens the soul.*
>
> *Unknown*

It is unfortunate that we often see acts of kindness as acts of duty and obligation, thus replacing the joy that is built within every kindness with drudgery and indifference.

When a person moves his limbs in the air, he uses up energy without creating much work. However, when he gets into the water and moves his limbs, he swims! Such are the acts of kindness. In performing the acts of kindness, we need to immerse ourselves in the stream of sanctifying grace and move in the realm of the Holy Spirit. And when we do, we reap much joy and blessing, for ourselves and for others.

We derive happiness when we help restore health to a person's body or soul, but the greatest joy and blessing come from the happiness habit of helping others find holistic health of their body, soul and spirit. In leading others to spiritual health through the regeneration and sanctification of their spirit, we help them find eternal health and happiness.

We said earlier (in the chapter on **Transformation**) that the key difference between reformation and transformation is that in the latter, the reformed becomes the reformer. The litmus test of transformation is therefore this - in your pursuit of health and happiness, are you helping others to find theirs?

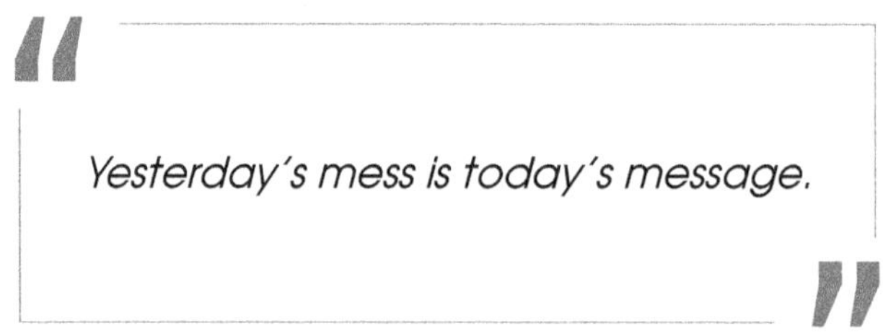

The single and clearest evidence of spiritual health is the brimming over of your spiritual health to the lives around you. In delivering you from your spiritual death, it is not God's idea to get you out of the mortuary to spend the rest of your life in the ICU until Christ's second coming. As mentioned earlier, I repeat for emphasis that God wants to get you up and out of the mortuary, and send you out as spiritually healthy people into the streets and alleys to bring the spiritually dead to Him, in order that He can also get them up and out of the mortuary to bring in more dead spirits.

If you have been spiritually regenerated, yet happiness escapes you, you are probably in need of regaining the meaning to life and re-finding meaningful engagement in life. Look no further than the happiness habits. Invest your time, energy and effort in performing acts of kindness, in particular helping others in their journey to spiritual health.

Grace upon Grace

The journey to spiritual health has indeed been one of grace upon grace - universal grace, enabling grace, regenerating grace and sanctifying grace. Out of His fullness, God leads us into His fullness, patiently and gently. God's purpose is to transform every person into the image of His Son. His Spirit lives in us to transform us into Christlikeness, with ever-increasing glory.

In the beginning, God created man and woman in His image. In our sinning, we missed the mark or target of being God's image-bearers. In the continuing, God is re-creating man and woman into the image of His Son - through His Spirit that works in us to regenerate and sanctify us. Yet as beautiful as this story is, it is incomplete.

Our story does not end here, in fact it will not end. It continues into the next world.

GLORIFYING GRACE

The world as we know it will not last forever. When Jesus

returns to earth, He will regenerate it and rule His Kingdom on earth forever. We will all receive a new body when Jesus returns - those who have died will be resurrected with the glorified spiritual bodies and those still alive will be changed in the twinkling of an eye to the same new spiritual bodies. Our new heavenly bodies will never, never die or perish but live forever.[39]

I think that Resurrection (whatever it exactly means) is so much profounder an idea than mere immortality. I am sure we don't just 'go on'. We really die and are really built up again.

C.S. Lewis

Such is the Christian hope of ultimate spiritual health! Our spiritual health is in three stages - In our regeneration, we have been healed. In sanctification, we are being made well. And in our glorification, we shall be made fully whole.

Let us not forget what this full spiritual health means! It is the complete integration of our physical, mental, emotional and spiritual health into total wellness. It also means we will receive our new spiritual bodies which will reveal us as who we truly are - the children of God! Full spiritual health really means we fully partake in God's divine nature and become a son of God!

The Son of God became a son of man so that we might become a son of God. Praise God for His glorifying grace. Hallelujah!

> *The Greek has three words for life -*
> *Bios, Psyche, and Zoe.*

Bios refers to the physical life. We get the word biology from it. If you want a happy and healthy **bios**, focus on improving your **wok**, **walk** and **watch**.

Psyche refers to the psychological life or the human soul - the mind, emotion and will. We get the word psychology from it. If you want a happy and healthy **psyche**, focus on improving your **thoughts**, **talk** and **torque.**

Zoe refers to the spirit or the spiritual life. The Greeks use **zoe** to refer to the eternal or divine life uniquely possessed by God. In the Bible, this word is used to describe Jesus – 'In him was life, and that life was the light of all mankind.'[30] This is also the same Greek word Jesus used to make His promise to us, 'I came that they may have life, and have it abundantly.'

If you want **zoe** - eternal life or the divine life possessed by God, focus on improving your spiritual health by becoming like His Son, Jesus!

Appendix 1

Mentally Healthy Foods that Help Produce
The Following in Your Body:

Antioxidant	Spinach, red grape, dark chocolate, strawberry and goji (wolfberry).
Curcumin	Turmeric powder and curcumin tablet.
Magnesium	Dark chocolate, almond, cashew, pumpkin seed and tofu.
Omega-3	Salmon, sardines, mackerel, cod liver oil and walnut.
Potassium	Pumpkin seed, banana, soya bean, potato and spinach.
Selenium	Pork, chicken, soya bean, oat and mushroom.
Serotonin	Egg, banana, tofu, cheese and salmon.
Vitamin D	Egg yolk, salmon, sardine, tuna and mushroom.
Zinc	Pumpkin seeds, meat, dark chocolate, almond and cashew nuts.

Appendix 2

SIMPLE MEDITATION

BODY first

Step 1

Choose a quiet place. Get comfortable. You can sit in a chair with your back straight and your feet firmly on the ground. Place your hands (palm facing upward) on your lap. Check to make sure you have relaxed shoulders. Turn on a 5-minute piece of meditation music. You should be able to find one on YouTube.

Step 2

Close your eyes. Breathe in (count of 4) slowly through your nose to fill your belly with air (feel your belly rise). Hold for a count of 2. Breathe out (count of 6) slowly through your mouth or nose, whichever is more relaxing to you (you should feel your belly lower as you breathe out). Focus on your breath and continue this 4-2-6 breathing until you get into a rhythm.

The MIND follows

Step 3

Once you are in a rhythm, as you breathe in, recite with your mind slowly, 'Everything will be okay in the end.' As you breathe out, recite with your mind, 'If it's not okay, it's not the end.'

Slowly and gradually, progress to 'I have done this before' (breathe in), 'I can do it again' (breathe out).

Continue until the music stops.

Progressively increase your meditation to 10 and 15 minutes on the second and third week respectively.

CHRISTIAN MEDITATION STAGE 1

BODY first

Step 1

Choose a quiet place. Get comfortable. You can sit in a chair with your back straight and your feet firmly on the ground. Place your hands (palms facing upward) on your lap. Check to make sure you have relaxed shoulders. Turn on a 5-minute piece of meditation music. You should be able to find one on YouTube.

Step 2

Close your eyes. Breathe in (count of 4) slowly through your nose to fill your belly with air (feel your belly rise). Hold for a count of 2. Breathe out (count of 6) slowly through your mouth or nose, whichever is more relaxing to you (you should feel your belly lower as you breathe out). Focus on your breath and continue this 4-2-6 breathing until you get into a rhythm.

The MIND follows

Step 3

Once you are in a rhythm, as you breathe in, pray with your mind slowly, 'Lord Jesus Christ.' As you breathe out, pray with your mind, 'Have mercy on me.'

Step 4

Slowly and gradually, as the Spirit leads you, progress to 'Lord Jesus Christ' (breathe in), 'Son of God' (breathe out), 'Have mercy on me' (breathe in) and 'A sinner' (breathe out).

Continue until the music stops. Proceed to do your Quiet Time (QT) reading for 5 to 10 minutes.

'Lord Jesus Christ, Son of God, have mercy on me, a sinner.' is the classical form of the **Jesus Prayer.**

Optional Reading: https://www.svots.edu/saying-jesus-prayer

CHRISTIAN MEDITATION STAGE 2

Step 1

Choose a quiet place. You can sit comfortably in a chair with your back straight and your feet firmly on the ground. Place your hands (palms facing up) on your lap. Check to make sure you have relaxed shoulders. Turn on a piece of 10-minute meditation music.

Step 2

Do the 4-2-6 breathing to get into the rhythm of breathing deeply and slowly.

Step 3

Once you are in a rhythm, pray the Jesus' Prayer – as you breathe in, pray with your mind slowly, 'Lord Jesus Christ.' As you breathe out, pray with your mind, 'Have mercy on me.'

Slowly and gradually, as the Spirit leads you, progress to 'Lord Jesus Christ' (in), 'Son of God' (out), 'Have mercy on me' (in) and 'A sinner' (out).

Gradually proceed to –

'Lord Jesus Christ' (in), 'My Lord' (out), 'Have mercy on me' (in), 'Rule over my ...' (out).

'Lord Jesus Christ' (in), 'My Saviour' (out), 'Have mercy on me' (in), 'Save me from ...' (out).

'Lord Jesus Christ' (in), 'My King' (out), 'Have mercy on me' (in), 'Remember me when you come into your kingdom' (out).

Step 4

As the Spirit leads you, pray the Lord's Prayer slowly, in keeping with 4-2-6 breathing:

Our Father in heaven,
hallowed be your name,
your kingdom come,
your will be done,
on earth as it is in heaven.
Give us today our daily bread.
And forgive us our debts,
as we also have forgiven our debtors.
And lead us not into temptation,
but deliver us from the evil one.

For yours is the kingdom and the power
and the glory forever.

Continue the *Jesus' Prayer* until the music stops. Proceed to do your QT reading.

CHRISTIAN MEDITATION STAGE 3

Step 1

Choose a quiet place and get into a comfortable and relax sitting position. Turn on a 15-minute piece of meditation music.

Step 2

Do the 4-2-6 breathing to get into the rhythm of breathing deeply and slowly.

Step 3

Once you are in a rhythm, pray with your mind slowly the Jesus' Prayer.

Gradually proceed to –

'Lord Jesus Christ' (in), 'My Lord' (out), 'Have mercy on me' (in), 'Rule over my …' (out).

'Lord Jesus Christ' (in), 'My Saviour' (out), 'Have mercy on me' (in), 'Save me from …' (out).

'Lord Jesus Christ' (in), 'My King' (out), 'Have mercy on me' (in), 'Remember me when you come into your kingdom' (out).

Step 4

As the Spirit leads you, pray the Lord's Prayer.

Step 5

Invite the Spirit to fill you:

Come Holy Spirit (in). Come (out).

Come Holy Spirit (in). Pour out the Father's love into my heart (out).

Come Holy Spirit (in). Fill me with your Presence (out).

Come Holy Spirit (in). Fill me with your Peace (out).

Come Holy Spirit (in). Fill me with your Power (out).

Come Holy Spirit (in). Come (out).

For it is not by might (in), not by power (out).

But by your Spirit, Lord (in). So come, Holy Spirit come (out).

Come Holy Spirit (in). Come (out).

Continue the *Jesus' Prayer* until the music stops.

Proceed to do your QT reading.

- *Benjamin Franklin: An American Life* by Walter Isaacson

- *Blink: The Power of Thinking Without Thinking* by Malcolm Gladwell

- *Chicken Soup for the Soul* by Jack Canfield & Mark Victor Hansen

- *For One More Day* by Mitch Albom

- *Lord of the Rings* by J. R. R. Tolkien

- *Reclaiming Virtue* by John Bradshaw

- *The Chronicles of Narnia* by C.S. Lewis

- *The Five People You Meet in Heaven* by Mitch Albom

- *The Power of Positive Thinking* by Norman Vincent Peale

- *The Purpose Driven Life: What on Earth Am I Here For?* by Rick Warren

- *The Road Less Travelled* by M. Scott Peck

- *The Time Keeper* by Mitch Albom

- *Tuesdays with Morrie* by Mitch Albom

- *What the Dog Saw* by Malcolm Gladwell

Appendix 5

Answer to Game Number 1:

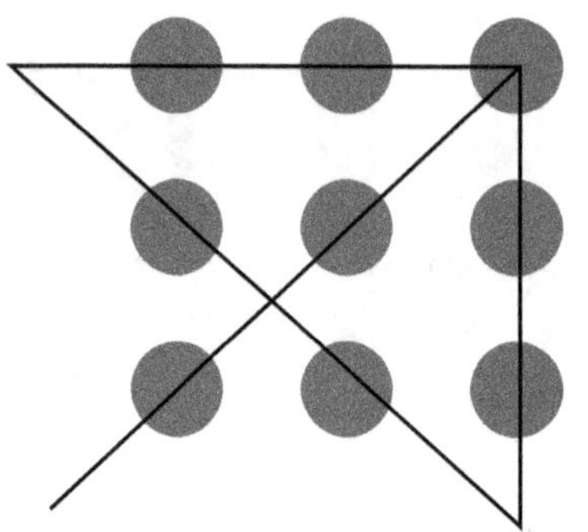

Connect nine dots

with four lines

without lifting your pencil

Solution Focused Therapist/Coach:

Name	Email Address	Telephone
Egero Wellness	egerowellness@gmail.com	9863 8339
Debbie Hogan	admin@sf-academy.com	6456 9280
Tony Ong	reception@counsel.org.sg	6536 6366
Simon Lee	simon.tp@briefacademy.com	6829 2287

Appendix 6

Employ 'I messages'.

'I messages' are irrefutable statements about the communicator's feelings, thoughts, observations, perceptions, and reactions. When confronting someone, talk in terms of yourself, for example, 'I think,' 'I feel,' 'In my experience,' 'for myself,' 'I need,' 'I've observed.'

State your request clearly.

Be honest and direct. Do not over-explain or apologize.

Focus on the offending behaviour involved, not the person.

Be specific in your description of the behaviour and the effect it had on you.

Use appropriate non-verbal behaviours.

Show the intensity of your feelings. Look the other person in the eye. Speak clearly, without hesitation, leaning toward the listener.

Source: Saint Joseph's University. (n.d.) Confrontation Skills. Retrieved July 7, 2020, from https://sites.sju.edu/counseling/self-help-resources/confrontation-skills/

Other Books by The Author

Praying the Psalms for the Half Full Soul consists of 150 short devotions grafted from the Psalms, based on the author's devotion to the Psalms and his work with youth and families. It is intended to nurture the mental wellness of youths by nourishing their spiritual life through reading and praying the Psalms. Youths are equipped with many tools to help them navigate through life. However, no toolbox is complete if it is missing the tool of prayer. This book hopes to help the youths acquire the tool of prayer by learning to pray the Psalms.

This book is also for adults who work with teenagers or have teenage children. They will find it a useful resource to enter the youth's world and face the common issues that threaten the youth's mental and spiritual health.

In his second book, *The Devil Goes for Life Coaching*, Charlie cleverly creates a satirical style of dialogue between the devil and its life coach to reveal some of the age-old tactics that the devil uses in distracting and deceiving believers of Christ, even causing them to unknowingly fall victim to its cunning ways and subtle methods. Charlie's professional background as a counsellor/psychotherapist and his past experience as a Church pastor come through strongly in this book. He takes advantage of modern-day challenges and contemporary Singaporean society to play out the devil's schemes in order to draw out warnings for serious followers of Christ. Do spend some time reading this highly entertaining book, and come away with greater clarity and resolve that you will put on your spiritual armour at all times, and be alert, as the devil is indeed waiting to devour his next victim.

PART-1 BEGINNING OUR JOURNEY

1. Robbs, K. (2016, January 10). The Feeling Wheel. Verbalists: My Language Network. https://verbalistseducation.com/2016/01/10/see-the-magical-vocab-wheel-that-will-help-you-find-the-perfect-word-to-express-your-feelings/

Chapter One Changing Our Wok

1. Diabetes: The rice you eat is worse than sugary drinks. (2019, November 24). The Straits Times. https://www.straitstimes.com/singapore/health/diabetes-the-rice-you-eat-is-worse-than-sugary-drinks

2. For a better understanding of this, check out the five-minute video: Bohorquez, D. (2017, October 25). How does our gut talk to our brain? (Video). TED Archive. YouTube. (https://www.youtube.com/watch?v=utFG8GEvmfg&t=2s

3. Davison, K.M., Lung, Y., Lin, S., Tong, H., Kobayashi, K.M., Fuller-Thomson, E. (2019). Depression in middle and older adulthood: the role of immigration, nutrition, and other determinants of health in the Canadian longitudinal study on aging. BMC Psychiatry, 19, 329. https://doi.org/10.1186/s12888-019-2309-y

Chapter Two Changing Our Walk

1. Seow, J. (2019, June 27). 1 in 2 Singapore residents feels stressed out by the thought of doing nothing: Survey. The Straits Times. https://www.straitstimes.com/business/one-in-two-singapore-residents-feel-stressed-out-by-the-thought-of-doing-nothing-survey

2. Donnelly, L. (2019, September 11). Social media linked to increased risk of mental health problems. The Telegraph. https://www.telegraph.co.uk/news/2019/09/11/social-media-linked-increased-risk-mental-health-problems

3. Lim, K. (2019, November 12). Children exposed to digital devices at an early age may have emotional and behavioural difficulties: Study. TODAY. https://www.todayonline.com/singapore/children-exposed-digital-devices-early-age-may-have-emotional-and-behavioural-difficulties?

4. LaMotte, S. (2019, November 4). MRIs show screen time linked to lower brain development in pre-schoolers. CNN Health. https://edition.cnn.com/2019/11/04/health/screen-time-lower-brain-development-preschoolers-wellness/index.html

5. To avoid dementia, exercise better. (2019, November 17). TODAY. https://www.todayonline.com/world/avoid-dementia-exercise-better?

6. Beyer, M. (2019, November 17). Depression: 35 extra minutes of exercise daily slashes risk. Medical News Today. https://www.medicalnewstoday.com/articles/327037

7. Domonell, K. (2016, January 13). Why endorphins (and exercise) make you happy. CNN Health. https://edition.cnn.com/2016/01/13/health/endorphins-exercise-cause-happiness/index.html

8. Lagos, L. & Singh, J.R. (2019, December). How playing sports benefits your body … and your brain. (Video) Ted-Ed. https://ed.ted.com/lessons/how-playing-sports-benefits-your-body-and-your-brain-leah-lagos-and-jaspal-ricky-singh

9. Lim, S. (2018, December 13). 6 common mental disorders affecting Singaporeans

today and where you can go to get help. Business Insider Singapore. https://www.businessinsider.sg/6-common-mental-disorders-affecting-singaporeans-today-and-where-you-can-go-to-get-help

10. Jones, B. & Wang, K. (2019, November 6). 2 experts debunk sleep myths, from snoring is just annoying to stay in bed if you can't fall asleep. Business Insider. https://www.businessinsider.com/sleep-experts-debunk-biggest-myths-snoring-falling-asleep

11. Shmerling, R. H. (2017, September 25). The latest scoop on the health benefits of coffee. Harvard Health Publishing. https://www.health.harvard.edu/blog/the-latest-scoop-on-the-health-benefits-of-coffee

12. Pearson, H. (2017, April). Lessons from the longest study on human development. (Video). TED2017. https://www.ted.com/talks/helen_pearson_lessons_from_the_longest_study_on_human_development?language=en

13. Curtin, M. (2018, October 23). Neuroscience Reveals 50-Year-Olds Can Have the Brains of 25-Year-Olds If They Do This 1 Thing. Inc. This Morning. https://www.inc.com/melanie-curtin/neuroscience-shows-that-50-year-olds-can-have-brains-of-25-year-olds-if-they-do-this.html

14. Giving thanks can make you happier. (2011, November). Harvard Health Publishing. https://www.health.harvard.edu/healthbeat/giving-thanks-can-make-you-happier

15. Achor, S. (2011). The Happiness Advantage: The Seven Principles of Positive Psychology That Fuel Success and Performance at Work. Ebury Publishing.

16. Barker, E. (n.d.). 7 Easy Happiness Boosters According to Harvard Research. https://www.bakadesuyo.com/2012/08/what-7-activities-does-harvard-happiness-expe/

Chapter Three Changing Our Watch

1. Aryana, M. (2010). Relationship Between Self-esteem and Academic Achievement Amongst Pre-University Students. Journal of Applied Sciences. 10(20), 2474-2477. https://scialert.net/abstract/?doi=jas.2010.2474.2477

2. Elite, H. (1999). The relationship between self-esteem and job performance (Thesis, Florida International University). Proquest Dissertations and Theses Global. https://search.proquest.com/docview/304578795

3. Smirnov, I. (n.d.). 9 Celebrities Who Struggled with Low Self-Esteem. https://business-motivationfamily.net/4-celebrities-struggled-low-self-esteem/

4. Baumeister, R.F., Campbell, J.D., Krueger, J.I., & Vohs, K.D. (2003, May 1). Does high self-esteem cause better performance, interpersonal success, happiness, or healthier lifestyles? Psychological Science in the Public Interest, 4(1), 1-44. https://journals.sagepub.com/doi/full/10.1111/1529-1006.01431

5. Rosenberg, M., & Pearlin, L.I. (1978). Social class and self-esteem among children and adults. American Journal of Sociology, 84(1), 53-77. https://www.jstor.org/stable/2777978?seq=1

6. Martin, S. (2017, May 8). Why highly successful people struggle with low self-worth (and how you can reclaim your self-worth). PsychCentral. https://blogs.psychcentral.com/imperfect/2017/05/why-highly-successful-people-struggle-with-low-self-worth/

7. Rick Warren shows God's value to 5,000 inmates. (n.d.). Preaching Today. https://www.preachingtoday.com/illustrations/2014/september/4092914.html

8. Sohn, P. (2016). Quarter-Life Calling: Pursuing Your God-Given Purpose in Your Twenties. FaithWords.

PART II CONTINUING THE JOURNEY

1. Plato, The Republic.
2. Colossians 2:20-23, Peterson, E.H. The Message (2002). NavPress.
3. Yirmeyah 17:9, Goble, P. Orthodox Jewish Bible (2002). Artists for Israel International.
4. Merritt, A.C., Effron, D.A., Monin, B. (2010). Moral self-licensing: When being good frees us to be bad. https://www.compassionate.center/docs/Merritt,_Effron_&_Monin,_2010,_SPPC.pdf
5. Tan, T. (2020, February 4). Pastor Philip Chan, co-founder of halfway house, The Hiding Place, dies of cancer at age 69. The Straits Times. https://www.straitstimes.com/singapore/pastor-philip-chan-who-dedicated-his-life-to-helping-drug-addicts-dies-of-cancer-at-age-69
6. Galatians 4:19, Colossians 1:28 and Ephesians 4:11-13, New International Version (2011). Biblica, Inc.
7. 2 Peter 3:18, Good News Translation (1976). American Bible Society.
8. Mello, T. (2019, July 12). Thinking of business like a bamboo tree can help you stay motivated. Here's why. Inc.com. https://www.inc.com/tommy-mello/thinking-of-business-like-a-bamboo-tree-can-help-you-stay-motivated-heres-why.html
9. John 12:24, New Living Translation (2015). Tyndale House Publishers.

Chapter Four Changing Our Thought

1. Robbs, K. (2016, January 10). The Feeling Wheel. Verbalists: My Language Network. https://verbalistseducation.com/2016/01/10/see-the-magical-vocab-wheel-that-will-help-you-find-the-perfect-word-to-express-your-feelings/
2. 4 Studies That Show How Your Thoughts Can Make You Sick. Power of Positivity. https://www.powerofpositivity.com/3-studies-that-show-how-your-thoughts-can-make-you-sick/
3. Powell, T. (2000). The Mental Health Handbook. Speechmark Publishing Ltd.
4. Pratt, K. (2015, November 6). 10 Cognitive Clarities (the opposite of cognitive distortions). HealthyPsych. https://healthypsych.com/10-cognitive-clarities-the-opposite-of-cognitive-distortions/
5. Romans, 12:2. New Living Translation (2015). Tyndale House Publishers.

Chapter Five Changing Our Talk

1. Ecclesiastes 4:12. New International Version (2011). Biblica, Inc.
2. James 3:5-6. New International Version (2011). Biblica, Inc.
3. Proverbs 16:24. New Living Translation (2015). Tyndale House Publishers.

Chapter Six Changing Our Torque

1. Rosamond, C. (2017, February 3). What is torque? All about torque: definition, equations, and units. Auto Express. https://www.autoexpress.co.uk/car-news/95110/what-is-torque-all-about-torque-definition-equations-and-units

2. Waldinger, R. (2015, December). What makes a good life? Lessons from the longest study on happiness. (Video) TED Talks. This has been viewed more than 13 million times.

3. Mineo, L. (2017, April 11). Good genes are nice, but joy is better. The Harvard Gazette. https://news.harvard.edu/gazette/story/2017/04/over-nearly-80-years-harvard-study-has-been-showing-how-to-live-a-healthy-and-happy-life/

4. Hari, J. (2015, January 27). Can connection cure addiction? Greater Good Magazine. https://greatergood.berkeley.edu/article/item/can_connection_cure_addiction

5. Saint Joseph's University. (n.d.) Confrontation Skills. Retrieved July 7, 2020, from https://sites.sju.edu/counseling/self-help-resources/confrontation-skills

6. Wachtel, T. (2016). Defining Restorative. 4.5. Compass of Shame. International Institute for Restorative Practices. https://www.iirp.edu/defining-restorative/compass-of-shame

7. Voskamp, A. (ca. 2018). In Facebook (Fan page). Retrieved July 7, 2020, from https://www.facebook.com/AnnVoskamp/photos/a.36946146306603 4/1497686953576807/?comment_id=1498896320122537

PART III COMPLETING THE JOURNEY

1. Romans 5:3, English Standard Version (2016). Crossway.

2. 2 Corinthians 6:10, English Standard Version (2016). Crossway.

3. 2 Corinthians 4:18, God's Word® Translation (1995). Baker Publishing Group.

4. Peterson, E.H. (2018). As Kingfishers Catch Fire: A Conversation on the Ways of God Formed by the Words of God. Hodder & Stoughton.

Chapter Seven Understanding Spiritual Health

1. Galatians 5:14. New International Version (2011). Biblica, Inc.
2. Psalm 19:7-8. New Living Translation (2015). Illinois, Tyndale House Publishers.
3. Psalm 104:14-15. New International Version (2011). Biblica, Inc.
4. Luke 24:30-31. New International Version (2011). Biblica, Inc.
5. Luke 24:41-43 & 45. New International Version (2011). Biblica, Inc.
6. Acts 1:4. New International Version (2011). Biblica, Inc.

7. Matthew 11:19. New International Version (2011). Biblica, Inc.

8. John 21:12, Mark 6:21. New Living Translation (2015). Illinois, Tyndale House Publishers.

9. 1 Kings 19. New Living Translation (2015). Illinois, Tyndale House Publishers.

10. Values-based Education Resources. (2020, June 15). In Facebook (Group page). Retrieved June 23, 2020, from https://www.facebook.com/groups/567475040078555/permalink/1582221555270560/

11. Scazzero, P. (2017). Emotionally Healthy Spirituality: It's Impossible to Be Spiritually Mature, While Remaining Emotionally Immature. Michigan, Zondervan.

12. Ong, Charlie. (2019). Praying the Psalms for the Half-Full Soul. Singapore, Genesis.

13. Psalm 13:2. New International Version (2011). Biblica, Inc.

14. Psalm 10:1. New International Version (2011). Biblica, Inc.

15. Psalm 88:4. New International Version (2011). Biblica, Inc.

16. Matthew 4:5-7. New Living Translation (2015). Illinois, Tyndale House Publishers.

17. Psalm 19:1. New International Version (2011). Biblica, Inc.

18. Matthew 4:8-10. New International Version (2011). Biblica, Inc.

Chapter Eight Begining the Journey of Spiritual Health

1. Matthew 5:45. New International Version (2011). Biblica, Inc.

2. Luke 6:35. New International Version (2011). Biblica, Inc.

3. Watson, J. C. (2002). Re-visioning empathy. In D. J. Cain (Ed.), Humanistic psycho-therapies: Handbook of research and practice. (p. 445-471). American Psychological Association. https://doi.org/10.1037/10439-014

4. Romans 7:18-19. New Living Translation (2015). Tyndale House Publishers.

5. John 3:1-8. New Living Translation (2015). Tyndale House Publishers.

6. Titus 3:3-7. New International Version (2011). Biblica, Inc.

7. John 3:16. New Living Translation (2015). Tyndale House Publishers.

8. 1 Corinthians 2:14. New International Version (2011). Biblica, Inc.

9. Ephesians 1:13-14. New International Version (2011). Biblica, Inc.

10. 2 Corinthians 5:17. New Living Translation (2015). Tyndale House Publishers.

Chapter Nine Improving Our Spiritual Health

1. 1 John 4:19. New International Version (2011). Biblica, Inc.

2. Genesis 3:1-3. New Living Translation (2015). Tyndale House Publishers.

3. John 1:1-4, 14. New Living Translation (2015). Tyndale House Publishers.

4. 1 John 4:7-9. New Living Translation (2015). Tyndale House Publishers.

5. Colossians 3:10 & 2 Corinthians 3:18. New International Version (2011). Biblica, Inc.

6. 1 Corinthians 12:13 & Galatians 3:26-27. New International Version (2011). Biblica, Inc.

7. Galatians 4:4-6 & Romans 8:14-17. New International Version (2011). Biblica, Inc.

8. Romans 8:15-25. New Living Translation (2015). Tyndale House Publishers.

9.   1 John 3:2. Peterson, E.H. The Message (2002). NavPress.

10. John 1:13, Ephesians 2:10, 2 Corinthians 5:17 & 2 Peter 1:4. New International Version (2011). Biblica, Inc.

11. Ephesians 4:13. New International Version (2011). Biblica, Inc.

12. Colossians 1:15. New Living Translation (2015). Tyndale House Publishers.

13. Romans 8:28-29. The Living Bible (1971). Tyndale House Publishers.

14. 2 Corinthians 3:18. New Living Translation (2015). Tyndale House Publishers.

15. 2 Corinthians 1:22 & Ephesians 1:15. New International Version (2011). Biblica, Inc.

16. 1 Peter 2:24. New Living Translation (2015). Tyndale House Publishers.

17. Ephesians 1:7-8. Peterson, E.H. The Message (2002). NavPress.

18. Isaiah 61:8. New International Version (2011). Biblica, Inc.

19. 2 Corinthians 5:21. The Living Bible (1971). Tyndale House Publishers.

20. 1 Peter 3:18. New Living Translation (2015). Tyndale House Publishers.

21. 1 John 2:2. New International Version (2011). Biblica, Inc.

22. Gumbel, N. Bible in One Year 2020. Bible.com. https://www.bible.com/reading-plans/17704-bible-in-one-year-2020-with-nicky-gumbel/day/75

23. Gumbel, N. The Three Tenses of Salvation. Bible in One Year. https://www.bibleinoneyear.org/bioy/commentary/1005

24. 1 John 1:8-9. New International Version (2011). Biblica, Inc.

25. Romans 8:9-11. Peterson, E.H. The Message (2002). NavPress.

26. Ephesians 1:19-21. The Living Bible (1971). Tyndale House Publishers.

27. 1 Corinthians 6:19. New International Version (2011). Biblica, Inc.

28. 1 Corinthians 2:6-16. New International Version (2011). Biblica, Inc.

29. John 10:10. New American Standard Bible (1995). The Lockman Foundation.

30. John 1:4. New International Version (2011). Biblica, Inc.

31. Philippians 4:11-13. The Living Bible (1971). Tyndale House Publishers.

32. Peck, M. Scott. (1993). Further Along the Road Less Travelled: The Unending Journey Toward Spiritual Growth. Simon & Schuster.

33. Leviticus 11:44, Matthew 5:48 & 1 Peter 1:15-16. New International Version (2011). Biblica, Inc.

34. Colossians 1:28. New International Version (2011). Biblica, Inc.

35. Galatians 3:3. New Living Translation (2015). Tyndale House Publishers.

36. 1 Thessalonians 5:23. New International Version (2011). Biblica, Inc.

37. The People of the United Methodist Church. (2014, February 3). The Wesleyan Means of Grace. United Methodist Church. https://www.umc.org/en/content/the-wesleyan-means-of-grace

38. Spencer, L. (2018, December 1). A Wesleyan View of Grace "Sanctifying Grace". Alabama Gazette. https://www.alabamagazette.com/story/2018/12/01/religion/grace-to-the-third-power-a-wesleyan-view-of-grace-sanctifying-grace/1529.html#:~:text=It's%20by%20His%20sanctifying%20grace,preached%20a%20lot%20of%20times.&text=And%20sanctifying%20grace%20is%20what,power%20of%20God's%20Holy%20Spirit!

39. 1 Corinthians 15:42-56. The Living Bible (1971). Tyndale House Publishers.

9 789811 802010